Improving Secondary Science Teaching

John Parkinson

KU-050-848

RoutledgeFalmer
Taylor & Francis Group

LONDON AND NEW YORK

507.12
PAR

First published 2004
by RoutledgeFalmer
11 New Fetter Lane, London EC4P 4EE

Simultaneously published in the USA and Canada
by RoutledgeFalmer
29 West 35th Street, New York, NY 10001

RoutledgeFalmer is an imprint of the Taylor & Francis Group

© 2004 John Parkinson

Typeset in Palatino by Wearset Ltd, Boldon, Tyne and Wear
Printed and bound in Great Britain by TJ International Ltd,
Padstow, Cornwall

All rights reserved. No part of this book may be reprinted or
reproduced or utilised in any form or by any electronic,
mechanical, or other means, now known or hereafter invented,
including photocopying and recording, or in any information
storage or retrieval system, without permission in writing from
the publishers.

British Library Cataloguing in Publication Data
A catalogue record for this book is available from the British
Library

Library of Congress Cataloging in Publication Data
A catalog record has been requested

ISBN 0–415–25046–3 (pbk)
ISBN 0–415–25045–5 (hbk)

To my family

Impr
Scier

CARDIFF
CAERDYDD

CYNGOR CAERDYDD
CARDIFF COUNCIL
LIBRARY SERVICE

CARDIFF

26 APR 2005

29 SEP 2005

26/11/10.

13/12/10.

This book must be returned or renewed on or before the
latest date above, otherwise a fine will be charged.
Rhaid dychwelyd neu adnewyddu y llyfr hwn erbyn y dyddiad
diweddaraf uchod, neu bydd dirwy i'w thalu.

19Sg/54   LAB01

CLS

Improving S   ew
and experie   he
effectiveness   ng
methods use   n-
agement issu

   With und   to
learn; how   ol;
and the valu

- The impro
- Planning
- Promoting
- Dealing w
- Making u
- Learning

This timely   se
who are working to improve the management of science departments or their own
teaching practice. It will also be a valuable resource for science education researchers
and students on higher degree courses in science education.

John Parkinson taught science in secondary schools in England and Wales before
becoming a lecturer in education at the University of Wales, Swansea. He is Deputy
Director for the PGCE course and team leader for the MA course on school improvement.

ACC. No: 02300079

CONTENTS

FIGURES

TABLES

CHAPTER 1

The improvement process

Teaching is not to be regarded as a static accomplishment like riding a bicycle or keeping a ledger: it is, like all arts of high ambition, a strategy in the face of an impossible task.

Lawrence Stenhouse (DfEE, 1999: 95)

From time to time we all take stock of where we are and what we are doing and make decisions about the future. This is usually an *ad hoc* process, with the decisions being made on gut feelings rather than any clearly defined strategy. The purpose of this chapter is to examine some of the key tools and processes that will help science teachers evaluate their current practice and plan for improvement. The chapter draws heavily on the school effectiveness and school improvement paradigms, and examines how these impact on the work of the department and the individual teacher.

School effectiveness

The whole notion of school effectiveness is fraught with difficulty. How does one determine what is, and what is not, effective? Is something that is deemed to be effective in one situation going to be equally effective in another situation? A working definition of school effectiveness is:

> The extent to which any (educational) organisation as a social system, given certain resources and means, fulfils its objectives without incapacitating its means and resources and without placing undue strain on its members.
>
> (Reynolds *et al.*, 1996: 2)

The research into school effectiveness is very well established, and uses sophisticated data analysis to investigate situations and draw conclusions. For example, judgements can be made on the contribution made by the school to pupils' learning by examining attainment in year 7 (Y7) and comparing it with attainment in Y11. Factors such as gender, parental socio-economic status, parental education and parental ethnicity or racial background can be taken into account. In addition to academic outcomes, effectiveness research can provide useful information on factors such as attendance, behaviour, attitudes and the level of self-esteem. As a result of this research we have lists of factors associated with effective schools and, while there is a considerable amount of commonality between these lists, some contain additional items. The established key factors for effective schooling, as summarised by Reynolds *et al.* (1997: 128) and Stoll and Mortimore (1997: 18) are:

1 **Professional leadership.** The headteacher plays an important role in having an overview of all aspects of school life and provides the drive to shape the school into an effective learning environment. In an effective school, the headteacher works well with the senior management team, consults widely on key decisions, and promotes good feelings and collegiality between the teachers and non-teaching staff. Teamwork and collaboration between colleagues are seen as very important issues.

2 **Shared vision and goals.** In an effective school, staff work together towards the common goals. There is a sense of purpose, collegiality and ownership, leading to good co-operation and team work.

3 **An orderly environment and school coherence.** An orderly environment appears to affect achievement in a variety of ways:
   - it provides a disciplinary climate within which students' and teachers' opportunities to conduct task-related work are maximised
   - an orderly and purposeful atmosphere promotes a sense of efficacy among teachers and pupils, which in turn enhances teaching and learning performances
   - the consistency and stability associated with an orderly environment appears to promote higher achievement (Stockard and Mayberry, 1992). An environment that is attractive and comfortable also has benefits for pupils' learning.

4 **High-quality teaching and learning.** In an effective school the maximum amount of time in lessons is spent on teaching and learning. This requires reducing the time spent on administration, and organising transitions from one activity to another smoothly. The teaching has clarity of purpose, with both teacher and pupils knowing what is to be achieved. Learning is valued, and there is an expectation that academic progress will be made. In general, the literature suggests that the quality and pacing of instruction, the way in which teachers give information, the way in which teachers question pupils and wait for responses, and the way in which they handle class work and homework all influence pupil achievement. The findings regarding the quality of pacing of instruction have been most consistently replicated. As would be intuitively expected, pupils have higher achievement when more of the curriculum is covered and when more time is spent actively engaged in learning that is appropriate to their level.

5 **High expectations.** In an effective school, the teachers have high expectations of the pupils and these are clearly communicated to the pupils. Pupils are provided with work that will challenge them intellectually rather than letting them get into a routine of completing low-level tasks.

6 **Positive reinforcement.** This involves teachers identifying with what pupils do well and giving appropriate praise for their work or actions rather than adopting a negative approach where teachers only comment on poor behaviour and lack of good work. Discipline, when it is needed, should be clear and fair.

7 **Monitoring and enquiry.** Individual teachers keep good records of pupils' achievements and use these to identify problems in pupils' learning. On a whole school basis, assessment data from a variety of sources are used to evaluate the performance of the school.

8 **Pupils' rights and responsibilities.** This is concerned with developing the right sort of atmosphere in a school, where pupils can develop their sense of self-esteem and understand their rights and responsibilities in society.

9 **Learning for all.** Staff development is matched to the needs of the individual and the needs of the school.

10 **Partnerships and support.** Working with parents and the local community can help to extend and widen the learning experiences of the pupils, and raise awareness of individual needs and the level of support mechanisms available.

A list of key points such as this is of interest but of limited value when it comes to thinking about how to improve. A school may not be as effective as it should for a variety of reasons, some of which may relate to the above while others may not (MacBeath and Mortimore, 2001). The research so far only gives us an indication of what factors give rise to an effective school; it gives no indication as to the strength of each factor and, more importantly, no guidance on how to change an ineffective school into an effective one (Coe and Fitz-Gibbon, 1998).

School improvement

School improvement can be defined as:

> A systematic, sustained effort aimed at change in learning conditions in a school with the ultimate aim of achieving educational goals more effectively.
>
> (Reynolds *et al.*, 1996: 3)

Like school effectiveness research, school improvement research has a long and distinguished history. Its origins lie in the school development projects of the 1960s, when curriculum packages were prepared mainly by people not involved in school teaching. They failed to have an impact largely due to teachers' lack of understanding of what the projects were trying to do. In many respects they felt alien to the teachers' pedagogic knowledge, and the in-service training provided was unsuccessful in creating a sense of ownership between the teachers and the courses. The direction of school improvement has changed in many ways since then, moving from a top-down approach to one involving all members of staff in a school from the outset. The emphasis now tends to be on managing the process of change over a period of time, keeping things on track and monitoring progress towards the targets. This approach has been brought about by a joining of forces between the school improvement researchers, who mainly worked on a qualitative basis, and the school effectiveness researchers, whose work had a quantitative focus. The new era of improving school effectiveness is now with us, combining the use of data with plans for improvement.

In most schools, improvements are happening all the time. Teachers learn from one another, they pick up ideas from articles or courses that they have attended and they learn from their ongoing experiences in the classroom. But how do we increase the number of opportunities to improve, and how do we ensure that good practice is maintained? There are a number of relatively simple actions that can be taken to initiate improvement, such as:

1 **Attending courses.** Many teachers obtain all their new ideas about teaching through award bearing and non-award bearing courses. While some of these courses are very useful there are others that fail to meet teachers' direct needs and, as a result, the planned change or improvement is not implemented. School-based INSET is frequently used to ensure that a course is targeted to needs with the clear advantage that it can be based around authentic situations. However, if these types of courses are restricted to discussion between staff in the school, there is a danger that the level of improvement may be limited owing to the lack of innovative ideas from outsiders.

2 **Reflecting on what happens in the classroom.** Personal reflection on classroom events can play a significant part in helping individual teachers to improve their practice (see page 37).

3 **Sharing ideas with colleagues.** At departmental meetings, time is put aside to discuss pedagogy – what works and why it works, and what doesn't work. Key issues need to be discussed, such as: do pupils like the science they are being taught? Are both boys and girls achieving to their full potential? What is the uptake of science subjects post-16? In addition, colleagues need to share experiences and learn from teachers of other disciplines.

4 **Evaluating data, identifying weaknesses and taking action.** Schools generally maintain a plethora of data on each pupil, and sophisticated computer programs enable teachers to track an individual's progress. The computer can also be used to track teachers' performance, noting those who consistently get good results with their classes and those who don't.

5 **Research.** In most professions, practitioners tend to keep up to date with developments in their field. However, for a number of reasons this is not generally true of teaching, even though significant advances are being made every year in the field of science education research (for example, see Parkinson, 2003). Those that do keep up to date do so by reading magazines such as *School Science Review* and *Education in Chemistry*. In addition to reading about research, some teachers adopt a research-based philosophy in their teaching (see page 50).

6 **Involvement in the work of examination boards.** One way of improving examination results is to become a marker for one of the examination boards. There is no doubt that this gives insight into the types of questions that are set and the types of answers expected and, as such, should improve the number of pupils gaining A*–C grades. Some would argue that this is developing knowledge about how to work the system rather than helping to develop quality teaching and learning.

7 **Working in partnership with others.** Partnerships with parents, community representatives, the LEA, higher education establishments etc. can often bring a fresh

perspective to the work of the school and provide useful insights into how the school could improve.

8 **Use of a critical friend.** A critical friend may be a colleague from the school or someone external to the school, such as an LEA advisor. Such a person can help to review the work of a department or make a study of what happens in an individual's classroom through a period of focussed observation and support for improvement (see page 42).

9 **Listening to the pupils.** Listening to what the pupils say and watching their reactions to the work gives immediate feedback on the value of the lesson. However, the reactions of small groups of pupils can sometimes mask the feeling of the majority, and a more structured approach to eliciting pupil feedback has increased reliability.

10 **Taking on new responsibilities.** The very process of being put in a situation where you are asked to take on a new role within the school forces you to take a fresh look at the work you have been doing and consider if there are any changes that you might wish to include.

Understanding the resistance to change

There is no one fixed method for improving schools, as they all differ in terms of their culture, their needs and the personalities involved. The process of change from an ineffective situation to an improved one is by no means simple, and there are no 'quick fix' solutions. The basic process involves a school working its way through a series of phases, each with its own set of problems (see Table 1.1). Teachers are sometimes resistant to change, and may be heard saying such things as:

- How do you know it is going to work?
- Will it be any better than what we are doing at the moment?
- How much extra work will it be?
- Is this just another 'bandwagon' we all have to jump on to make sure we get through the threshold?
- Will we be given additional non-contact time to get things organised?

Fullan has made an extensive study of the process of change, and has indicated how difficult it is (Fullan, 1997). In this article he points out that a certain amount of vision is required to provide the clarity and energy for promoting specific changes. The people involved need to be committed and skilled in the change process as well as in the change itself.

Whitaker (1993) points out that managers need to be sensitive to three particular clusters of feeling that teachers may experience when confronted with change:

1 Loss
  - of firmly held beliefs and ideas
  - of established patterns and behaviours
  - of comfortable habits
  - of confidence and self-esteem.

Table 1.1 *Possible phases in the process of school improvement*

Phase	Characteristics	Some problems
Initiation • goal setting • policy making • planning • preparation	Why does the school need to change? What needs to be changed? Who should be involved?	Winning over the hearts and minds of the teachers. Considering the effect of changing one factor on the other factors
Implementation • pressure to change • monitoring and evaluating	Putting the change processes into action	Resistance to change (another job to do) Maintaining the momentum New priorities may arise from other directions (e.g. DfES, Ofsted)
Institutionalisation • review	The new processes become embedded into practice	Change in staff Change in school culture Reduction in 'drive' from the SMT

2 Anxiety
   • about required levels of understanding
   • about new skills
   • about what the future will be like
   • about being able to cope
   • about being seen as different.
3 Struggle
   • to survive intact
   • to acquire new competence
   • to gain respect and recognition.

As a science teacher you may tackle a change using the same sort of methodology used to deal with a scientific problem, and might expect that by altering the situation in a systematic manner you would get some meaningful results. However, because of the complex nature of change and the idiosyncrasies of human beings it is not always possible to transpose this model of operating on to the process of carrying out a change in procedures in the science department. One of the first hurdles to be negotiated is the development of a common understanding of what the change actually means. This may be clear in the originator's mind, but each member of the team (e.g. members of staff in the science department) may have a slightly different interpretation of what is involved. It may take some time to tease out the direction of the change and what you are going to do in order to be able to achieve your goals. This type of problem can reappear as you work through the change process and people begin to lose direction. Teachers have many different things influencing their daily work, and may wander off target either because they have lost sight of what they are supposed to be doing or because they have started to question the original assumptions made. In order to increase the chance of the improvement strategy being implemented successfully, it is worthwhile adopting a strategy that incorporates the following:

- Ongoing debate about the goals of the strategy and the methodology being used. This is for clarification and to make sure that everyone is on the right track. It would be wrong to alter the direction in the early stages.
- A clearly written plan using terms that everyone understands and principles that everyone agrees on. The plan is likely to change over time as new, unpredictable factors come into play.
- A recognition that significant change takes time, possibly two to three years in terms of departmental reform and five to six when the whole school is considered. Short-term goals or review points help to keep the process going.
- An understanding that people need pressure to change, even those who are extremely positive about the reforms.

Improvement projects

There have been many school improvement interventions and programmes in the UK and throughout the world, for example the:

- International School Improvement Project (ISIP) (Van Velzen *et al.*, 1985)
- Halton Effective Schools Project, based in Canada (Stoll and Fink, 1996)
- Improving the Quality of Education for All Study (IQEA) (Hopkins *et al.*, 1994)
- Schools Make a Difference Project (Myers, 1995)
- Improving School Effectiveness Project (ISEP) (MacBeath and Mortimore, 2001)

There are many common elements to these projects, such as an initial assessment of the school's current performance, the development of school improvement targets and implementation strategies, and a built-in method for monitoring progress. A key feature of the ISEP is the use of three groups of questionnaires to elicit information – one to parents, one to pupils and one to teachers – to get a clear view of all the factors involved.

The IQEA project is ongoing and has a reputation for helping schools to build a capacity for development and change. It is based on a six-phase plan, elements of which are common to other projects. These phases are as follows (Hopkins, 2001):

1 The school selects its own priorities for development and its own methods for achieving them, thus having ownership of the process. These may arise from the School Development Plan or some internal audit as described below.
2 The school collects appropriate data on its performance, e.g. examination results, PANDA data, quality and range of teaching and learning, internal conditions. Analysis of the data helps to identify what needs to be done.
3 A School Improvement Group (SIG) is established, comprising staff with different types of expertise, length of experience and level of seniority.
4 The SIG receive training related to:
    - teaching strategies
    - planning and providing staff development
    - conducting school-based research on school improvement.

5 A whole school staff development strategy is initiated, to include:
   • sharing of work done in departments
   • interdepartmental meetings to discuss teaching strategies
   • workshops
   • partnership and peer coaching
   • design and execution of collaborative enquiry activities.
6 In order to maintain the impetus of the improvement, there follows a period of:
   • careful planning of curriculum and teaching developments
   • organisation of staff development
   • strategies for sustaining the momentum across the school
   • evaluating the progress and successes.
   This leads to a way of working that is natural and fits with the school's aspirations.

Fundamental to this project is the involvement of the teacher in action research, a process of identifying key aspects of teaching and learning, putting into practice a plan for improvement and evaluating its implementation (see page 50). University staff are involved in an advisory role throughout, and feed in information from the ever-growing knowledge base on school effectiveness and school improvement. The whole process, from inception to securing an improved climate, takes about five years.

Harris (2000) has identified a number of features of school improvement programmes that have proved to be particularly successful. These are:

1 **Establishing a vision.** This involves all of the staff having a clear picture of where they would like the school to be in a fixed period of time.
2 **An extended view of leadership.** There is a view that everyone is involved. The head and members of the senior management team (SMT) function as the leaders and the decision-makers, but everyone has a voice and all will be required to take risks.
3 **Matching programme to context.** There is no 'off the shelf' school improvement package. A school must choose one that best fits its individual needs and situation and then adapt it accordingly.
4 **Focussing on specific pupil outcomes.** The most important outcome from an improvement strategy will be pupils' academic results, and the key to this is through a review of teaching practices.
5 **A multi-level approach.** All levels of the school organisation (whole school, subject departments, pastoral system, individual classroom teachers) need to be involved in the change.

Identifying the starting point

The initial starting point may be the issues for attention from an Ofsted inspection, the identification of problems through a study of the PANDA data, or simply a desire to improve the standards in the school. In most schools there is a wealth of data on pupils' achievement, such as key stage assessments and CATs scores, all of which can be used to predict future performance. However, having got all these numerical data, what do you do with them and how do you relate them to the activities that go on in the school? The data will identify:

- under-achieving departments and teachers
- departments and teachers that get better results than those predicted
- 'coasting' departments and teachers.

In order to get a fuller picture of a school's performance it is necessary to carry out a self-evaluation study (Saunders *et al.*, 2000) which, in addition to scrutinising the assessment data, involves:

- an examination of school policies and other similar documents
- the observation of teachers in the classroom
- structured interviews with teachers
- an examination of pupils' records
- an examination of pupils' work
- structured interviews with pupils
- structured interviews with adults other than teachers.

Saunders provides a number of schedules based on these sources of information to help compile the type of evidence required to give a clear picture of how a school is performing. This process takes you beyond simply looking at the numbers, to look at the personal characteristics that lead to the data. The numerical data may hide a number of facets of the school's work, which may come to light by examining case studies of pupils' progress through the school. Self-evaluation helps the head and the SMT to organise change.

Planning for improvement

Schools produce development plans to indicate how they intend to implement their policies and achieve their targets. A development plan looks at specific areas of the work of the school, e.g. the development of ICT, improving the level of literacy for key stage 3 (KS3) pupils. A different plan is prepared for each area that the school wishes to improve, and each contains the following information:

- a clearly written target related to the area of work to be improved
- a list of tasks or strategies to be used to achieve the target, together with a list of corresponding success criteria and dates by which the targets should be met
- the resource implications
- the in-service training requirements.

Figure 1.1 illustrates the cyclical process of development, from inception at school level, through departmental planning and staff development to classroom practice.

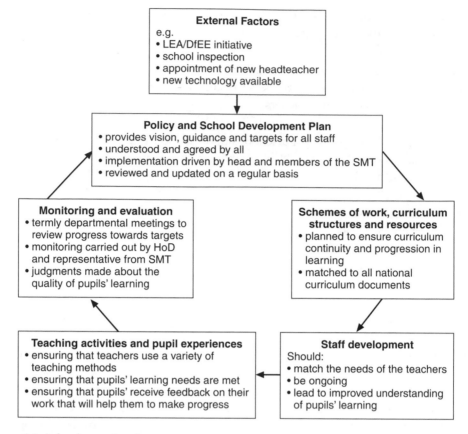

Figure 1.1 A development cycle

All schools have to complete an action plan following a Section 10 inspection. These are normally structured under the same type of headings used for the development plan but they focus only on the weaknesses identified in the inspection report, the key issues for action. In its guidance to schools, Ofsted (2001: 2) suggests that action plans are likely to prove successful if they concentrate on improving:

- the leadership provided by the headteacher and key staff, including governors, with particular emphasis on their strategies for raising standards;
- levels of attainment and the rate of pupils' progress;
- management, including pastoral care of pupils/staff, communication, financial planning, control and administration;
- systems to monitor and evaluate the school's performance;
- the pupils' behaviour, attitudes and work habits;
- the planning and organisation of lessons;
- the challenge and pace of teaching;
- the quality and range of opportunities for learning, including the development of policies, schemes of work, curricular planning, and assessment, recording and reporting;
- resources to address the above.

Fidler (1996) proposes that in certain circumstances (e.g. when a new headteacher is appointed, when a school is merging with another school, or when a school is put under special measures) it is important to carry out a more in-depth review and plan. He calls this process 'strategic planning', as it examines all aspects of the school's work and involves regular monitoring over a five-year period.

Evidence-based education

The proponents of evidence-based education question the usefulness of some of the school effectiveness research, arguing that you cannot simply take a list of effective teacher factors and apply these to other less effective teachers. Education is not like that; what works in one situation may not work in another. The centre for evidence-based education (E-BE) is the University of Durham (www.cem,dur.ac.uk), who define E-BE as:

> The support for and promotion of practices and policies that are based on good evidence about their effects (i.e. costs and benefits).
>
> (Coe *et al.*, 2000)

A key feature of the research methodology is the use of randomised controlled trials, which, they argue, gives much more meaningful results than the statistical correlations used in traditional school effectiveness research. Taking the example of the effect of class size on pupils' achievement, correlation studies show that pupils in large classes learn as much as, and often more than, pupils in smaller classes. When you come to think about it, maybe this is what you would expect the results to show because:

- when schools have a choice they tend to put more manageable pupils into large classes, allowing more difficult pupils to be taught in small groups
- more popular, 'successful' schools are likely to be oversubscribed and so have larger classes than those with lower levels of achievement.

When the research is carried out using pupils who are randomly allocated to classes of different sizes, it is possible to separate out the effects of class size from all the other related factors. When this is done it is found that pupils in smaller classes do learn more, although the size of the difference is not as large as one might have hoped for.

What can go wrong?

There are many reasons why efforts to improve fail to work, including the following:

- Some teachers are unwilling to understand what changes need to be made. They have an 'I don't want to know' attitude, and put up a mental barrier against anything new.

- Some teachers become disheartened when things start to go wrong and they lose confidence in the process (e.g. during the inevitable dip in progress in the early stages of the implementation phase).
- Some teachers feel they are drowning in the enormity of the tasks to be done.
- Some teachers fail to accept that any aspect of ineffectiveness is to do with them. These teachers would say that the problem lies in the low level of pupils' abilities and/or the low aspirations of their parents. They would argue that there is little that can be done about these factors.
- Some teachers cling on to 'tried and tested' methods.
- Some teachers don't see change as their responsibility – the 'my job is to get through the syllabus (it doesn't matter if they don't understand it)' approach.
- It can be difficult to move things on smoothly when there are different opposing factions in a school. A struggle for power can be detrimental to progress. Some individuals can get together to block the changes.
- Some teachers are simply worried that they will 'fail' in any new system.

School culture

A school's culture is difficult to describe, being a combination of the realisation of relationships, beliefs, attitudes and ideologies of all those that work in the establishment. It is shaped by its history, and by the influences of the local education authority, the community and the teaching staff. The headteacher and the SMT play an important role in building a professional culture that is responsive to change (Hargreaves and Dawe, 1990). These senior members of staff help to set the values for all, and attributes such as commitment and hard work can be made to filter through all aspects of school life.

Carrying out a school self-evaluation exercise, as described above, assist in bringing about a change in the culture of the school, helping to formalise and to extend existing processes of evaluating teaching and learning and data analysis (Saunders *et al.*, 2000). A school culture that is open and receptive to change is likely to have:

- staff who share a common vision for the school, who are forward looking and have high aspirations for themselves and their pupils
- an environment where standards are consistent, and morale and expectations are high
- an appreciation of the importance of progression in learning and a knowledge of how it can be achieved
- a high degree of collegiality, where staff are prepared to help one another to improve their teaching
- an understanding and commitment to professional development for needs of the individual and for the school as a whole.

Value added

It is worth remembering that when the concept of value-added data was first mooted as being a fairer way of judging schools than simply looking at the 'raw' scores it was ridiculed by the Secretary of State for Education, who condemned it as 'cooking' the results. It is only since 2000 that value-added measures have been provided in secondary school performance tables. Value-added analyses are currently being used to:

- 'compare like with like' in terms of schools' background and context
- represent pupils' progress rather than raw achievement
- identify which institutions are doing better/worse than predicted
- provide similar information about individual departments/year groups
- identify which pupils are performing above or below average.

(Saunders, 1997: 192)

Using information from the Autumn Package (DfES) and the confidential PANDA data for the school gives a clearer picture of how the school is performing in comparison with other similar schools. Value-added measures are a significant improvement on using the raw data, but the method is not without its problems and it is important to manage the translation of the data into improvement strategies with care (Saunders, 1999: 71).

References

Coe, R. and Fitz-Gibbon, C. (1998) 'School effectiveness research: criticisms and recommendations', *Oxford Review of Education*, **24**(4), 421–438.

Coe, R., Fitz-Gibbon, C. and Tymms, P. (2000) Promoting Evidence-Based Education: The Role of Practitioners. Paper presented at BERA conference, Cardiff, September 2000.

DfEE (Department for Education and Employment) (1999) *All our Futures: Creativity, Culture and Education*, London: DfEE.

Fidler, B. (1996) *Strategic Planning*, London: Pitman.

Fullan, M.G. (1997) 'Planning, doing and coping with change', in Harris, A., Bennett, N. and Preedy, M. (eds) *Organizational Effectiveness and Improvement in Education*, Buckingham: Open University Press.

Harris, A. (2000) 'What works in school improvement? Lessons from the field and future directions', *Educational Research*, **42**(1), 1–11.

Hargreaves, D. and Dawe, R. (1990) 'Paths of professional development; contrived collegiality, collaborative culture and the case of peer coaching', *Teaching and Teacher Education*, **6**(3), 227–241.

Hopkins, D. (2001) 'Meeting the Challenge' An Improvement Guide for Schools Facing Challenging Circumstances, at http://www.standards.dfes.gov.uk/schoolimprovement/meet_introduction_0.html.

Hopkins, D., Ainscow, M. and West, M. (1994) *School Improvement in an Era of Change*, London: Cassell.

MacBeath, J. and Mortimore, P. (2001) *Improving School Effectiveness*, Buckingham: Open University Press.

Myers, K. (ed.) (1995) *School Improvement in Practice: The Schools Make a Difference Project*, London: Falmer Press.

Ofsted (2001) *Action Planning for School Improvement*, London: HMSO.

Parkinson, J. (2003) 'Distillates', *Education in Chemistry*, **40**(3), 82.

Reynolds, D., Bollen, R., Creemers, B., Hopkins, D., Stoll, L. and Lagerweij, N. (1996) *Making Good Schools: Linking School Effectiveness and School Improvement*, London: Routledge.

Reynolds, D., Sammons, P., Stoll, L., Barber, M. and Hillman, J. (1997) 'School effectiveness and school improvement in the United Kingdom', in Harris, A., Bennett, N. and Preedy, M. (eds) *Organizational Effectiveness and Improvement in Education*, Buckingham: Open University Press.

Saunders, L. (1997) 'Value-added principles, practice and ethical considerations', in Harris, A., Bennett, N. and Preedy, M. (eds) *Organizational Effectiveness and Improvement in Education*, Buckingham: Open University Press.

Saunders, L. (1999) *'Value Added' Measurement of School Effectiveness: An Overview*, Slough: NFER.

Saunders, L., Stradling, B. with Rudd, P. (2000) *Raising Attainment in Secondary Schools: A Handbook for School Self-evaluation*, Slough: NFER.

Stockard, J. and Mayberry, M. (1992) *Effective Educational Environments*, Newbury Park, Ca.: Corwin Press.

Stoll, L. and Fink, D. (1996) *Changing our Schools*, Buckingham: Open University Press.

Stoll, L. and Mortimore, P. (1997) 'School effectiveness and school improvement', in White, J. and Barber, M. (eds) *Perspectives on School Effectiveness and School Improvement*, London: Institute of Education Bedford Way Papers.

Van Velzen, W.G., Miles, M.B., Ekholm, M., Hameyer, U. and Robin, D. (1985) *Making School Improvement Work*, Leuven/Amersfoort: ACCO.

Whitaker, P. (1993) *Managing Change in Schools*, Buckingham: Open University Press.

CHAPTER 2

Leading and managing the science department

The climate in a department should be such that any person, regardless of his or her position, is free to put forward a case for making a change.

(Hull and Adams, 1981: 116)

An effective school is made up of effective departments and effective teachers. In this chapter the characteristics of effective departments are examined, looking at the in-built structures and procedures required to generate a climate for improvement.

There are certain things that you would expect of an effective science department, such as good science examination results, year on year. However, there are other, perhaps less obvious, outcomes concerned with pupils' attitudes towards science. We want pupils to enjoy science, to be motivated and excited about what they do in their lessons and to leave school having a real understanding of a number of key scientific ideas. This is a job for the whole department through the setting of a philosophy of teaching that permeates all aspects of the subject. The work of one excellent teacher can be quickly neutralised by another whose presentation is thorough, but boring. Effective departments place pupils' learning at the very centre of their work (Harris et al., 1996), and learning is seen as something of immense value for both pupils and teachers and is an ever-present goal. Such departments also provide a caring environment where pupils are not afraid to approach teachers if they don't understand the work. You would expect to find an abundance of well-managed and properly maintained resources for pupils of all abilities to use. Effective departments will not want to rest on their laurels; they will be looking for ways of improving and looking for new challenges. We all know that teachers are constantly being faced with new demands from the DfES, parents and the community at large, and the 'new exciting challenges' as seen by some can be seen as 'yet another job to do' by others. An improving department looks at current practice, considers what needs to be done, and develops strategies to ensure that the new situation is reached as efficiently as possible through contributions of all members of the departmental team. The departmental arrangement creates territories within schools where groups of people spend time together, share materials and generally co-exist in a common 'comfort zone' (Goodson and Marsh, 1996). The key player in getting this team to work together is the subject leader or head of department.

Leadership and management

The head of department (HoD) needs to be both a leader and a manager, and, for the moment at least, it is worth distinguishing between these two aspects of the job. As a leader you are concerned with showing the way, setting up examples of good practice and encouraging others to follow. Leadership is involved with issues such as:

- the establishment of a vision of science education and its place in pupils' overall school experience (based on your own philosophy of education and the school's aims)
- being a role model for members of the department in terms of teaching and professional duties (being positive, cheerful and encouraging)
- the recognition of the importance of everyone's contribution to team work (departmental, pastoral and whole school, listening to other people's points of view)
- being knowledgeable about science in general and your subject specialism in particular
- being knowledgeable about teaching methods and assessment techniques
- keeping up to date with developments in science education and government initiatives.

As a manager you are concerned with being in charge, making decisions and taking responsibility. Management involves issues such as:

- planning, implementing and evaluating changes
- communicating with others (e.g. headteacher, governors, other heads of department, parents)
- dealing with conflict within the department (e.g. people who fall short of the job requirements, disagreements between staff)
- the appraisal of staff and support for CPD
- the monitoring of examination results and the responsibility for target setting for staff and pupils
- the control of the departmental finance and the deployment of resources
- the selection of new members of staff
- the responsibility for the health and safety of all members of the science department and the pupils taught.

Being the HoD requires distinctive skills. The Teacher Training Agency (TTA) (1998) has introduced a set of standards outlining the skills it considers necessary for subject leadership. These can serve as a guide for professional development and help teachers to monitor their own progress. They can also act as a stimulus for investigating the effectiveness of the department in meeting a range of departmental issues. Table 2.1 takes some of the standards for professional knowledge and understanding, and poses some questions that relate to the role of the HoD. Working as a HoD with a group of professional adults is clearly quite different from teaching science to a group of young people, and there is not necessarily a correlation between the skills required for the

Table 2.1 *Examples of professional knowledge required by subject leaders (National Standards for Subject Leaders, TTA, 1998)*

Issues of concern to the HoD	Questions related to the issues of concern
School goals	What does it say in the school development plan that specifically affects the science department? How can the science department contribute to the aims (mission statement) of the school?
Relationship with other subjects	Where does curriculum overlap occur, and what are the consequences for teaching science? (e.g. links with geography, maths, English, D&T) What skills do pupils learn in science that are of use in other curriculum areas?
KS3 National Strategy	What is the impact of the KS3 strategies in literacy and numeracy on pupils' learning in science? How does science contribute to pupils' progress in literacy, numeracy and ICT? What is the impact of the KS3 National Science Strategy on the work of the department?
Subject knowledge	How do you keep up to date with developments in science? How do you keep up to date with the subject knowledge requirements for the different courses being taught?
Pedagogical content knowledge	What does the latest Ofsted/Estyn report say about the teaching of science, and how will this affect your department's work? What professional journals/magazines/newspapers do you read to keep up to date with developments in science teaching?
Assessment	Where can you obtain suitable data to compare the progress of pupils in your science department with similar pupils? How is pupils' progress in science monitored throughout their time in school? What strategies are employed in the case of under-achievement?
ICT	What use is made of ICT in helping the pupils to learn science? How is ICT used to help with departmental administrative duties?
Governing body	How is the governing body informed of the work of the science department?
SEN	What are the implications of the Code of Practice for the science department?
Spiritual, moral and ethical issues	What opportunities are available in the science curriculum for raising these important issues? How well prepared are members of the department to deal with these issues?
Preparation for adult life	How does the work of the science department prepare pupils for lifelong learning? How does the science department try to develop positive attitudes towards science among its pupils?
Health and safety	Are all members of the department aware of their responsibilities with regard to health and safety? Who is qualified to give first aid? Is all the safety equipment in proper working order, and are all the safety manuals and HAZCARDS easy to find?

two jobs. The HoD has to have an appreciation of the contribution each of the branches of science brings to the teaching of the whole subject and gauge how this affects timetabling and resource allocation. In addition to work within the department, the HoD also has to represent the department's interests in the wider context of the school. While science is one of the 'big three', along with English and mathematics, there are inevitably, power struggles whenever there is competition for limited resources, and the HoD must be able to hold his or her own in such a conflict. However, an effective HoD will not simply fight the science own corner in order to reap benefits for the department. In making whole-school decisions, the HoD needs to focus attention on the whole curriculum experienced by the child. In addition, at HoD level discussions need to take place as to how subjects can contribute to areas of school life that are less easy to pinpoint, such as the aesthetic, moral and spiritual needs of the individual. As with any job within teaching, it is not easy to write a list of what the job of head of department entails. It is multifarious, and changes to meet new demands; it involves dealing with people, systems and materials. It is not easy for the HoD to satisfy the demands made by the SMT and at the same time keep the respect of departmental colleagues (Dillon, 2000).

An effective leader is someone with vision, someone who can identify the weaknesses in a department and devise strategies for eliminating them. Harris *et al.* (1996: 33) provide us with a list of characteristic traits of effective leaders gathered from previous research:

- a sense of responsibility
- concern for task completion
- energy
- persistence
- risk-taking
- originality
- self-confidence
- capacity to handle stress
- capacity to influence
- capacity to co-ordinate the effects of others in the achievement of purpose.

Perhaps we can add one more to this list: the capacity to delegate. This doesn't mean giving other members of the department tasks the HoD cannot or does not want to do, but a sharing of responsibility between staff and an appreciation of the different areas of expertise within the group. In a review of different types of leadership, Day (1999: 86) discusses the characteristics of *liberating leaders*, and notes that this type of approach blends in well with current thinking. A culture of collaboration, listening to what members of the team have to say and keeping in tune with the feelings of the department helps to develop self-esteem and raise achievement, and to produce a bonded department (Goodson and Marsh, 1996).

In her research into ineffective departments, Harris (1998) has identified two extreme forms of leadership style that result in poorly run departments. At one end of the scale there are the *laissez-faire* leaders who leave the department to run itself, and at the other there are the *authoritarian* leaders who refuse to delegate and are reluctant to pass on information to colleagues (Table 2.2). The general characteristics of ineffective departments were found to be:

- inappropriate leadership and management styles
- lack of vision for the department and the departmental subject(s)
- poor communication within the department
- poor organisation
- inadequate systems for monitoring and evaluation
- non-collegial departmental climate
- no leading professional within the department
- absence of professional development and learning
- insufficient focus upon teaching and learning.

There has been a steady shift of emphasis in the responsibilities of heads of departments over the years from one where administration and taking a lead role in professional development was at the forefront to one where key managerial tasks are the prominent feature (Wise and Bush, 1999). Unfortunately, in many cases these heads have neither been given the time to accommodate their expanded role nor the training required for effective leadership (Turner, 1996). Brown *et al.* (2000) have identified five key issues that need to be addressed to support departmental heads in their involvement in school improvement. These are:

1 Time – particularly time to complete tasks that can only be done in school.
2 Curriculum stability – there have been too many changes, and heads of departments are sceptical about government promises to reduce change.
3 Professional development – the lack of time and money for CPD and the range of possibilities for professional development.
4 Lack of vision – insufficient quality of vision from the headteacher and SMT. In addition, the departmental heads argued that their vision was undervalued and their professional judgement insufficiently recognised by the SMT, governors and external bodies.
5 Lack of communication – concern about the lack of involvement in the major decision-making processes and having to implement the decisions made by others.

Table 2.2 *Different types of heads of department (Harris, 1998)*

Laissez-faire HoD	Authoritarian HoD
• HoDs talked in terms of shared responsibility and devolution of tasks	• HoDs talked in terms of ownership of the department and leading from the front
• Absence of departmental planning and cohesiveness	• HoDs were over-controlling, over-anxious and reluctant to delegate
• Departments lacked internal cohesion	• HoD became isolated
• Teachers either worked in isolation or formed cliques	• Low level of support, interaction and communication between departmental members

Planning for departmental improvement

The approach to planning promoted by the DfES and others (see page 9) is one of analysing the situation and setting targets for improvement. This has a certain logic that is likely to appeal to most science teachers. However, there will be some who prefer to start the process from the standpoint of their vision of the department and the desired goals to be achieved in the future. This approach tends to be more inspirational and motivating, as it is focussed on positive ideals and not on 'what sort of things have we been doing badly?'. A possible drawback is that the approach may lead to isolated developments and subsequent mismatch with the overall school improvement policy. At some stage in the planning procedure it is important to marry up departmental concerns with whole-school issues.

The idea of having a vision for the science department is useful in that it helps to identify those things that are really important (see examples in Table 2.3). It can be related to fundamental things to do with teaching science (e.g. the appropriateness of the curriculum for the less able, the relevance of the science taught, conceptual development) rather than the day-to-day issues, which are equally important but need to be put on one side to ensure that they don't stifle creative thinking. Initial ideas about the future of the department are likely, but not exclusively, to be formulated by the HoD, and the next stage in the process must be communicating these to all members of the team in a way that encourages personal ownership of the ideals (see the section on teamwork below).

It is useful to go through a number of clearly defined steps to analyse the current situation, to ensure that a clear and balanced view is obtained. If the data-gathering is left too open there is the possibility that people will follow their pet idiosyncrasies, making it difficult to see the whole picture. A good way of starting this is to carry out a SWOT analysis, identifying the **S**trengths, **W**eaknesses, **O**pportunities and **T**hreats facing the department (Table 2.4). Starting with a list of what the department is good at helps to create the right sort of atmosphere for positive planning and persuades people to be more open about identifying weaknesses. Doing this at whole-department level can produce a wealth of information and identify issues that might not have occurred

Table 2.3 *Possible plans for the future*

Now	In the future
Pupils are 'spoon fed'	Pupils take more responsibility for their own learning
Pupils do not respond positively to science	Pupils enjoy science and have a positive attitude towards the subject
Pupils fail to appreciate the nature of science as a subject	Pupils understand the nature of the subject
54% of pupils get A*–C grades in science	60% of pupils get A*–C grades in science
Pupils use ICT for writing up investigations and data-logging	Pupils use ICT in a variety of ways to help them learn science
Formative assessment strategies are not well developed	Pupils receive oral and written feedback on how to improve

Table 2.4 *An example of a SWOT analysis identifying the current state of the science department*

Strengths	Weaknesses
Members of science team work well together	Number of pupils choosing A-level physics
Good ICT facilities in all laboratories	Pupils' ability to write up investigations
Good liaison between Mrs P and SENCO	Quality of the software available for KS3
Detail in KS3 scheme of work	Text book for KS4 does not cover all aspects of
Teachers teaching their subject specialism	the GCSE specification
Improvement in KS3 results	Method of recording pupils' progress at both
Helpful technical staff	key stages

Opportunities	Threats
Improved reading ability of pupils in Y7	Decrease in departmental budget
Helpful KS3 science strategy advisor	School inspection in two years
PGCE student to start next term	Miss T promoted to SMT (reduction in science
Mr K to start MA course	teaching staff)
Health and safety course for technicians run by LEA	Mr J looking for new post

to the HoD. However, there are sensitive issues, such as weaknesses in a teacher's performance, that it would be inappropriate to raise in an open forum. In order to ensure that all aspects of the department's work are considered it is appropriate for the HoD to produce a private SWOT analysis, taking the points raised by members of the department and adding confidential information. Clearly, the more precise you are in the statements made, the less confusion there is likely to be when the points are revisited at a future date and the easier it will be to identify an improvement strategy. Statements such as determining a weakness as the 'teaching resources at KS4' need to be refined to identify which resources are poor. Further auditing of the current situation can be done through other departmental review mechanisms, e.g. structured group discussions, and through an ongoing process of monitoring teaching performance and use of resources. The auditing process is complete only when you are happy that you have clarified what is wrong with the present system and have communicated this to all members of the departmental team.

The next stage is to look at the evidence from the audit and the existing whole-school documents (e.g. School Development Plan, Action Plan, Mission Statement, policy documents) and start to put together an improvement plan for the department. This is a matter of prioritising issues and making decisions about when things should be done. There are two useful mechanisms for doing this, a force-field analysis and a priority analysis (Field *et al.*, 2000). In a force-field analysis, each issue is examined and consideration is given to factors (and their relative strengths) that will help to push forward the improvement and those that will oppose the change. In Table 2.5, an example of an appraisal of the situation with regard to using ICT in science identifies the strength of the driving forces that could lead to an improved situation, together with the problems that face the department. The next stage would be to consider how best to make use of the departmental strengths e.g. the expertise of the new staff and the liaison with the ICT co-ordinator to help to reduce or eliminate some of the problems. A priority analysis (Table 2.6) is helpful in determining when things should be done by giving some sort of value to the urgency of dealing with the situation and its

Table 2.5 *Force-field analysis for the introduction of ICT into KS3 (s, strong; m, medium; w, weak force)*

 Driving forces    Restraining forces

Driving forces	Restraining forces
What and who will help in achieving the targets?	What or who will prevent or slow down the process?
Three 'new' computers in all labs (s)	Difficulty in booking computer room for whole-class work (m)
One set of data-logging equipment available for each lab (m)	Always some computers and/or printers not working (s)
Good support from ICT co-ordinator (s)	Three members of the department show no commitment to using ICT in their lessons (m)
Everyone has received some ICT training (m)	
The two NQTs have considerable ICT expertise and are enthusiastic about using computers (s)	The quality of the training has not always been of a high standard (m)
Opportunities for using ICT appear in the SoW (m)	ICT activities have been added on rather than fully integrated (s)
Department can book the interactive whiteboard and data projector (m)	Opportunities for using interactive whiteboard and data projector have not been identified as yet (s)
New software purchased annually (m)	Booking system is in chaos (m)
Pupils are enthusiastic about using ICT (s)	Software purchase takes a significant part of the budget (m)

Table 2.6 *Making judgements to help prioritise issues*

Issue	How urgent?			How important?		
	not very	moderate	very	not very	moderate	very
Number of investigations in Y7						
Pupils' understanding of graphs in Y11						
The lack of resources for teaching circuits in Y8						

degree of importance. In making decisions about the relative urgency and importance you may need to consider each of the groups of people you are dealing with – e.g. the pupils, the SMT, members of the science department, parents. An item that can be classified as 'not very important' from the standpoint of one group may be 'very important' from another point of view. Your professional judgement will help you make the crucial decisions, bearing in mind that the pupils are the most important group for you to consider.

Having analysed the situation and decided on the priorities, you are now in a position to plan for change. This is best done by composing some sort of action plan listing what is going to be done, by whom and by when. Other than in cases involving confidential issues, it is important that all the steps are identified and are clear to everyone. It is then a matter of people working towards their goals and closely monitoring what is going on. Clarity can be improved by using the target-setting principles and writing the action plan in such a way that the goals are SMART, i.e.

Specific	e.g. increase the number of investigations in Y7 from three to five
Measurable	i.e. involve numerical values
Achievable	need to take into account a whole range of school factors
Realistic	e.g. judged by comparing performance with other departments
Time-related	i.e. set a deadline.

Progress will not be smooth, it may exhibit spurts and periods of sluggish movement, perhaps even to an extent that the change may be seen to be having a negative effect. It is a matter of believing in your convictions and having the courage to see it through. Keeping a check on the progress can be done through a variety of methods, such as:

- observing one another's lessons to identify examples of good practice that can be shared
- analysing assessment data
- holding review meetings to determine each member of the department's perspective on the situation
- asking a member of the SMT to review progress.

Observing colleagues teach and co-teaching is a relatively new phenomenon. In the past, teachers have been reluctant to observe colleagues and have preferred to monitor through a process of checking exercise books, lesson plans and assessments. The introduction of the National KS3 strategy and collaborative teaching during initial teacher education has given increased emphasis to the idea of teachers working together in a classroom. Teachers are beginning to see the benefits of providing feedback to each other in a professional and non-threatening way.

A slightly different approach to auditing was taken by a new HoD. As a new member of staff, he was required to turn the department around following a very poor report from a previous Ofsted inspection. Carr and Storey (2001) report on how the involvement of an outsider can help. Working with a university colleague, the HoD identified strengths and weaknesses by asking members of the department to complete a review form indicating their views about:

- areas in which the department was very successful/successful
- areas in which the department was successful but which members of the department would like to see developed
- areas in which the department was unsatisfactory and which members of the department viewed as requiring attention.

The returned audits were analysed by the university colleague and were followed by a series of interviews to increase the depth of understanding of the issues. Four key interrelated issues for improvement were identified and a plan was drawn up to meet the concerns. This illustrates how an external person, acting as a critical friend with no

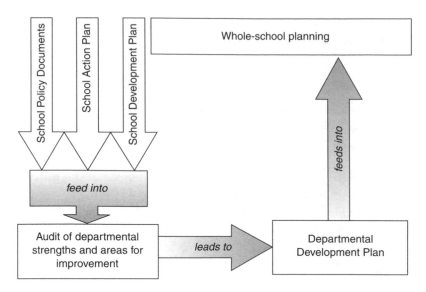

Figure 2.1 *Inter-relationship between departmental and whole-school planning*

predetermined interest in the situation, can bring in new ideas and a fresh perspective on the situation.

This process of planning for departmental improvement is the backbone of school improvement, and may be the initial stimulus for change within the whole-school environment. There is a synergy between what goes on at both levels, so it is not simply a matter of departments being told what to do; departments influence the key decision-making and planning for the whole school (Figure 2.1).

From planning to policies

It is important that policy writing isn't seen as just another piece of bureaucracy that has to be done to satisfy the powers that be. Policy writing serves a number of purposes, it can:

- help to determine the nature of the department's work
- act as a focus for departmental discussion, initially in formulating the policy and later in reviewing work
- help to provide consistency in approach
- identify how the department relates to whole-school policies and the mission statement
- indicate to other interested groups (e.g. the SMT, governors, parents, Ofsted) that the department knows what it is doing.

There are no fixed ideas as to what should be present in a policy, but it should initially contain some indication of what the department sees as important, phrased in terms of vision, aims and objectives. This should be followed by a description as to how these aims are to be achieved, perhaps with some examples and cross-referencing to other departmental, school or public documents (e.g. schemes of work, the National Curriculum, Ofsted reports, School Development Plan, LEA policies). The National College for School Leadership (NCSL) has produced a number of sample policies that are worth consulting to help you plan one to fit your situation (see http://www.ncsl.org.uk/index.cfm?pageid=managing-policies-index).

A science department may have policies on each of the following issues:

- health and safety
- teaching and learning
- practical work
- ICT
- the control of pupils' behaviour
- assessment and monitoring of pupils' progress
- out of school visits.

Policies can help to hold together cross-curricular issues within the school, such as literacy, numeracy and ICT. The document should give an indication as to how and where the issue could be incorporated into the teaching, and signify the level of commitment the department can offer. In the case of ICT, a policy statement will help to co-ordinate the way in which pupils are taught in timetabled ICT lessons with ICT in science (Kennewell *et al.*, 2000).

Developing a change-friendly culture

It is more than likely that not everyone will see the need for change from the same point of view as the HoD, and there may be a number of members of the department whose initial reaction will be to put up barriers. Teachers, like other learners, differ in their preparedness to engage in change and the rate in which they implement it. This preparedness is related to teachers' implicit beliefs about teaching and learning and their relevant conceptual knowledge (Munro, 1999). Scott and Jaffe (1989) have produced a useful model of possible phases that people go through when asked to change their practice, and the four phases are listed below with an indication as to what a HoD could do to counter the resistance (Field *et al.*, 2000: 136):

1 **Denial.** This is characterised by a non-acceptance that the change is necessary. For example, the teacher might say:

> You are misinterpreting the results (from the Ofsted inspection, examination scores etc.)
> We don't need to do this now (the problem will resolve itself in time)
> It's not our problem (it is a whole-school issue and there is nothing we can do about it)
> We don't have the resources

The HoD should be forceful in:

- pointing out that the evidence indicating that a change is necessary is correct and is directly relevant to the work of the department
- indicating why the change needs to take place now to help the current generation of pupils
- reminding staff that change is a necessary part of teaching in order to meet the needs of individuals.

2 **Resistance.** This is characterised by a non-acceptance that the new order will be no better than the present situation. For example, teachers may say:

> How do you know it will work?
> Let's form a working party
> We tried this once before and it didn't work
> It won't work because ... (goes on to give a list of reasons as to why the initiative is doomed to failure)
> I think this is a good idea but ... (gives a list as above)
> I have been doing it this way for years and I'm too old to try anything new
> I am not sure I can do that; it's not my style.

The HoD should:

- listen carefully to what the teacher says and offer praise for the good work he or she does at present (try to maintain the teacher's self-esteem)
- be sensitive to the situation and avoid getting into arguments over whether the change will work or not
- present any evidence to show how similar changes have worked elsewhere.

3 **Exploration.** This is characterised by an interest in the possible benefits of the change. For example, teachers may say:

> OK, let's give it a go, but ... (I'm not going to accept any responsibility if it fails) (do it on a small scale first)
> Why don't we ... (The teacher starts to make suggestions for the way forward)

The HoD should:

- maintain enthusiasm and optimism about the change, and get things moving as soon as possible
- involve all members of the department associated with the change
- continue to be positive even when it looks like things are not working out as planned.

4 **Commitment.** This is characterised by a willingness to be involved with the change and a commitment to see it through. Teachers:

- look for guidance from the HoD, support materials and Inset courses
- consider adjusting aspects of their work (e.g. time, priorities) to incorporate the change
- make positive comments about the change.

The HoD should:

- set time aside to support and encourage members of the department (listening carefully to what they have to say)
- make sure that adequate resources are in place when required.

Gray and Wilcox (1995) propose that in order for change to work, teachers need to consider:

- choosing a medium to long-term timescale – not just a few months
- collegiate ownership – for improvement to take off, a body of staff within the school needs to agree that here is a problem that needs to be tackled, that there are some strategies that could be explored, and that they will search out the solutions for a while
- prioritising – directing staff energy and time towards the problems, and targeting problems by identifying that some are more important than others.

There is a danger that some people will believe that bringing about a change will solve a multitude of problems. For example, a department may decide to introduce CASE into KS3 with the hope that it will improve examination results. This may or may not result in the desired outcome due to many other factors within the school. Any one change will have an impact on the way other things are done within the department. How does the introduction of CASE affect the way that teachers function in other lessons, and how often are pupils given the opportunity to put thinking skills into action? Measuring the success of the change is therefore quite difficult, and you should not be disheartened if the initial results do not match your expectations.

Team building

In an effective department colleagues work together as a team to achieve common goals, and there is a spirit that everyone is working towards things that will benefit the whole group in addition to the benefits brought to individuals through closer collaboration. A good team uses the skills and attributes of the individual members, and features most of the following characteristics (Kemp and Nathan, 1989):

1 **Shared clear objectives and agreed goals.** Members of the team have a common vision of science teaching and what the department is trying to achieve.
2 **Clear procedures.** Procedures should be in place for academic, pastoral and administrative work.
3 **Regular progress reviews.** A forward-looking department needs to check periodically that it is keeping on track.
4 **A good leader.** The HoD leads by example and encourages all members of the team to use their strengths for the benefit of the department.
5 **Open lines of communication.** Members of the team talk to each other about teaching and learning issues.
6 **A climate of support and trust.** Members of the team feel comfortable in giving and receiving help and advice.
7 **Recognition that conflict is inevitable.** Members of the team are not always going to agree, but such differences of opinion are normal and it is better to discuss these openly than bottle up resentment.

8 **Concern about the personal and career aspirations of its members.** Members of the team are encouraged and supported in their continual professional development.

Teamwork is recognised as being an important issue in terms of threshold assessment, and it is up to the HoD to encourage staff to take collective responsibility for improving the teaching in the department. Teachers by their very nature rarely boast about their talents, and are frequently unaware of the contributions they can make to the department as a whole. Smith (2000) suggests that in preparing for threshold assessment, teachers should identify the range of activities they are involved with in a school and follow this up with a review of all the teams, working parties, committees etc. that each individual belongs to. In this analysis Smith suggests that teachers identify their contribution to the work of the team and how they help the team to achieve its goals. This type of activity helps to raise personal awareness and promotes a sense of responsibility and ownership of the work of the team. Ownership can be further enhanced by giving members of the team specific tasks to do and by remembering to thank them for their contributions. Everyone in the team should be seen as important; it is all too easy to forget to include someone in the discussions, possibly a new member of staff or someone who is generally quiet in meetings. Frequently new contributors can put new perspectives on old arguments and help to turn things around.

Technicians are important members of the science team, and are crucial to the successful running of the department. Experienced technicians not only prepare equipment for practical activities, they will also try out experiments, test equipment, order new stock and help to organise the teacher's day. It is no wonder that there is wholesale panic when the technician is absent. It is crucial that technicians are involved in the decision-making process whenever the issue under discussion impinges on their work. Sometimes this will be in a formal situation and other times it may be informal, but on the whole, in an effective department there will be a sense of community and co-operation. Busher and Blease (2000) describe this as a collaborative culture based on:

- trust between people
- delegation of functions depending on people's abilities to carry them out, rather than on status
- values of co-operation and shared purpose
- particular styles of leadership which emphasise inclusivity of purpose
- a sense of belonging to a community.

As HoD, you are going to identify things that need doing within the department. For example, you may have identified weaknesses in the KS3 science scheme and you would like to change it. It is likely that some members of the team will also have identified the same points, but there will be others who are happy with what they do, probably because they have all the materials prepared for the existing scheme. Simply telling the members of the department that you are going to replace the old scheme with a new one is very likely to result in resentment and resistance. You will have to prepare a good case, identifying the faults in the existing scheme and pointing out the advantages of the proposed scheme. It might be that there are several new schemes to choose from, and if so members of the team could be given the responsibility of identifying the advantages themselves in preparation for a departmental meeting. In any case it is a good idea to ask members of the group to work on specific tasks on the new resource, such as:

- the match with the current NC requirements
- the overall philosophy behind a book and how it presents science as a subject
- the variety of teaching approaches used
- the types of practical work suggested and the resources required
- the reading level
- how the book promotes literacy, numeracy and ICT
- how the book caters for different ability groups.

The tone of the review meeting needs to be very positive and centred on the new opportunities the proposed scheme can bring to the department. This could be followed by looking at what can be salvaged from the old scheme. This bringing in of what is good from the existing work helps to limit the rearguard action and gives a sense of not having to start completely from scratch.

Departmental meetings play a useful role in keeping members of the team informed, and provide an opportunity for discussion and transmitting a sense of vision. You may find it useful to consider the following points when organising and running these meetings:

1 Prepare an agenda to avoid people rambling during the meeting, and make sure that you stick to it.
2 Keep items of information to the minimum, as these can be disseminated more efficiently by other means.
3 Make sure that you have thought through the discussion items, particularly the controversial ones, and have supporting documentation to hand.
4 Have a time limit for the meeting and keep to it; hopefully this will sharpen people's thinking.
5 Start the meeting on time, even if not everyone is there. If you wait until everyone arrives, people will be late coming to the next meeting.
6 At the end of each key point (agenda item), summarise the decisions.
7 Keep a record of the decisions of the meeting. It is important that someone takes the minutes – preferably not the chairperson, who will need to concentrate on managing the meeting. Some of the decisions may be in the form of action points, with the name of the key person next to the point. At the next meeting, these points should be checked for completion of the work.

As mentioned earlier, conflict is inevitable. However, there are things that individuals can do in order to maintain an agreeable atmosphere. For example, simple daily routines, such as the manner of greeting colleagues, can make a significant difference to the harmony of the department. Gold (1998) points out that important messages about including or excluding people from shared activity can be conveyed by the following:

- whether or not a greeting is given
- where it is given
- whether it is accompanied with a smile
- whether eye contact is made
- who initiates it
- the tone of voice employed.

In summary, to run an effective team a HoD needs to:

- establish clear lines of communication
- foster trust
- build bridges between individuals through developmental activity
- delegate leadership tasks
- seek support
- be a team player as well as a team manager (Harris and Hammond, 2002).

Time management

Finally in this chapter we return to the problem that faces us all; the lack of time. It is very easy to get into a situation where you become inundated with work and start to lose your effectiveness as a HoD. You have got to ask yourself why has this happened and what are you going to do about it. Here are a few suggestions:

- You may have taken on tasks because you thought you were the only person in the department who could do them. This is probably not true. You could delegate work to others either because you see that they have the time to do it or because you see that it would be useful for their professional development. Cutting back on your workload will probably result in you being a better manager. Ofsted has given guidance for teachers on the use of support staff to save time on routine administrative tasks (see http://www.teachernet.gov.uk/remodelling).
- Prioritise what you have to do. Consider how long you should realistically take to do each task.
- You need to have an efficient way of dealing with the large amount of paperwork that will come your way. Reduce clutter and keep your desk as clear as possible. Throw away or redistribute all paper that is not of direct relevance. Only file papers if you will need to refer to them later. Try to deal with requests for information straight away; don't let your in-tray get too full.

References

Brown, M., Rutherford, D. and Boyle, B. (2000) 'Leadership and school improvement: The role of the head of department in UK secondary schools', *School Effectiveness and School Improvement*, **11**(2), 237–258.

Busher, H. and Blease, D. (2000) 'Growing collegial cultures in subject departments in secondary schools: working with science staff', *School Leadership and Management*, **20**(1), 99–112.

Carr, B. and Story, A. (2001) 'The role of the head of faculty in school improvement', *Management in Education*, **15**(5), 23–24.

Day, C. (1999) Developing Teachers: The Challenges of Lifelong Learning, London: Falmer Press.

Dillon, J. (2000) 'Managing the science department', in Osborne, J. and Monk, M. (eds) *Good Practice in Science Teaching*, Buckingham: Open University Press.

Field, K., Holden, P. and Lawlor, H. (2000) *Effective Subject Leadership*, London: Routledge.

Gold, A. (1998) *Head of Department*, London: Cassell.

Goodson, I.F. and Marsh, C.J. (1996) *Studying School Subjects: A Guide*, London: Falmer Press.

Gray, J. and Wilcox, B. (1995) *'Good School, Bad School', Evaluating Performance and Encouraging Improvement*, Buckingham: Open University Press.

Harris, A. (1998) 'Improving ineffective departments in secondary schools', *Educational Management and Administration*, **26**(3), 269–278.

Harris, A. and Hammond, P. (2002) 'Team leadership', *Managing Schools Today*, 33–34.

Harris, A., Jamieson, I. and Russ, J. (1996) *School Effectiveness and School Improvement: A Practical Guide*, London: Pitman.

Hull, R. and Adams, H. (1981) *Decisions in the Science Department*, Hatfield: ASE.

Kemp, R. and Nathan, M. (1989) *Middle Management in Schools: A Survival Guide*, Hemel Hempstead: Simon & Schuster.

Kennewell, S., Parkinson, J. and Tanner, H. (2000) *Developing the ICT Capable School*, London: RoutledgeFalmer.

Munro, J. (1999) 'Learning more about learning improves teaching', *School Effectiveness and School Improvement*, **10**(2), 151–171.

Scott, C. and Jaffe, D. (1989) *Managing Organisational Change*, London: Kogan Page.

Smith, R. (2000) *Performance Management and Threshold Assessment, Pack 2: Class and Subject Teachers*, Cambridge: Pearson.

TTA (1998) National Standards for Subject Leaders, London: TTA. http://www.canteach.gov.uk/publications/community/standards-sen/subject.pdf.

Turner, C.K. (1996) 'The roles and tasks of a subject head of department in secondary schools in England and Wales: a neglected area of research?', *School Organisation*, **16**(20), 203–218.

Wise, C. and Bush, T. (1999) 'From teacher to manager: the role of academic middle manager in secondary schools', *Educational Research*, **41**(2), 183–195.

CHAPTER 3

Self-improvement

Like it or not, we are living in a time of immense technological change; the world of education is being asked to grapple with challenges and opportunities which almost boggle the imagination.

Lord Puttnam of Queensgate (DfEE, 1999: 21)

Just how do teachers get better at their job? If you ask teachers this question, many of them will give you the reply that it comes with experience or you learn on the job. To a large extent this is true, but certain teachers don't make a great deal of progress in their learning and some get very fixed ideas about what constitutes a good lesson, even though this may be far from the truth. In many instances teachers' progress tends to hit a plateau. Teaching, along with most other facets of life, is changing at a very rapid pace, and teachers need to think about how they improve their effectiveness to meet the new demands. This chapter provides you with a framework for evaluating your teaching and reflecting on what you do.

Making judgements about your own performance

In the main, teachers tend to work in isolation in their own classrooms and thus have difficulty in making judgements on the effectiveness of their own teaching (CST, 2000). There will be times when the teacher is observed by a senior colleague or an inspector, but is this one-off 'performance' typical of his or her usual classroom work or is it a 'special' lesson? In the present climate, effectiveness is commonly associated with measurable outcomes such as examination results and staying-on rates. However, clearly other things that cannot be easily measured, such as enjoyment and attitude towards the subject, are equally important. Effectiveness can also be judged in terms of teachers' responsibilities, such as:

- the degree of co-operation with colleagues and the SMT
- the completion of routine administrative tasks
- the level of organisational competence (extracurricular activities, field trips, parents' evenings etc.)

- the extent to which the teacher is ready to react positively to unexpected demands from colleagues, the education system or pupils.

More commonly effectiveness is seen in terms of personal achievements or character-istics, such as:

- pupils' performance in examinations
- classroom control
- completing the course in the time allocated
- being open minded about the 'flavour of the month' initiative
- being a warm, encouraging, courteous person with a sense of humour
- the frequency of using good teaching strategies.

(Brown and McIntyre, 1992: 22)

A teacher needs to know what is effective on a day to day basis – what sort of teaching is likely to lead to good results, an enjoyable classroom atmosphere and interest in science. Some teachers have very fixed views about the make up of a good lesson, based on their experience, their views about what is important in science and their perspective of pupils' learning. In order to obtain a more objective view of your effec-tiveness it is worthwhile looking at characteristics that have been identified by research as working well. In addition to some fairly obvious factors, such as good attendance and punctuality, there are a number of key teaching strategies that have been identified. These have been put in the form of a self-evaluation checklist in Table 3.1. This shouldn't be treated as a simple tick-box exercise but as an opportunity to think about each of the issues and to ask yourself why you do certain things and don't do others. Following on from that, it could be used to help you identify targets for improvement. In addition to this it is worth taking into account things that pupils like and dislike about their lessons, many of which are summarised in Table 3.2. From the list of dislikes it is clear that teachers are not getting the right sort of message across about science, and much of this book is devoted to planning and teaching methods that make science an interesting subject to study. It is a combination of the positive factors listed in the two tables, when used consistently over a prolonged period of time, that gives rise to effective teaching. A good teacher creates an environment where pupils are keen to learn, and provides them with the means to do it.

Hargreaves and Fullan (1992) point out that teachers require the following in order to make effective teaching possible:

- sufficient opportunities to learn and acquire the knowledge and skills of effective teaching
- opportunities to develop personal qualities; the commitment and self understanding essential to becoming a sensitive and flexible teacher
- a working environment that is supportive and not restrictive of professional learn-ing and continuous improvement.

Table 3.1 *A self-evaluation checklist on teacher effectiveness (based on Harris et al., 1996: 60; Teddlie and Reynolds, 2000: 146)*

Main question	Subsidiary questions	Always	Sometimes	Never
Do you maximise the use of the lesson time?	Do you start and finish lessons on time? Do you minimise the time spent on administration? Do you minimise the time spent on discipline? Are transitions between activities carried out efficiently? Do you pace the learning appropriately?			
How well organised are you?	Are lessons planned in sufficient detail? Are all your resources to hand during the lesson? Are you knowledgeable about the subject content?			
How clear are you?	Does everyone understand your explanations? Do you convey the learning objectives to the pupils? Do pupils know what is expected of them?			
How effectively do you monitor pupils' progress?	Do you ask appropriate questions of most pupils in a lesson? Do you give time to pupils to respond and do you listen carefully to what they say? Do you provide useful written feedback to pupils, including targets? Do you teach pupils how to monitor their own progress?			
Are the tasks set for pupils appropriate?	Do you organise and structure the tasks to help pupils work through them? Are pupils kept on-task during the lesson? Do you set tasks that address higher-order as well as lower-order objectives? Do the tasks promote progression in pupils' learning? Are tasks set that teach pupils metacognitive strategies?			
Do you create a learning atmosphere?	Are pupils willing to ask you questions? Does the teaching room have a pleasant working ambience?			
Are you reflective?	Do you evaluate your lessons and plan for improvement? Do you discuss teaching strategies with colleagues? Do you put into practice ideas and suggestions from INSET courses? Do you work towards the targets identified in your appraisal meeting?			

Table 3.2 *Pupils' likes and dislikes (based on Brown and McIntyre, 1992; Osborne and Collins, 2001)*

Pupils' likes
- Practical work
- Certain science topics (e.g. human biology); aspects conceived as being more modern, such as the effects of drugs on humans; mixing chemicals and seeing the effects for themselves (particularly liked the element of danger); space
- The creation of a relaxed and enjoyable atmosphere in the classroom
- The retention of control in the classroom
- The presentation of work in an interesting and motivating way – good teachers are enthusiastic about their subject
- Teachers who provide conditions that help pupils understand the work
- Clear instructions about what they have to do and what they should achieve
- Teachers who know their pupils and understand their capabilities
- Teachers who help when a pupil has difficulties (an approachable teacher) and teachers who encourage pupils to raise expectations of themselves (being challenged and stimulated to learn more)
- Teachers who listen and make fair decisions
- Teachers who are knowledgeable about their subject and teachers that have personal talents that they bring to the life of the school

Pupils' dislikes
- The apparent 'low tech' nature of some of the subject matter, e.g. the blast furnace
- The sense that they have to rush through the curriculum (there isn't enough time, everything has to be done in a rush)
- The remoteness of some aspects of science (particularly aspects of chemistry, e.g. the periodic table)
- Copying (seen as 'boring writing')
- Being told to accept things rather than have them explained
- The emphasis on learning lots of facts
- The repetition of work
- A lack of time for discussion and putting forward your own views
- Lack of opportunity to be creative (work done within fairly tight limits, pupils not given the opportunity to express themselves)
- The fragmentation of the curriculum (poor links between the different components of a science course)

Getting over the brick wall

Changing your teaching methods is rightly seen as a risky operation. Teachers can become very content with what they do, and while they may be prepared to drop things (e.g. do less practical work) they are reluctant to take on something new (e.g. use ICT). When people are faced with the prospect of change there is always apprehension, and questions in their mind about the likelihood of success or failure. As shown in Chapters 1 and 2, change for groups of people and institutions can come up against considerable resistance and are thus quite difficult to implement. Here we are concerned with changing personal practices and, as long as you don't have the attitude depicted in the left-hand column of Table 3.3, you are likely to find the process of implementing new ideas refreshing and rewarding (see right-hand column of Table 3.3). The initial stages are going to be difficult, and you may feel that you are constantly banging your head against a brick wall as you try to get everything together and elicit help from your colleagues. Munro (1999) has identified six conditions that are necessary for teacher change. They are when teachers:

Table 3.3 *Attitudes towards change (Newton and Tarrant, 1992; Whitaker, 1993)*

Comments made by those resistant to change	Positive reasons for change
We tried this before and it didn't work	It can be interesting and exciting
We don't have the time	It encourages teachers to reflect on the
We don't have the resources	effectiveness of what they do
We've managed so far without it	It ensures that the teaching matches
It won't work in our department	developments in the curriculum
Let's wait until things settle down	It can help to promote teamwork as members of
We've always done it this way before and no one	the department work together to implement the
has complained	change
You can't teach an old dog new tricks	It fosters personal and professional development
Not that again!	It helps to give teachers greater confidence in
	their own ability

1 Have the opportunity to learn through active construction processes
2 See that their existing implicit knowledge about learning is valued
3 Frame up goals or challenges for learning
4 Have the opportunity for individual and collegiate collaborative activities
5 Engage in self-direction and systematic reflection on their practice
6 Explore and demonstrate new teaching procedures in their classroom.

As an individual, a number of things must come into play if change is to happen (Figure 3.1). You must feel motivated to initiate the change. This frequently comes from working in a culture where people recognise the need for improvement, but it can also come from personal drive and ambition. Empowerment is about taking on the responsibility for personal growth in the realisation that it is up to us as individuals to develop our own creativity. Having the right level of resources and time are important factors in bringing about change. Sometimes they are not easy to come by, and those who are less motivated quickly abandon the change process. Throughout this chapter there are references to the important role played by other individuals in helping you to think things through and keep you focussed. In addition to all this, you need to develop the skills associated with recognising and understanding what goes on in a classroom – which is something that can be more difficult than it may at first appear.

Teacher as learner

Teachers entering the profession come equipped with a number of coping procedures that they have practised during their PGCE course. They have routines that work for them, they have built up a number of response strategies that enable them to deal with classroom situations, and they have a view about the purpose of teaching pupils science. Many, if not all, of these new teachers will have been introduced to the ideas of adopting a reflective approach to their teaching and learning from their experiences. The introduction of the induction year and early professional development gives ample opportunity to extend these principles and provide a sound basis for continued teacher learning.

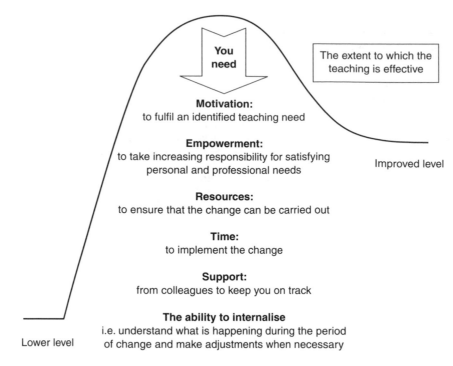

Figure 3.1 *Significant factors required for change in effectiveness*

Learning about teaching is not as simple as many outside the profession seem to think. It is the number of closely interconnecting strands of teacher knowledge together with an understanding of individual personal traits that makes learning about teaching so challenging. Shulman (1987) has identified seven knowledge bases that teachers draw on in their daily work (see Figure 3.2), and each area of knowledge is insufficient on its own for effective teaching to occur. Pedagogical-content knowledge can only be achieved if the teacher has a sound understanding of the types of knowledge listed on the left-hand side of the figure and the nature of the interplay between them. Each of the areas is likely to be the basis for some professional development during the course of a teacher's career. It is sometimes assumed that teachers have good subject knowledge; after all they have a degree in science. However, most science teachers have significant gaps in their understanding of some science concepts when they enter the profession, and do not fully appreciate the nature of science as a field of learning. An individual can go on teaching the 'wrong science' for years unless there is some means of identifying these deficiencies. Some types of knowledge, such as general pedagogical knowledge and knowledge of educational contexts, are built up over time, and the general assumption is that teachers become expert as a result of being in classrooms for so long. However, experience alone does not necessarily result in an understanding of the issues, and nor does it necessarily provide the teacher with the wherewithal to improve. Perhaps the most common type of professional development is concerned with keeping up to date with the revisions in the curriculum and examination specifications, together with the new teaching resources that accompany

Subject knowledge Knowledge of science content, the links between concepts and an understanding about the nature of the subject	Pedagogical-content knowledge Knowing how to teach science effectively, e.g. explain concepts, select appropriate models
General pedagogical knowledge Knowledge of dealing with pupils, e.g. classroom management, developing appropriate relationships	
Curriculum knowledge Knowledge about the National Curriculum, public examinations, the school's SoW, textbooks etc.	
Knowledge about learners Understanding the needs of the different types of learners in any one class	
Knowledge of educational contexts An understanding of educational institutions and situations, e.g. different types of schools, learning outside school, learning cultures	
Knowledge of educational goals and values An understanding of the aims of education and the philosophy of education	

Figure 3.2 *Types of teacher knowledge according to Shulman (1987)*

these changes. The take-home message from these updating courses is frequently concerned with 'what new things should be taught' and 'what things are no longer required'. What tends to be missing is an emphasis on any change in the overall philosophy of the course and how it should be taught. For example, Scientific Enquiry, in its various incarnations since the introduction of the National Curriculum in 1989, has never been fully implemented in most secondary schools. Teachers, like other learners, differ in their preparedness to engage in change and the rate at which they implement it (Munro, 1999).

Unlike their pupils, teachers don't have the luxury of day to day lessons on how to teach, so much of their learning must be through self-reflection. A teacher needs to develop the ability to be able to 'read' what is going on in the classroom and make judgements on the value or effectiveness of particular actions. This involves the use of what can be simply described as 'with-it-ness' type of intelligence. The teacher has not only got to take in the situation but also to see through what is happening and draw reasoned conclusions. The essence of 'with-it-ness' is probably a mixture of:

- recognising relationships between individuals
- appreciating that there are many factors that affect pupils' behaviour
- knowing the best time to do certain things in a lesson
- picking up signals from pupils' body language or behaviour

- appreciating the importance of being fit and healthy
- understanding situations and knowing how to deal with them
- analysing teaching and know what to do to improve.

A considerable amount of research has been carried out over the last 30 years or so emphasising the importance of critical reflection on teachers' learning. Donald Schön has performed much of the work and the term 'reflective practitioner' (Schön, 1983) is a common phrase used in education, which is synonymous with good practice. According to Schön, reflective practitioners display knowledge-in-action, reflection-in-action and reflection-on-action (Table 3.4). In many respects this is a very useful model for teacher development but there are a number of drawbacks (Bell and Gilbert, 1996), including the possibility that such a process tends to indicate that the problem is due to the teacher, department or school. However, the problem may not be resolvable by individuals; it may be something that is more deep-seated in the social and political system. Reflection-on-action works best when there is someone available to support the learning – someone who can scaffold the learning (see page 96) by giving the right sort of input, asking the right sort of questions and directing the 'learning teacher' to appropriate resources. Such a person can be called a tutor, a mentor or a coach. Each title can have a slightly different meaning in terms of the nature of the relationship: tutoring, on the whole, involves supplying information and making comments on the teaching; mentoring involves more listening, understanding and helping the teacher to reflect; and coaching goes one step further and involves support and guidance at classroom level.

Reflection is an ongoing process, sometimes taking place on a rather shallow level due to lack of time, but at other times involving considerable thought and discussion with others. Because of the lack of time so often cited by teachers there can be a

Table 3.4 *Types of reflection*

	Characteristics	How formed
Knowledge-in-action	The actions, recognitions and judgements that teachers know how to carry out spontaneously. The actions are intuitive, tacit and intangible	Teachers are frequently unaware that they have 'picked up' these ideas about teaching. They may originate from experience in the classroom or out of the classroom
Reflection-in-action	This is where the teacher thinks about the knowledge-in-action event and questions why a particular course of action was taken. It is a process of 'thinking on your feet', quickly making decisions and acting on them	The process can come from experience or by learning from others (observation of teaching followed by discussion). It requires the teacher to have a reasonable degree of intuitive and intellectual intelligence
Reflection-on-action	This takes place after the event. Ideally it involves some sort of systematic analysis of what has happened. Unlike reflection-in-action, it opens up the possibility of talking to others about teaching. It could lead to changes in beliefs about teaching	This can arise through the recall of reflection-in-action events. It can serve as a means of looking at teaching over a period of time, perhaps through the use of some form of diary or record of activity

tendency to adopt a 'quick fix' approach to personal learning. This shouldn't necessarily be dismissed out of hand as a poor approach, as it can sometimes lead to positive results and perhaps act as a stimulus for further reflection when time allows. Examples of a number of shallow approaches to learning are given in Table 3.5; all are typical of an individual rushing to get on with things and not having time to think more deeply about the issues involved. There is of course another, more worrying, group of people who don't even adopt this shallow approach. These are those that don't really want to know; they are happy just to get through the day and show little concern for improvement. These people construct a massive brick wall against change, and it will take considerable effort, cajoling and perhaps even pressure to make them move.

Not surprisingly, the process of reflection closely matches generally accepted views about learning, as illustrated by Kolb's cycle of learning (see Figure 3.3). The first key stage is the planning process – deciding on what is going to be taught, the teaching methods and what evidence you are going to be looking out for in order to structure your analysis and subsequent lesson reflection. The next stage is putting into practice those ideas that have been carefully thought through beforehand. It is at this point that you make decisions about whether to follow the original ideas or change tack and adopt a different strategy, which leads to the task of making sense of all that has gone on. New teachers are advised to focus on one or two aspects of the lesson (Parkinson, 2002) and to be aware that judgements can be clouded by incidents such as breaches of discipline. Experienced teachers may wish to continue this practice rather than trying to make sense of the complex interweaving events that usually take place in any one lesson. The best sort of evidence to look at is concerned with the activities that the pupils carry out. Such things as behaviour, enthusiasm, on-task time, quality of responses to questions and quality of written or oral work are all good indicators of the level of success of your teaching. You then have to make sense of the information you have collected and start to ask yourself the 'why and what' questions – e.g. 'Why did this happen in this way?', 'What did I do to instigate this course of action with the pupils?', 'What was the value of a particular task in helping pupils to learn?', 'Why did the pupils enjoy the work? (did the task allow them time to talk to their friends, or was the task an enjoyable and valuable learning experience?). The analysis can be signific-

Table 3.5 *Levels of involvement with learning about teaching*

Shallow approach	Deep approach
Teacher accepts ideas without question, and has the desire to get the right results and keep others (e.g. HoD) happy	Teacher has an extended understanding of the issues and is able to identify what is personally relevant
Teacher looks for a 'hints and tips' approach to teaching, and wants quick solutions to problems	Teacher engages with the ideas over a prolonged period
Teacher thinks about his or her practice and makes some changes, but does not see the need to discuss practice with others	Teacher systematically reflects on his or her practice and works with a coach in planning and implementing improvements
Individuals in a department work alone to improve their work	There is a culture of professional learning within the department. The development of all members of the team is seen as important

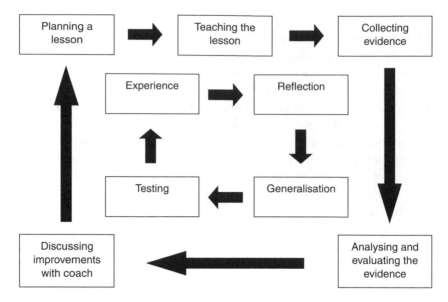

Figure 3.3 *Kolb's Learning Cycle (inner loop) with cycle of reflective teaching (outer loop)*

antly improved through the help of a critical friend, mentor or coach. If the person can observe the lesson and give feedback on this basis all the better, but in reality this is only going to happen infrequently. More often than not you are going to have to describe the lesson and discuss your suggestions for improvement. The role of the coach is to ask you questions to try to get you to think more deeply about your actions and to ensure that you have thoroughly questioned yourself about the focussed areas of reflection. The main job of the coach is not to provide answers, but to get you to think through each situation.

The model of learning that underpins the processes described about is one that science teachers are very familiar with; that of constructivism. Even before prospective teachers embark on a PGCE course, views about what teaching involves are clearly present in an individual's mind. Throughout their year of training, by a process of taught sessions, practical teaching, observation of experienced teachers and tutor intervention, the students are constantly confronting ideas that make them question their original assumptions. They begin to construct new knowledge about teaching strategies, and start to develop a self-identity as a teacher of science. This process continues throughout a person's teaching career; not always uniformly, as there may be times when the conditions are such that progress is halted or even reversed. Most of our knowledge about teaching comes about as a result of personal construction based on our experiences of teaching alone. Bell and Gilbert (1996) argue that knowledge can also be constructed in a social context where the second person casts doubt on embedded meanings and understandings. The second person (mentor or coach) can:

- show the direction to new interpretations
- provide the scaffolding for new learning

- help raise the teacher's awareness of his or her thoughts, beliefs and ways of coming to know about the processes of teaching and learning (i.e. develop a teacher's metacognitive skills)
- make changes in his or her own understanding of teaching and learning through the social interaction that takes place with the learning teacher.

Identifying what needs to be improved

It is not always up to the individual to decide on professional development needs. As illustrated in Table 3.6, the teacher may need to work on improvement strategies decided upon by the government, the local authority, the school or the science department. There can be a feeling of resentment when some of these initiatives, particularly those from external agencies, conflict with other interests you have in the school. However, for the most part these new strategies are devised by people with considerable experience in education and a strong commitment to making improvements on a large scale. Chapter 2 discussed how these innovations and developments can be incorporated into the department, and this section will look at personally identified needs.

As a reflective practitioner, you will be able to pinpoint aspects of your work that need improving with relative ease. This might be a sufficient basis for planning for improvement, or you may wish to think about it further in terms of prioritising work, how the changes might impinge on other aspects of your work etc. One way of doing this effectively is to complete some sort of self-review checklist, starting with a clear identification of what it is you want to develop (see, for example, Table 3.7).

Reflection on your day to day teaching may not reveal all aspects of work that are in need of change, and it may be the case that you need to look at your job overall. To a large extent teachers' job descriptions are fairly vague; you have to do everything, but there will be aspects of your work that you take special responsibility for. It is worth periodically reviewing your job specification with your line manager and identifying your strengths and weaknesses in terms of the roles you have to adopt. Changes in the type of work you do or taking on new challenges can sometimes provide you with that new lease of life that is important to everyone at various stages of their professional work.

Up to now this section has referred to things that are relatively straightforward, either because they can easily be observed (such as teaching techniques and the management of pupils) or because they are concerned with the introduction of new curricula or teaching innovations. However, if you probe a little deeper into what is happening in the department you may discover that there are other, more fundamental, things that might need changing. The way we teach, the approach we have to science, our use of ICT and the attitude we have to pupils are all based on the inbuilt beliefs we hold. We do things in a particular way because of these strongly held beliefs. It may be that it is at this sort of level that you need to address what needs to be improved. In a study carried out in Australian schools, Baird (1999) asked teachers questions such as 'What is it, to be a science teacher?' and 'What is science teaching?' in order to help them

Table 3.6 *Identifying professional development needs*

Origin	Who or what determines the need?	Method of determining development needs
Individual level	• Identified as something to enhance personal teaching • Supporting professional development • Helping with career progression	• Self-review using a pre-prepared checklist • Analysing present job specification • Arising from discussions with HoD • Arising from an appraisal interview • Following an observation session • Completing a questionnaire about INSET needs
Departmental level	• The curriculum • The staff involved with the course and their range/level of expertise • The resources available • Roles and responsibilities in the department	• Annual departmental review • Structured group discussion based on agreed issue • Departmental team self-review using a pre-prepared checklist • Departmental development plan
School level	• The curriculum • The headteacher and members of the SMT • The resources available • The management of all aspects of the work of the school • The organisation of the school	• School development plan • Action plan arising from Ofsted or Estyn inspection • Using a review instrument devised by an external agency
LEA or National level	• The National Curriculum • External examinations • Financial considerations	• Determined externally

Table 3.7 *Self-review checklist for personal professional development*

Questions to ask yourself	Things to consider
What aspects of my work do I do well?	Identify those things you are good at. This helps raise your self-esteem and puts you in the right frame of mind for planning for improvement
What aspect(s) of my work do I need to develop?	Are these absolutely clear? If they are vague, you may spend a lot of time doing things that don't help you to meet your goal(s)
How should I prioritise the work I plan to do?	If there are a number of things that you need to work on, it is advisable to list them in order of priority and to target one thing at a time
Have I got a clearly defined plan for improvement?	It's no use being woolly about this; you must have a carefully thought through plan that will enable you to meet your objectives
How will the changes I make affect the department and the school?	Maybe this is the time to be selfish and only think of yourself, but clearly you need to think of any impact your change may have on the rest of the team
What support will I need?	Sometimes support can be readily available, but you may find it necessary to work on people and cajole them into helping (e.g. being your coach) or releasing the finance for courses
How will I be able to monitor my progress?	You need to have some mechanism for checking on how things are going, e.g. feedback from pupils' work
What could go wrong and how would I deal with it?	It is a good idea to prepare for things going wrong, but you will find it impossible to contemplate all eventualities
What is the timescale for my improvement project?	You must have a clearly defined time limit, otherwise the job will either never get started or will never finish

reflect on their perspectives of teaching. One of the conclusions that he came to was that this type and level of reflection should form an important part of the professional discussion that takes place within the science department.

Managers play a vital role in helping individuals to identify their needs and in providing the support and resources to ensure that the needs are met. In carrying out their duties they need to have a sensitive understanding of staff needs and aspirations. Each person involved in a work team is likely to have a different pattern of needs and aspirations, and it is important to build a relationship based on trust and support. If people feel appreciated and valued, they tend to work with greater commitment and a more purposeful sense of direction (Whitaker, 1997).

Performance management

Performance management was introduced into all maintained schools in England and Wales in autumn 2000 to improve the effectiveness of teaching and leadership (DfEE, 2000). Schools are required to prepare a school management and performance policy outlining the school procedures and the rights and responsibilities of all individuals concerned. Procedures are based around a performance cycle, which is not too dissimilar to the processes outlined in Figure 3.3 but is described as consisting of three phases:

1 **Planning.** Starting from the teacher's job description, four to six objectives are identified as targets for improvement during the coming year. The objectives must be concerned with both pupil progress and professional development. In the case of subject leaders, leadership/management objectives must also be identified.
2 **Monitoring.** The team leader carries out lesson observation and provides constructive feedback to the teacher (see the section on peer coaching below).
3 **Reviewing performance.** The team leader reviews the teacher's overall performance for the year and identifies further areas for development.

Baker (2001) stresses the importance of the teacher taking responsibility for identifying personal strengths and weaknesses and planning ways of achieving continuous learning and development. He proposes that in order to do this, teachers need to conduct a self-review against the threshold standards and maintain a file of evidence throughout the year (see professional development record below).

In the autumn term of 2001 and the spring term of 2002, Ofsted undertook a survey of schools to determine the extent to which performance management had been implemented (Ofsted, 2002). A number of areas were identified as being in need of further development for teachers and subject leaders. In particular, the following points were made:

1 The links between the school development plan and individual teachers' objectives were generally weak.
2 Weaknesses with regard to pupils' progress objectives included:
   • Some teachers did not have objectives relating to pupils' progress
   • Some teachers' objectives were not measurable and were not well supported by clear criteria to indicate what specifically should be achieved
   • A significant number of the objectives lacked challenge.
3 The professional development objectives written by some teachers were unclear. They were written in terms of activities or tasks rather than targets and they often did not detail the strategies or the support needed.
4 One of the weakest features of performance management practice was the production of training plans to enable teachers to meet their objectives.

A pupil progress objective is probably best written in a way that matches the principles outlined in the SMART acronym (see page 23), for example:

- to increase the number of pupils achieving A*–C in Double Award Science from 54% to 60% by the end of this academic year.

Other objectives, such as to improve the quality of pupils' written work or to strengthen the nature of practical activities, are perfectly valid in terms of helping pupils to make progress, but will only satisfy performance management criteria if they are measurable. When the objective refers to examination results the success criteria are apparent, but when the objective refers to more nebulous things (such as quality of work) the success criteria need to indicate how this will be measured. For example, it could involve the introduction of a number of graded exercises where pupils were required to write about science. Pupils would be required to complete these exercises and their progress would be monitored. The success criteria would stipulate the exact nature of the desired improvement.

A professional development objective is likely to be written in terms of an improvement in teaching, classroom management and control, assessment or an aspect of pastoral responsibilities, for example:

- to improve personal effectiveness in using ICT in science teaching.

The success criteria would need to make this more quantifiable by indicating how the effectiveness is measured. The linked training plan would give the outline details of courses, teacher observation, working groups etc. that would be required to bring about the improvement.

Appraisal

Appraisal is one of the mechanisms that help teachers to identify their strengths and weaknesses, and to work out what is required to make progress. If not set up or carried out properly, appraisal can give rise to all sorts of tensions. Appraisers may be worried about saying the wrong thing and causing offence, while appraisees may consider that they are being judged and that aspects of their work may be brought into question. If the appraiser is concerned about upsetting the appraisee, then there is a danger that little of value will come out of the meeting. The appraisee needs to go into the meeting with the understanding that nobody is perfect and that the purpose of the meeting is formally to identify strengths and weaknesses and try to find realistic ways forward. The appraisal process:

- is not a substitute for regular feedback (this should be done by the line manager from time to time)
- should be seen as a strengthening of existing communications between colleagues in the school, rather than reinforcing barriers between managers and others
- should not be problem-centred (problems with individual performance should be pursued when they arise)
- is a confidential process, and issues should only be pursued outside when both parties agree.

The appraiser should be someone who knows about your work and has probably observed you teach; also someone who either has the authority to make things happen or is confident that any recommendations made for staff development will be acted on. The appraisal process is considerably weakened when it is not possible to provide the training needs identified as important in the meeting. It may be the case that the appraiser will need to put to one side the friendships that exist in many schools where the community is closely knit and there is a significant amount of camaraderie between staff. This has got to be a purely professional job, with a clear agenda for the meeting and focussed discussion based on the evidence available. The main job of the appraiser is to ask questions and listen to the answers and, rather than contradicting anything that the appraisee says, to ask for clarification or justification of the statements. In order to promote discussion, the appraiser could describe some aspects of the observed lesson(s) or talk about some of the work done by the appraisee.

The appraisee needs to do a certain amount of preparation in readiness for the meeting. For example, the appraisee needs to:

• agree the appraisal meeting agenda
• have a clear view of what his or her present job entails (i.e. produce a job description)
• identify ways in which the job has changed since the last appraisal meeting (may need to refer back to documents produced at the time of that meeting)
• identify his or her main strengths and weaknesses in relation to all aspects of school work (expect to be asked probing questions)
• identify the progress made towards the targets documented at the last appraisal meeting
• list any organisational obstacles that are hindering progress
• find out about any courses or supporting organisations that could help in the realisation of the improvement plan, together with costings if possible.

If the appraisee hasn't thought things through properly there is a likelihood that opportunities will be missed and, as the appraisal process only happens infrequently, missing this chance could have a considerable negative effect on career progression.

Choosing the place where the appraisal meeting is held is important, as it is all part of setting the right sort of tone. It needs to be comfortable (i.e. not sitting on laboratory stools) and quiet (i.e. no disturbance from pupils, other teachers or telephones). This is an important time for the appraisee, who must be put at ease from the start of the meeting, and the whole thing mustn't be rushed. The appraisee expects the meeting to be highly confidential unless there are matters that you both agree require discussion elsewhere. As a result of the discussion, there will be:

• a written summary of the main points discussed and the targets for the next period
• an agreed written plan as to how the targets should be achieved, indicating any training needs and how these should be met.

The last, and most important, step in the whole process is making sure that the plans are put into action. It is not uncommon for the plans to be safely filed away and the hectic life of school to go on as normal. What a waste.

Types of professional development

In Chapter 1, the following types of professional development strategies were identified:

1 Attending courses
2 Reflecting on what happens in the classroom
3 Sharing ideas with colleagues
4 Evaluating data, identifying weaknesses and taking action
5 Research
6 Involvement in the work of examination boards
7 Working in partnership with others
8 Use of a critical friend
9 Listening to the pupils
10 Taking on new responsibilities

In this section two of these strategies, courses and research, will be developed further. The other types of professional development are dealt with elsewhere in this book.

The DfES and the General Teaching Councils are intent on encouraging teachers to be involved in personal and professional development from the outset of their career through a process of induction followed by Early Professional Development (EPD) and moving on to Continuing Professional Development (CPD). Funding is available for teachers to go on courses and carry out school-based CPD activities (DfEE, 2001a). All manner of organisations are now offering courses for teachers, and so, in theory, you should be spoilt for choice. However, before you go out and spend your money, you need to consider how closely the course matches your particular learning needs. This is not always easy to find out, particularly when the advertising flier contains a minimal amount of information and a snazzy, but often meaningless, title. You will find it worthwhile making enquiries about the course content, ensuring that it is relevant, at the right level, and contains a good mixture of input and discussion. As I am sure you are well aware, 'workshop' experiences can be extremely variable, and in many cases you can end up knowing just as much as when you started. The DfEE has produced a guidance document outlining a code of practice for CPD (DfEE, 2001b). It identifies the following principles that should be met by high quality courses. They should:

- meet identified individual, school or national development priorities
- be based on good practice – in development activity and in teaching and learning
- help raise standards of pupils' achievements, including those with special educational needs
- respect cultural diversity
- be provided by those with the necessary experience, expertise and skills
- be planned systematically
- be based, where appropriate, on relevant standards (e.g. subject leaders, SEN, SENCOs)
- be based on current research and inspection evidence
- make effective use of resources, particularly including ICT

- be provided in accommodation which is fit for purpose
- provide value for money
- have effective monitoring and evaluation systems, including seeking out and acting on user feedback to inform the quality of future provision.

There is a number of other issues that organisers would do well to consider in terms of the planning and running of the course, such as:

- collaborative planning, involving course leaders and the prospective participants, in order to make sure that CPD needs are met
- careful preparatory briefing for participants several weeks ahead of the course, with opportunities for pre-course work where appropriate
- a programme that is structured but has enough flexibility to allow for modifications in the light of monitoring and formative evaluation
- a programme that is orientated towards experience, practice and action and using, as appropriate, methods like action research, performance feedback and on-the-job assistance
- a 'sandwich' timetable including course-based and job-based experiences to facilitate this approach
- careful debriefing after the course and sustained support, ideally with on-the-job assistance, where new skills are being implemented.

(Bolam, 1987 cited in Bradley, 1991: 86)

For some people the short, non-award bearing courses will satisfy their needs, but others may wish to make a longer commitment to CPD and embark on a university-based Master's programme. There are a number of advantages of this type of approach and, while all courses are different, it is likely that you will:

- be taught how to carry out classroom-based research and recognise valid and invalid data
- receive guidance about writing proposals for such things as GTC awards
- have the opportunity to carry out independent supervised studies where you can perform school-based research under the guidance of a university tutor
- have access to a university education library and all that that entails.

Going on courses enables you to meet people with similar interests and aspirations. It can help you to get away from the culture of teacher isolation and individualism that is prevalent in some schools and can sometimes lead to reduction in drive and creativity (Hargreaves, 1994).

The most common type of research is action research. This involves the teacher:

- identifying an area of study, e.g. the effectiveness of the written feedback given to pupils in Year 10
- designing a plan to investigate the issue
- carrying out the investigation and drawing conclusions from the results.

The aims of this sort of work are:

- to improve your own practice
- to improve your understanding of your practice
- to involve others who will be affected by your practice.

Action research is very much teacher-driven and teacher-owned. It is not subject to the same sorts of constraints as more formal education research, and is more concerned with what works for a particular individual with a particular group of pupils. There may be outcomes that are transferable to other situations, but you shouldn't be surprised if what you have found to work with one class doesn't work with another. Figure 3.4 illustrates the nature of the stages that a teacher will go through, and indicates that it is a cyclical process – a path of continuing improvement. It may be that the same issue will need to be revisited, but it is more than likely that the teacher will identify another issue of interest and start a new cycle of investigation.

Action research takes reflective practice one step further through the process of carrying out a systematic enquiry, leading to an outcome that goes beyond finding a solution to a problem. The process can open up a teacher's eyes to different perspectives on a situation and provide new insights into personal effectiveness, helping him or her to understand why some things work and others don't.

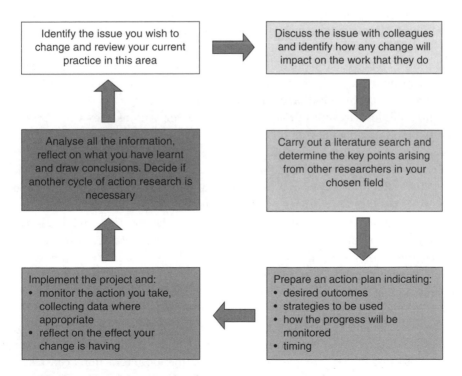

Figure 3.4 *The stages in an action research cycle*

Peer coaching

Peer coaching is the term adopted by Joyce and Showers (1995) for the process whereby one teacher helps another to improve by helping that teacher to identify strengths and weaknesses and develop strategies for improvement. The two teachers involved must have a special working relationship with one another. More often than not the line manager (Head of Department) is not the appropriate person for this role, as the person being coached may see this as threatening. The success of the whole enterprise is heavily dependent on the quality of personal and interpersonal skills of those involved, together with the development of mutual trust, confidence and respect. Coaching involves:

- observing teaching
- analysing performance and providing feedback
- identifying strategies for improvement
- monitoring change in performance
- consolidating improvements.

(West-Burnham and O'Sullivan, 1998)

Most teachers are initially uncomfortable with being observed by their colleagues, and even the observers feel somewhat out of place. For some this stems back to their period of initial teacher education, where observation is seen in judgemental terms and as the passing or failing of the PGCE course. Peer observation is entirely concerned with colleagues helping colleagues to get better at doing their job, and both the teacher being observed and the observer can benefit a great deal from the experience. Observed teachers can find out things about their teaching that they were completely unaware of, and confirm beliefs that were half formed. Observers may get fresh ideas that they could use to improve their own practice, and there will be certain incidents in the lesson that will prompt reflection on their teaching.

The first step in carrying out an observation is for you 'as the observer' and the person to be observed to decide on the focus of the session. Classroom situations are very complex, and you may find that if you try to monitor all that goes on during a lesson you will end up with nothing of significant value. Simply saying that the lesson went well and the pupils appeared to enjoy what they were doing is of little benefit to the observed teacher, who is trying to gain a greater insight into the extent of pupils' learning. In this instance you may want to focus on the class as a whole, looking at such things as time on-task, the level at which the pupils interact with the teaching resources, the involvement of boys compared to girls. Alternatively, you may wish to look at the work of individuals, picking out a more able or a less able pupil for special study and looking at the learning experiences presented in the lesson.

The next thing to consider is where you are going to sit. You have got to be as unobtrusive as possible and yet able to see the whole class. Sitting at the back of the room is often best, trying to adopt an 'I'm not interested in you' stance towards the pupils. They need to forget that you are there so that authentic interactions can take place between the class and the teacher.

A record of the lesson needs to be taken in order that there is a basis for the follow-up discussion. One way of doing this is to video record the whole or parts of the lesson. While this is hardly unobtrusive, it does provide a very good record of what went on and is probably the best method for collecting evidence about teaching activities for detailed analysis. However, you need to be aware that pupils sense that they are being filmed and frequently play to the camera. Audio recording is less conspicuous, particularly if the small Dictaphone-type recorders are used. However, they are only likely to pick up reasonable quality sound within the small area surrounding the recorder and, without taking proper notes, it is sometimes difficult to relate parts of the recording to actual scenarios that happened during the lesson. One word of advice: if you choose to use either of these techniques, have some spare batteries with you. Recording on paper is the most common approach, as it is less 'fussy' than using pieces of technology. However, it does require you to be on the ball all the time, paying careful attention to what is happening in different parts of the classroom. One way of doing this sort of recording is to write a description of what happens at pre-determined key points in the lesson, without making any judgements as to the effectiveness of the procedures taking place. Another method is to use a checklist or observation schedule. Using these you can collect a lot of information about the lesson and frequently get a high level of detail. For example, if your focus is on questioning, you can 'measure' the number of different types of questions used, the distribution between boys and girls, the time on the activity and the response/wait times etc. There are a number of different types of observational schedules in use, for example those used by institutions involved with initial teacher education to monitor PGCE students' progress towards the competencies set by the DfES. Muijs and Reynolds (2001) illustrate two observation instruments that have been reliably used in research to provide both quantitative and qualitative information. They point out the importance of training in the use of these types of schedules to ensure that observers rate things consistently. Some teachers might want to devise their own type of schedule, which is carefully focussed on the issues being studied. The process of devising this can be an extremely useful part of the pre-observation discussion.

Now we move from the uncomfortable scenario to the downright difficult: how to give feedback to a colleague. The initial reaction may be to skirt round the issues and avoid saying anything that might cause offence. An equally unsuitable approach is to assume that you have all the right answers and to proceed by telling the observed teacher where he or she went wrong. You need to be cognisant of the fact that we all see life through different windows, and there will be aspects of the lesson where you see it from one perspective and the observed sees it from another. A more appropriate course of action is to make some general comments about the strengths of the lesson and then to revisit the focus of the observation, followed by a report outlining what you observed. This can be done in stages, with opportunities for comment from the observed teacher and some questions from you to determine the reasons why the actions were taken. You need to bear in mind that during the lesson the teacher is busy interacting with the pupils, often making decisions based on pedagogic knowledge built up over time. You need to think carefully about the questions you ask to make sure that they are not done in an inquisitorial fashion but in a way that shows genuine interest and understanding of the situation. In some cases the pedagogical knowledge may be so deep rooted that it may be difficult for the observed teacher to explain his or her actions. The feedback you give must be accurate and devoid of criticism, and there should be a recognition of the interrelationships that frequently occur in lessons – such as when the teacher does something because of another incident that occurred some time ago. It is through this process of questioning and dialogue that the targets and strategies for improvement are identified. Set a time interval for the strategies to be implemented, and put plans in place for a follow-up observation. However, you as coach don't disappear in the intervening period; you are there, either physically or at the end of a telephone, to provide ongoing support and encouragement.

In summary, the role of the coach is to:

- ask questions
- help set targets
- advise on the action to be taken
- help to review progress
- give encouragement and help to identify success (i.e. be a critical friend).

Professional development record

There is a danger that the self-improvement strategies described in this chapter will be carried out piecemeal by teachers, reacting to situations as they happen. This may lead to a situation where, over time, the teacher makes limited overall progress due to the disparate nature of the issues covered. In order to help a teacher develop as a rounded professional it is important to consider long-term planning and to address questions such as:

- Where do I want to be in 2, 5, 10 years' time?
- What should I be doing in order to meet my goals?
- What sort of record of my work should I be keeping to show my progress?

One way of planning for career-long learning is to maintain your own personal development plan or professional development record (DfES, 2001). In addition to providing a structure for medium- and long-term development and a focus for self-reflection, the record may also be used as:

- a record of evidence for new jobs, promotion etc.
- a basis for discussion at appraisal interviews.

There is no fixed way of producing a record and no standard format for presenting it but, because of the changing nature of your job as a teacher and of teaching in general, it is advisable to maintain an electronic version and print it out from time to time. The record may contain the following types of information (DfES, 2001):

- Review of experience (perhaps a CV and/or something providing more detail on courses that have been significant to you)
- Learning achieved (identify significant learning experiences, from courses, research, classroom situations etc.)
- Planning future development (an action plan based on personal, departmental and school needs)
- A collection of evidence (assemble items such as certificates of attendance on courses, assessment data to show pupils' progression, reports from classroom observations, records of school visits you have supervised).

Day (1999: 106) points out a number of important values that should underpin the design of a record. It should:

- be owned by the teacher and **not** the school
- focus upon enhancing teachers' self-esteem and confidence by recognising achievement
- provide means of feedback on learning to teachers through reflection and analysis of key learning moments
- encourage the planning of short-, medium- and long-term development
- enable teachers to evaluate their learning
- not be too time consuming
- be portable
- provide opportunities for development discussions with others
- be more than a simple accumulation of data
- be of use to teachers in individual development and school accountability processes.

While the main purpose of collecting all this information in a personal development record is to help you to monitor and plan your improvement, there is no doubt that we are moving into an age where records of this nature are seen as very important when there is a dispute between the employer and employee.

References

Baird, J.R. (1999) 'A phenomenological exploration of teachers' views of science teaching', *Teachers and Teaching: Theory and Practice*, **5**(1), 75–94.

Baker, C. (2001) *Preparing for Performance Management*, London: The Royal Society of Chemistry. http://www.chemsoc.org/pdf/LearnNet/rsc/Perf_Manage.pdf.

Bell, B. and Gilbert, J. (1996) *Teacher Development: A Model from Science Education*, London: Falmer Press.

Bradley, H. (1991) *Staff Development*, London: Falmer Press.

Brown, S. and McIntyre, D. (1992) *Making Sense of Teaching*, Buckingham: Open University Press.

CST (Council for Science and Technology) (2000) *Science Teachers: A Report on Supporting the Profession of Science Teaching in Primary & Secondary Schools*, London: CST. http://www.cst.gov.uk/.

Day, C. (1999) *Developing Teachers: The Challenges of Lifelong Learning*, London: Falmer Press.

DfEE (Department for Education and Employment) (1999) *All Our Futures: Creativity, Culture and Education*, London: DfEE.

DfEE (Department for Education and Employment) (2000) *Performance Management in Schools: Performance Management Framework*, London: DfEE.

DfEE (Department for Education and Employment) (2001a) *Learning and Teaching: A Strategy for Professional Development*, London: DfEE.

DfEE (Department for Education and Employment) (2001b) *Good Value CPD: A Code of Practice*, London: DfEE.

DfES (Department for Education and Skills) (2001) *Helping You Develop: Guidance on Producing a Professional Development Record*, London: DfES.

Hargreaves, A. (1994) *Changing Teachers, Changing Times*, London: Cassell.

Hargreaves, A. and Fullan, M. (1992) *Understanding Teacher Development*, London: Cassell.

Harris, A., Jamieson, I. and Russ, J. (1996) *School Effectiveness and School Improvement: A Practical Guide*, London: Pitman.

Joyce, B. and Showers, B. (1995) *Student Achievement through Staff Development: Fundamentals of School Renewal* (2nd edn) White Plains, NY: Longman.

Muijs, D. and Reynolds, D. (2001) *Effective Teaching: Evidence and Practice*, London: Sage.

Munro, J. (1999) 'Learning more about learning improves teacher effectiveness', *School Effectiveness and School Improvement*, **10**(2), 151–171.

Newton, C. and Tarrant, T. (1992) *Managing Change in Schools: A Practical Handbook*, London: Routledge.

Ofsted (2002) *Performance Management of Teachers*, London: Office for Standards in Education.

Osborne, J. and Collins, S. (2001) 'Students' views of the role and value of the science curriculum: a focus-group study', *International Journal of Science Education*, **23**(5), 441–467.

Parkinson, J. (2002) *Reflective Practice in Science 11–18*, London: Continuum.

Schön, D. (1983) *The Reflective Practitioner. How Professionals Think in Action*, London: Temple Smith.

Shulman, L. (1987) 'Knowledge and teaching: foundations of the new reform', *Harvard Educational Reform*, **57**, 1–22.

Teddlie, C. and Reynolds, D. (2000) *The International Handbook of School Effectiveness Research*, London: Falmer Press.

West-Burnham, J. and O'Sullivan, F. (1998) *Leadership & Professional Development in Schools*, London: Pitman.

Whitaker, P. (1993) *Managing Change in Schools,* Buckingham: Open University Press.

Whitaker, P. (1997) 'Changes in professional development: the personal dimension', in Kydd, L., Crawford, M. and Riches, C. (eds) *Professional Development & Educational Management*, Buckingham: Open University Press.

CHAPTER 4

Planning for continuity and progression

Time for an HMI to move to another table

The inspector was visiting a class of infants. Spotting an empty chair at one of the tables she sat down and wrote a few words in her notebook. This was observed by the pupils sitting at the same table. The conversation was opened by one of them.

'Who are you?'

'I'm the inspector.'

'What did you do in your book?'

'I wrote some words.'

'Can you do joint-up writing?'

'Yes.'

'Do you start your sentences with a capital letter?'

'Yes.'

'Well, you're sitting at the wrong table.'

(Evans, 1998: 23)

In a number of places in this book I refer to the problems that can arise when pupils are presented with mixed messages about science. Pupils can become confused when one science teacher tells them one thing and another teacher tells them something that is either slightly different or even completely contradicts the first teacher. **Continuity** is about consistency of pupils' experiences, and it requires teachers to have shared views on issues such as:

• the nature of science and how this is reflected in teaching
• the aims of science education
• the use of signs, symbols and the language of science
• teaching and learning styles
• expectations of pupils' work and behaviour
• methods of assessment and feedback given to pupils.

Progression is concerned with providing experiences for pupils that enable them to make progress in their learning. In most cases this will involve steadily increasing the demands of the work, presenting pupils with new challenges and more complex tasks, but in some instances it will involve revisiting previously learnt ideas to ensure that there is a firm foundation for learning new concepts. Progression requires teachers to have an understanding of issues such as:

- pupils' prior learning
- the conceptual demand of science concepts
- methods of reinforcing previously learnt concepts
- setting targets and monitoring learning.

Discontinuities can occur at any stage of pupils' school experience, as they move to the next academic year or even as they change from one science teacher to another within a year. However, the most significant discontinuity is the transition from primary to secondary school, when pupils not only have to cope with being taught by new teachers but also have to deal with coming to terms with working in a new environment and making new friends. Estyn (1999: 2) reports that:

> In around two-thirds of the primary and secondary schools, planning to promote continuity and progression in pupils' learning from KS2 to KS3 is largely undeveloped.
>
> The lack of adequate curricular links between most primary and secondary schools contributes directly to underachievement by a substantial minority of pupils in KS3.

It is this business of curricular links that has continued to cause problems and still remains largely unresolved. However, it doesn't stand alone and there are a number of interrelated issues that all require attention if progress is going to be made. Galton *et al.* (1999) have identified five hurdles or 'bridges' that pupils face when they make the transition between the two phases of education: the bureaucratic bridge, the social bridge, the curriculum bridge, the pedagogic bridge and the management-of-learning bridge. The key features of these are summarised in Table 4.1. Most, if not all, schools do an excellent job in ensuring that pupils settle in well into their new learning environment through such things as induction days and welcoming activities. The pastoral care programme frequently helps pupils to come to terms with relating to different teachers, and in most cases they quickly adapt to their new situation. The other areas are a little more difficult to deal with, and require some careful planning and commitment on behalf of the SMT and members of the science department. The investment in time and effort in getting information about pupils to the relevant teachers, designing a curriculum that helps pupils to make good progress and helping pupils to become more effective learners is bound to have significant dividends in the long term.

The problem of cross-phase continuity is not restricted to the UK. Studies carried out in Australia (Speering and Rennie, 1996) showed that primary pupils' expectations of secondary science were rarely met. Pupils expected science to be exciting, fun, hands-on and challenging. However, the lessons turned out to be a mixture of didactic teaching, note-taking and working from textbooks. As a consequence, the enthusiasm for science was found to decrease rapidly. Studies in the USA (e.g. Yager and Yager, 1985) have

Table 4.1 *Transition between primary and secondary schools*

From primary	To secondary
The bureaucratic bridge The school has useful information on pupils, such as: • assessment data • their backgrounds • special needs information	The problems facing the secondary school are: • getting the information to the right people • using the information effectively
The social bridge Pupils' concerns about: • being bullied in the secondary school • getting lost • the amount of homework • making friends • getting on with new teachers	The problems facing the secondary school are: • providing an environment where pupils are not afraid to ask questions • presenting the school as an interesting and exciting place to be
The curriculum bridge The problems include: • variation in coverage and emphasis of the NC • variation in primary teachers' knowledge of science	The problems facing the secondary school are: • the lack of reliability of NC teacher assessment as perceived by secondary teachers • repetition of work in the secondary school
The pedagogic bridge Pupils generally experience one teaching style (that of the form teacher)	Pupils have to cope with a number of different teaching styles. Some pupils find it difficult to come to terms with the different demands made on them
The management-of-learning bridge Pupils get used to a particular way of learning, guided by the teacher	New learning strategies are required to meet the demands of learning a wider range of subjects and increases in the level of difficulty

also found that attitudes generally become less positive as pupils progress through the school system. In a study of the learning environments of primary classrooms and secondary laboratories carried out in Australia, Ferguson and Fraser (1988) found that the change in environment had an effect on cohesiveness and the feeling of belonging to a particular class. Large laboratories can make some pupils feel distant from the teacher.

The National Curriculum and continuity

The problem of continuity has been with us for some time but it was probably first drawn to the attention of the majority of science teachers during the time of the Secondary Science Curriculum Review (SSCR) in the early 1980s through local meetings and a key discussion document produced by Jarman (1980). A later publication (Barber and Mitchell, 1987) pointed out problems such as secondary teachers' lack of understanding of primary school work and their negative attitude towards the teaching of science at that level. Patronising comments about the type of work done in primary schools were not uncommon, and in some areas this led to a complete breakdown of

---

Things to consider

Below is a number of strategies that are currently used to help pupils during the time of transfer. What does your school/department do?

Social bridge
To help, the school can:

- have a programme of PSE lessons on bullying and an anti-bullying policy
- hold induction days with activities to help people make new friends
- provide reassurance from older pupils (e.g. asking Y7 pupils to talk to Y6 pupils)
- plan the composition of form and teaching groups.

Curriculum bridge
The department can:

- organise cluster group meetings to exchange information and share ideas
- prepare an agreed common SoW that goes across the two phases.

Pedagogic
The problem can be minimised by teachers observing one another and learning from good practice.

Management of learning
Teachers can:

- make pupils more aware of themselves as learners through specific sessions on learning and its link to achievement
- track pupils' achievement over a period of time to ensure that they are being stretched.

---

communication. In this pre-national curriculum period, science was not taught in all primary schools and the amount of time spent on the subject varied considerably. In a document spelling out plans for the future, the government recognised this as a key issue that needed to be resolved in order to ensure equity and the provision of a balanced science course for all pupils:

> Continuity: as science education develops in primary and middle schools, it is increasingly important for the schools to which pupils subsequently transfer to give attention to building on the foundations already laid...
>
> (DES and WO, 1985: 5)

The introduction of the Science National Curriculum in 1989 provided a framework for broad and balanced science for all pupils between the ages of 5 and 16 based on the principle of continuity in learning, as illustrated in this statement from the Department for Education and Science (1987: 4):

> A national curriculum will secure that the curriculum offered in all maintained schools has sufficient in common to enable children to move from one area of the country to another with minimum disruption of education. It will also help children's progression within and between primary and secondary education and will help to ensure the continuity and coherence which is too often lacking in what they are taught.

Gorwood (1991) recognised that although the NC could solve some of the problems associated with transfer, it was unlikely that a curriculum alone would help with the significant problem of lack of communication between teachers. He identified a problem which still prevails today; that of transferring information about pupils from the primary school to those secondary teachers who need it for planning purposes. This was supported by Dawson and Shipstone (1991), who reported that only 4 per cent of the primary teachers in their survey passed on records. However, they found that liaison between primary and secondary colleagues had begun to improve in the years leading up to the NC, with the result that attitudes had become more positive and secondary teachers had greater confidence in their primary colleagues' abilities to teach science. In a longitudinal study carried out in Northern Ireland, covering the period just before and just after the introduction of the NC, Jarman (1997) reported that there were some changes in the approach to liaison. Most of the secondary teachers in the survey recognised an increase in the science knowledge and skill of their incoming pupils, and some had attempted to establish contact with their primary counterparts. However, only a few had taken any account of children's learning experiences in the planning and preparation of their secondary programmes.

Science in the secondary school

During the period from 1989 to the present, science teachers have had to cope with at least seven National Curriculum consultation reports and four statutory orders. Alongside this, teachers have had to tolerate the implementation of a system of regular inspections and come to terms with a system that puts a great deal of emphasis on examination results. The impact of these changes has been investigated by Jenkins (2000), who asked science teachers from a large sample of schools in England and Wales to complete a comprehensive questionnaire. Only the responses from teachers with over 10 years' experience were included in the analysis. The results are summarised in Table 4.2. On the positive side, the data indicate that teachers now spend more time on clarifying their lesson objectives and on detailed planning of lessons. The NC has also resulted in greater collaboration between science colleagues, and this has helped to increase the coherence of the science curriculum. In addition, teachers have

Table 4.2 *Components of teachers' work that have changed with the introduction of the National Curriculum (Jenkins, 2000)*

Increased	Decreased
Overall time for teaching science	Freedom in choice of teaching activities
Detailed planning of lesson	Time spent on laboratory work
Use of 'bought-in' courses	Range of laboratory activities
Use of textbooks	Enjoyment of science by pupils
Use of worksheets	
Emphasis upon schemes of work	
Clarity of lesson objectives	
Teaching outside specialist subject	
Collaboration with other science staff	
Demands placed on technical staff	
Range of teaching strategies	
Amount of 'feedback' to pupils	
Monitoring of pupils' progress	
Emphasis on homework	
Coherence of the science curriculum	
Use of differentiated activities	

given greater emphasis to schemes of work and have also made more use of textbooks, worksheets and 'bought-in' courses. Some of the teachers in the survey were concerned about the reduction of their freedom to choose courses that were, in their opinion, more appropriate for the pupils in their charge. Some of the chemistry teachers resented the inclusion of earth sciences in the NC. An interesting feature of a number of the replies was concerned with the amount of time spent on laboratory work, with teachers commenting on the increased pressure to complete the content of the curriculum, resulting in less time for practical work. Many of the teachers were critical of investigations, and thought that they restricted the work they could do and limited the number of exciting practicals that could be carried out. Some of the teachers thought that a lot of the fun had gone out of science and that school science was now less enjoyable for both pupils and teachers. Jenkins draws two main conclusions from the research. First, the work of secondary school science teachers has become increasingly directed towards meeting the demands of assessment. Second, science teachers see themselves as having less freedom to choose the kind of work they would like to undertake with their pupils and, as a consequence, respond more negatively to their needs.

Science in the primary school

Secondary teachers are sometimes unaware of the substantial pressures that come to bear on their primary colleagues. In addition to having to deal with the NC changes in science, each teacher has also had to cope with the changes in the other ten subject areas (eleven in Wales). They are also charged with the sometimes difficult job of helping children to integrate into a school environment and develop the key social skills of being a member of a class. Primary teachers are now also subject to external examination pressures, requiring them to devote considerable time and energy in the build up to key stage testing. Primary headteachers are placed in difficult situations when they have to make decisions as to the amount of time that can be allocated to each NC subject and to other worthy activities, such as the national literacy and numeracy strategies. In an ASE survey (ASE, 1999) looking at the effect of the literacy hour on the teaching of science, primary school teachers indicated that:

- they felt under more pressure since the introduction of the literacy hour
- the average number of hours dedicated to teaching science at KS1 and KS2 had declined
- the literacy hour could be used as a context for teaching some science.

The time allocated for science has been a persistent problem. Harris (1996) reported that there was considerable variation in science teaching time, with most schools allocating an hour and a half for infants and two hours for juniors, but some schools allocating less than one hour. She goes on to say that in many primary schools the accommodation for teaching science was inadequate. In the cases where this was a problem, the headteachers highlighted the lack of space for practical activities, no facilities for work involving water, and lack of storage space. Harris makes the point that pupils' perceptions of science are often coloured by the facilities that are available to teach it and the way in which the subject is taught. In a study of pupils' views of science carried out in the early 1990s, Jarman (1993) determined that pupils only thought they were doing 'real science' once they had started their secondary education and were allowed to use Bunsen burners and other 'sophisticated' equipment. Some schools have used the 'lack of facilities' argument as an excuse for doing very little practical work, concentrating their teaching on what has to be learnt for the KS2 tests (Harlen, 1998). Ofsted (1999) has been very critical of the substantial amount of time spent on revision for the KS2 tests in Y6. In order to encourage KS2 teachers to spend more time on investigative work, QCA (2000) and ACCAC (2000) have instructed teachers to double the weighting for Sc1 in comparison to the other attainment targets when they make their teacher assessment decisions (see QCA website at http://www.qca.org.uk/ca/tests/ara/KS2_appendixa.asp).

Under the present system, primary school teachers have to be generalists. On the whole their academic background tends to be more inclined towards arts-related subjects, and for some a significant mind shift is required for teaching science. In a study of Scottish primary teachers Harlen and Holroyd (1997: 100) identified a number of misunderstandings held by the teachers, such as:

- giving an inappropriate analogy (e.g. the eye works like a camera)
- attributing properties that do not correspond with reality (e.g. glass attracts heat)
- proposing a mechanism for which there is no evidence (e.g. there is a substance that is mid-way between liquid water and gaseous water)
- equating everyday language with scientific language (e.g. the greenhouse doesn't cool down until you open the door and let the cold in from outside)
- believing that 'some' means 'all' (e.g. all gases burn, as they do in gas fires).

While some of these problems can be ironed out fairly quickly, the researchers came to the conclusion that others could only be resolved through more intensive in-service training. Teachers continue to have difficulties with science and, in particular, they lack confidence in teaching work associated with Sc1 and Sc4 (Kruger *et al.*, 1990; Council for Science and Technology, 2000). This lack of confidence can lead teachers to adopt various coping strategies which, if used regularly, can have a limiting effect on pupils' learning. Teachers need to be able to engage pupils in dialogue about scientific concepts and help them improve their scientific vocabulary. Teachers who have a background in science are much more likely than others to ask pupils subject-relevant questions and more causal questions (Newton and Newton, 2001). The Welsh Schools Inspectorate has identified this aspect of language and learning as a significant issue for primary schools:

> There is a general need for a better focus on good talk and a greater concern for precision of language in written work, including the gradual and sensitive intro-duction of technical vocabulary that accords with pupils' experience.
>
> (OHMCI, 1999: 19)

However, the situation is gradually improving, and all new entrants to the profession must attend courses on science during their period of training and satisfy the course leaders that they have the knowledge and skills to teach the subject effectively.

In spite of all these problems, pupils generally enjoy their work in science in the primary school, particularly the practical aspects of it (Asoko, 2002), and many achieve a high level of understanding (87 per cent reached level 4 in the KS2 national tests in 2002). A growing number of primary schools are abandoning the con-straints of the literacy hour and moving towards more topic- and project-based work, creating opportunities for pupils to learn in a more integrated and creative fashion (TES, 2002).

Teaching methods

Classroom practice in the two phases of education has been carefully researched through the ORACLE (Observational Research and Classroom Learning Experiences) Project. The first study was carried out in the period 1975 to 1980 and is reported in Galton and Willcocks (1983), and the second study was carried out in 1996 to 1998 and is reported in Hargreaves and Galton (2002). The overall conclusion drawn from the studies is that science teaching has changed little over the last two decades. Galton (2002) identifies the following key issues:

- science teaching in both primary and secondary classrooms is largely done on a whole-class basis
- teachers tend to not use an enquiry-based approach (less enquiry-based work is carried out in the secondary school, and the general approach used is one of 'teacher direction' rather than 'guided discovery')

Things to consider

1 Finding out about primary practice
   - The first step must be to establish a liaison group between the secondary school and its feeder primaries. Once a relationship of mutual trust has been established, it should be possible to discuss issues such as curriculum content and teaching style.
2 Teaching methods in secondary science
   - Make teaching style the sole topic for a departmental meeting, and ask members of staff to report on the methods they use. Discuss the strengths and weaknesses of the transmission mode of teaching. How can pupils be encouraged to work things out for themselves? How can the cognitive demand on pupils be increased?
   - From time to time, e.g. at the end of each term, consider asking the pupils to write a short account of their likes and dislikes of the work they have been taught. This will give you an indication of the extent to which the course is living up to pupils' expectations of science. It will help you in coming to a decision about the balance of activities used in your teaching.

The medium- to long-term aim is to improve the quality of the teaching pupils experience in the two phases of education. It will require a clear policy and guidance on how changes can be made. Peer observation will initially be valuable in highlighting problems with current teaching styles, and at a later stage it will be a useful way of monitoring the effectiveness of the change.

- more open-ended questioning is used in primary classrooms (closed questioning tends to predominate in secondary)
- teachers in both phases spend a significant amount of the time when they are interacting with pupils making statements, mainly statements of fact (in comparison with teachers of other curriculum areas, secondary science teachers spent more time telling pupils what to do and giving them information rather than asking questions)
- science lessons after transfer typically involve short periods of practical activity followed by extensive periods of writing up experiments, during which time there is little interaction between the pupils and the teacher
- the cognitive demand made in most secondary science lessons is fairly low.

The dip at KS3

Although the dip in pupils' progress during KS3 is something that has only been identified recently, there is no reason to believe that it is a new phenomenon. It is more likely that it has been with us for some time and we are only now coming to realise that something needs to be done about it. The dip may be caused by a number of factors, some of which can be corrected and some of which are attributable to the natural maturation process, for example:

- the nature and content of the KS3 curriculum
- the quality of the teaching
- pupils' attitudes towards school and the learning of science in particular.

The dip has been identified by Ofsted (2000: 1):

> Whilst there have been improvements, standards in Key Stage 3 science have not been raised as much as they should have been, in view of the progress made in Key Stages 1 and 2. Lower-attaining pupils, in particular, make little progress during the key stage.

The data in this inspection report don't indicate that there is a dramatic dip. As shown in Table 4.3, the percentage of unsatisfactory lessons is slightly higher in secondary than in primary schools. Alongside this, pupils' achievement could be interpreted as being slightly lower in the secondary sector.

If test results are taken as the indicator of pupils' achievement, then, as pointed out by Galton *et al.* (1999), it is unfair to compare pupils' attainment in the high stakes tests at the end of KS2 with tests carried out in Y7, which are likely to be perceived by pupils as being of lower importance. It is common practice for secondary schools to test Y7 pupils shortly after arrival at the new school (McCallum, 1996). This is justified by the need to have accurate baseline assessment for target setting and value-added analysis (Ellis, 1999). It is perhaps only at the end of KS3 that it would be interesting to look at individuals' progress in comparison with the KS2 results. While recognising the decisions made by secondary schools in this respect, Ofsted believes that this 'represents a considerable duplication of effort when Year 6 pupils have already been assessed in most aspects of the core subjects at the end of Key Stage 2' (Ofsted, 2002a: 3).

There are many changes that take place as pupils work their way through KS3. As the excitement of being in a new school environment wears off there are social

Table 4.3 *The quality of teaching and pupils' achievement in science as determined by school inspection in 2000–2001; the values relate to the percentage of schools receiving a full inspection (Source: Ofsted, 2002b)*

Key Stage	Inspection rating	Quality of teaching	Pupils' achievement
2	Excellent–very good	7	6
	Good	55	41
	Satisfactory	33	40
	Unsatisfactory–poor	5	13
3	Excellent–very good	7	7
	Good	54	38
	Satisfactory	31	42
	Unsatisfactory–poor	8	14

pressures in developing and maintaining friendships, and pressures in keeping to the accepted codes of dress, mannerisms and attitudes towards all adults. There is a lot going on in pupils' minds at this stage, all of which impinges on their approach to science, and therefore in any consideration of the dip at KS3 it is worth bearing in mind attitudinal factors. The research concerned with values of pupils' attitudes referred to in this section is all taken from studies carried out in the UK. This is to avoid any criticism that attitudinal research carried out in other countries may not be relevant to a study of UK pupils, who will have been brought up in a different culture and educational system and will have followed a different curriculum.

The determination of a person's attitude towards a subject is extremely complex, partially because of the nature of attitudes (sometimes ephemeral and sometimes long lasting) and partially because of the research instruments we use. Most commonly attitudes are measured using a questionnaire, where pupils are presented with a series of statements and are asked to indicate their level of agreement using a five-point scale from 'strongly agree' to 'strongly disagree'. The following are examples of the sort of statements used: 'I think science is interesting'; 'I like doing experiments in science lessons'. The questionnaires are answered by a large population of pupils and the responses are analysed statistically, giving a generalised view of groups of pupils (e.g. grouped by gender, age, type of school). The research also often involves the use of follow-up interviews with a sample of pupils from the target groups, to give a check on the data and to obtain a further insight into pupils' views. This methodology produces statistically sound data, but has been criticised for a number of reasons:

1 The disparate collection of items on a questionnaire leads to a variety of attitudinal information, which cannot result in the production of a scale and cannot yield a meaningful score (Gardner, 1975)
2 It cannot take into account the instability of attitudes (Ramsden, 1998)
3 Questionnaires fail to expose pupils' views and, as a result, do not provide the type of information that is useful in understanding the root causes of the attitudinal stance (Osborne, 2001).

Bearing in mind these criticisms, the broad picture obtained from a number of studies is fairly consistent and appears to be generally stable, showing little variation to match the changes that have occurred in the science curriculum over the last 20 years or so. It appears that pupils' enthusiasm for science starts progressively to decline with age in primary schools (Murphy and Beggs, 2001; Pell and Jarvis, 2001). However, attitudes still tend to be positive round about the age of 11, and there appears to be little change as pupils move from Y6 to Y7 (Bricheno, 2001). As pupils work their way through KS3, attitudes decline by a significant amount (Smail and Kelly, 1984; Doherty and Dawe, 1988). A study carried out since the introduction of the NC has shown that science is the least popular of the core subjects at KS3 (Hendley *et al.*, 1995). However, most KS3 pupils retain a positive attitude towards science, with the involvement in practical work being the most significant factor in promoting this attitude (Parkinson *et al.*, 1998).

Ofsted findings match the general picture (Ofsted 2000: 10) but, if anything, paint a slightly more positive picture:

> ... pupils' attitudes and behaviour in science are good or very good in three-quarters of schools. Response in lessons deteriorates slightly during Key Stage 3 but remains good in the large majority of lessons. Pupils' attitudes are most positive when they are involved in practical work and least so when writing up experiments as a routine. Response is best when pupils are involved in lessons.

In comparison, a less positive picture about pupils' overall attitude to learning was given by the Chief Inspector in his Annual Report in 2002 (Ofsted, 2002b: para 63):

> The fall-off in pupils' attitudes to learning between Year 7 and Year 8 continues to be a distinct feature, and is not reversed until Year 10.

Any differences between the Ofsted and data analysis viewpoints regarding the change in attitude over the key stage may be related to the method of collecting the data. The statistical method, for all its faults, is completely dispassionate, while the Ofsted results are based on inspectors' opinions whilst watching lessons. Although direct observation can provide valuable direct evidence of classroom reaction, there is the possibility that the presence of an inspector, and any bias he or she may have when making the observations, will have an effect on the result.

As all teachers are well aware, some pupils start to rebel during KS3 and may begin to truant. Clearly pupils cannot make satisfactory progress if their attendance is poor and, as pointed out by Ofsted (2002b), truancy remains a consistent problem. Some researchers argue that the curriculum is a cause of pupil dysfunction and absenteeism (Kinder *et al.*, 1999), with science being one of the main subjects likely to cause pupils to truant (Reid, 1999). While some blame may be attributed to a centrally set curriculum, the problem is more likely to be associated with how it is translated into classroom practice (Galton, 2002).

Things to consider

Teachers are able to get a feeling about pupils' attitudes towards science by monitoring:

- pupils' willingness to be involved in activities
- interest shown in topics, as indicated by the statements they make and the questions they ask
- the quality of their work and the results they get in examinations.

When you see a deterioration in attitudes, who or what do you blame? What strategies could you use to turn the situation around?

The key stage 3 strategy for science

Following the successful implementation of the KS2 national strategies in literacy and numeracy, the DfES launched the KS3 strategy in September 2001 with the introduction of strategies for English and mathematics (see http://www.standards. dfes.gov.uk/keystage3/). In the following year, strategies for science, ICT and teaching and learning in the foundation subjects were launched. The aim of the strategy is to build on improvements, particularly in literacy and numeracy, attained in the primary school and develop a KS3 curriculum that is challenging, demanding, vigorous and inspiring (DfES, 2002a). In order to do this, the DfES has:

1 Published a series of resources (both web- and paper-based)
2 Worked with LEAs and funded the appointment of special advisory teachers
3 Provided funding to schools for:
   • CPD, e.g. to attend sessions provided by the LEA on the KS3 science strategy
   • transition activities, e.g. to support staff release to visit primary schools
   • summer schools, e.g. for new Y7 pupils
   • Y7 catch-up programmes, e.g. to provide extra staffing to help run sessions for pupils who have not reached a satisfactory level
   • Y8 mentoring programmes, e.g. to provide funding in order that schools can provide occasional one-to-one support for disaffected pupils
   • Y9 booster classes, e.g. to fund extra lessons for pupils who are between levels 4 and 5.

The activities and philosophy of the strategy are based on four important principles:

1 **Expectations.** This is concerned with raising teachers' expectations of all pupils and setting challenging targets for pupils to achieve. This will accomplished by activities such as:
   • auditing and developing the teaching of science by monitoring the progress of pupils, reviewing attitudes and behaviour, reviewing schemes of work, examining the quality of teaching and the use made of assessment (see 'Auditing a Subject at Key Stage 3, on the DfES website)
   • providing advice and support for teachers.
2 **Progression.** This involves both strengthening the transition between KS2 and KS3 (see DfES, 2002b) and ensuring that pupils make good progress throughout KS3. This will be accomplished by activities such as:
   • helping teachers to understand how to support progressive development of science concepts through KS3
   • providing advice and financial support for transition projects in science
   • raising awareness of the science taught at KS2.
3 **Engagement.** Pupils need to be encouraged to find out about science; their curiosity needs to be aroused. Pupils need to be active learners in lessons rather than passive receivers of information. In order to promote these ideals, the strategy provides support for:

- helping pupils to develop thinking skills
- helping teachers to use assessment more effectively
- widening the variety of teaching techniques used.

4 **Transformation.** This is a determined effort by the DfES to improve the teaching of science at KS3, and has involved a large expenditure of funds to provide teachers with relevant CPD and the support of science consultants.

All schools in England are encouraged to become involved in the strategy (there is no plan at present for Scotland, Wales and Northern Ireland to become involved, although each nation may feature KS2–KS3 continuity as one of its national priorities). In addition, all new entrants to the profession will receive some training about the initiative.

It would appear obvious that an important issue such as cross-phase continuity should be included in initial teacher education and training (ITET) courses, but this has not always been the case (Gorwood, 1989). Parkinson and Woodward (1996) argued that it should form a key component of all courses and that, where possible, student teachers from both phases should meet in joint sessions to discuss aspects of continuity. It is vital that the prejudices held by some secondary teachers are eradicated as early as possible. Those involved in ITET will be pleased that the National Strategy has recognised the importance of educating new teachers about continuity and has provided information and support for all those involved in PGCE courses. Hopefully, from September 2003 onwards we should see a new breed of teachers who are fully aware of strategies to deal with curriculum continuity.

Things to consider

When completing the DfES document *'Auditing a Subject in Key Stage 3'* (DfES, 0756/2001):

- How do you involve all members of the science department in completing the audit?
- Are you sure that all your action points are achievable? How will you be able to monitor the situation to check that you are getting there?
- What criteria did you use to select from your list of action points to produce the final action plan?

Passing on information

Not long after the introduction of the NC, Gorwood (1991) pointed out that teachers in 'linked' primary and secondary schools rarely came into contact with one another and that in some cases there was a feeling of mutual distrust. Secondary schools have continued to be critical of the range, quality and reliability of the information they receive from primary schools (e.g. Kaur, 1998; Ofsted, 2002a). Some secondary teachers are concerned about the accuracy of the levels achieved by pupils in the KS2 national tests, believing that the tests are easier than those at KS3 and are a less reliable measure of pupils' attainment in science (see page 163). However, it is not quite as simple as comparing one key stage test result with another. Each key stage test is based on the NC for that key stage and, while there may be some conceptual aspects that overlap, the content of the two programmes of study are different. Therefore, a level 4 at KS2 means something completely different to a level 4 at KS3.

On advice from secondary schools, most primary schools restrict transfer information to NC levels and test scores, based on the assumption that most secondary teachers will not have enough time to read and act upon more detailed information (Ofsted, 2002a). A common transfer form was introduced by the DfEE in 2000 (available at http://www.dfes.gov.uk/com_trans/) to support this. The DfES recommends that the file, containing data on teacher assessment, national test scores and attendance record, is transferred electronically. While this may increase the efficiency in terms of transfer of information from one school to another, there may still be problems associated with confidentiality and ensuring that the information reaches (and is read by) appropriate subject teachers. The level of bureaucracy related to the recording and transmission of results, even using computer technology, can be time consuming and can add to teachers' already significant burdens. Many teachers feel that important tasks such as this cannot be delegated to administrative staff (TES, 2002), and it appears that it will remain a part of teachers' workload unless the unions are able to make radical changes to teachers' contracts (e.g. NUT, 2001).

At present it would appear that the person with responsibility for liaison with the primary schools is the head of Y7 and/or a member of the SMT who is given this responsibility as part of his or her job description (Ofsted, 2000a). Sometimes the information gathered by this process does not filter down to classroom teachers, and even when it does some teachers do not use it in their planning (Schagen and Kerr, 1999). This, once again, points to the need to have a designated person in the science department with responsibility for liaison.

Things to consider

- What can be gained by working with other departments to produce a consistent strategy for liaison with primary schools?
- How could this tie in with the school policy on cross-phase transfer?
- What information is required for departmental planning?
- What do individual teachers need to know and how should the information be made accessible to them?

Maintaining motivation and enthusiasm for science

Some teachers tend to respond to perceived pupils' anxieties about the work in a new secondary school by providing them with a comfort zone, where pupils are presented with relatively mundane tasks over a period of several weeks. These might involve activities such as copying out the safety rules, learning how to draw scientific apparatus, and practising some laboratory skills such as how to use certain measuring instruments. Moving up to the 'big school' is a major event for all pupils, involving a mixture of emotions. Lucey and Reay (2000) carried out a study to monitor pupils' thoughts and feelings about the transfer by carrying out a series of focus group meetings and observations of groups of pupils during the period leading up to leaving primary school. The research indicated that pupils tended not to be worried about their new situation. In cases where there was worry, this was generally overcome by the thought that there would be someone at the secondary school who would be willing to give them help and support. In most cases there was a real sense of excited anticipation of looking forward to new experiences. Hawkey and Clay (1998) also noted that primary school pupils expect secondary science to be interesting and exciting, providing them with opportunities to learn something new. However, according to this study, many of the pupils repeated primary school work and made very little progress throughout the whole of Y7. According to Ofsted (2000a: 11), the following topics are often repeated in secondary school:

• plant structure and conditions for growth
• use of keys
• food chains
• separating mixtures
• simple electrical circuits.

It is terribly sad to lose the impetus that is so often present at the start of a new stage of pupils' lives, and teachers need to think of ways of maintaining motivation, such as:

• avoiding repetition by ensuring that someone in the department is given the responsibility for cross-phase liaison and continuity of the KS3 curriculum (suggestions for tasks and activities are given in Table 4.5, later in this chapter)
• avoiding 'boring' tasks such as copying information, e.g. the laboratory safety rules (consider building these up as they are relevant to the situation in hand, encouraging pupils to think about safety and put forward their suggestions)
• providing pupils with challenging situations (consider setting pupils tasks that require them to use their previous knowledge in new contexts)
• providing pupils with practical experiences that they are unlikely to have come across in the primary school (consider using good quality equipment that works)
• listening to pupils' reactions to the tasks you set and considering them in planning for the future.

A tremendous amount of numeric data is available on each pupil, and this is often used to challenge pupils through the process of target setting. Some schools plot pupils' tests scores against predicted scores based on either KS2 test results or CAT scores. Pupils who fall below the expected line can be given remedial support or the opportunity of a retest, and pupils who do better than expected can be given more demanding tasks.

Data from key stage tests can also be used to motivate staff into helping to reach departmental targets for external examination results (see Table 4.4). Using the Autumn Package and PANDA data (similar data are available for Wales on the National Assembly website), it is possible to compare your school with similar schools across the country. Other useful exercises include:

- comparing this year's results with last year's (trends over time)
- comparing boys' and girls' results
- looking at the progress made by groups of pupils based on their base-line data (how has the department catered for the less able and the most able?)
- comparing the progress of pupils in different teaching groups.

Having carried out the analysis, the next task is to decide how to use the information to improve the teaching in order to raise the standards for the following year.

Table 4.4 *Percentages of pupils reaching key levels for each of the core subjects from 1995 to 2002 (Sources:* Statistics of Education: National Curriculum Assessments of 7, 11 & 14 year olds, available at http://www.dfes.gov.uk/statistics/, *and* Educational Development Plans 2002–2007, available at http://www.standards.dfes.gov.uk/word/EDP2guidance_311001)

Year	KS2 percentage of pupils achieving level 4 and above			KS3 percentage of pupils achieving level 5 and above		
	English	Maths	Science	English	Maths	Science
1995	49	45	70	55	57	56
1996	57	54	62	57	57	57
1997	63	62	69	57	60	60
1998	65	59	69	65	59	56
1999	71	69	78	63	62	55
2000	75	72	85	64	66	62
2001	75	71	87	65	66	66
2002	75	73	86	66	67	66
	2004 target (Eng. and maths) = 85%			2004 target (Eng. and maths) = 75%		
				2004 target (science) = 70%		
				2007 target (Eng. and maths) = 85%		
				2007 target (science) = 80%		

Things to consider

- Are you making valid use of the data you have?
- Do the data assume (incorrectly) that the gap between each level is the same?
- If you use sub-levels (e.g. level 5c or 4.2), are you sure that everyone knows what it means?
- Do you convert topic test results from percentages into levels? How do you justify this?
- Bearing in mind that the levels obtained in the KS2 tests are based on the KS2 NC and those obtained in the KS3 tests are based on the KS3 NC, how valid is it to compare these two numbers?

Curriculum continuity

Although a substantial amount of the literature on continuity is concerned with science, the problem also occurs in other subjects. The other core subjects come in for criticism from Ofsted (2002a: 2):

> The secondary schools were not building well enough on what their Year 7 pupils had achieved in English and mathematics in Year 6. They generally did not know, in sufficient detail, what their new pupils could do, and they had not set targets for improving attainment during Year 7.

Huggins and Knight (1997) have reported on problems in history concerned with differences in ideologies linked with differences in beliefs about standards and the nature of school history. Williams and Howley (1989) have given an account of the problems facing geography teachers in terms of the differences in curriculum content in the two phases, and the lack of priority given to subject-related liaison activities.

Nott and Wellington (1999) have painted a very gloomy picture of cross-phase liaison in science. Their survey of over 400 secondary schools revealed that:

- a minority of secondary schools consulted the KS2 programme of study when planning work for KS3, and only a quarter of the secondary schools bothered to liaise with their primary partners
- about a quarter of the secondary schools used (a) KS2 test results or (b) information from the schools, but only an eighth used both information and the test results
- about an eighth of the secondary schools used knowledge of the KS2 schemes of work from their partner primaries.

The first stage towards effective liaison is to set up cluster group meetings comprising the science co-ordinators from each of the feeder primary schools and the secondary science person with responsibility for liaison. These need to take place on a regular basis two to three times a year in order to keep the momentum going and to ensure that all the business is dealt with thoroughly. Initially the meetings will be focussed on finding out what goes on in the two phases, but the focus must change to looking at ways for improving the situation. This will involve give and take on both sides – something that is not always easy to achieve. It needs to be made clear from the outset that the purpose of doing this is to create a curriculum that will be more attractive than the current one, leading to better academic results. The meetings should move on to produce action points that need to be implemented in all the schools, followed by a review process to determine the effectiveness of the changes. Table 4.5 illustrates how this process could take place when the focus for change is one topic, chemical reactions in this example. Table 4.6 goes on to illustrate some strategies that could be employed to improve liaison.

The preparation and use of a scheme of work (SoW) is the usual method for ensuring continuity of the curriculum. A SoW provides all members of the department with a common approach to teaching and assessment. It can help to maintain a consistency of approach in such issues as language across the science disciplines, policy on investigations, and ensuring that pupils receive similar messages about the nature of science (NoS) from all teachers. The SoW is likely to contain information such as:

- a sequence of lessons indicating teaching activities, together with an indication of the time allowed to teach each section
- tasks for pupils, including homework and out-of-school learning
- links to previous work so that teachers can appreciate what pupils have already been taught

Table 4.5 *Suggestions for improving continuity*

- Identify a member of staff who is responsible for co-ordinating KS3 work
- In addition to liaising with the special needs co-ordinator about the learning needs of less able children, consider identifying and meeting the needs of gifted and talented pupils
- Collaborate on the planning and reviewing of schemes of work (be aware of the problems that can arise by rigid adherence to a published resource)
- Try to ensure that KS3 work is not carried out in the primary school. Able children in the primary school could be offered opportunities to apply their scientific knowledge and skills in a challenging context[1]
- Use cross-phase projects such as:
  The British Association Young Scientists (BAYS) Young Investigators award scheme, which is aimed at pupils in the 8–13 age range
  Consider using the ASE passport project (see CD-ROM *'Who am I?'* sent free to all UK schools during Science Year).[2] For further details see Ryan, 2002
- Each year QCA and ACCAC produce reports on the results of the KS2 and KS3 national tests indicating areas of science where there are weaknesses in pupils' knowledge, understanding and skills. This information could be used as a starting point for a discussion of pupils' weaknesses in the partner schools and how these could be eliminated

Notes
1 For example, see 'Science challenges for able pupils in KS2', from Hertfordshire School Improvement and Advisory Service at http://www.thegrid.org.uk/learning/science/teaching/challenges.htm
2 Also available on the Web, at http://www.sycd.co.uk/who_am_i/startfil/home.htm

Table 4.6 *A framework for curriculum planning at a cluster group meeting*

Planning for continuity
At the meeting
The discussion could focus on a particular topic, e.g. chemical reactions, and issues could be raised about the focus of the work in the two sectors. For example:

- Decide on examples of solids, liquids and gases that will be used in the primary school to illustrate the states of matter
- How will the secondary school build on this foundation and introduce the particle model of matter?
- Decide on a common understanding of the use of models and theories in science teaching
- What emphasis will be given to making accurate observations and looking for evidence during each key stage?
- Discuss which chemical reactions should form the basis of the work in the primary school
- What are there opportunities for differentiation, and how will these affect continuity?

Identify a small number of targets and the timescale in which these targets should be met.

Implementation phase
Wherever possible, all members of the cluster group should be involved in implementing the targets to help create a sense of teamwork and responsibility towards the common goals.
To what extent do the revised activities work in terms of:

- pupil achievement
- pupil enjoyment
- challenging pupils to think
- providing pupils with the opportunity to make progress at a rate that matches their intellectual capability?

How do the changes affect other parts of the curriculum?

Review phase
Have the changes improved the continuity of the curriculum?

- common misconceptions held by pupils
- key words and phrases
- guidance on differentiation
- suitable resources and opportunities for using ICT
- assessment opportunities.

Clearly these are lengthy and time consuming documents to prepare, and teachers will be tempted to take short cuts such as adopting a published set of textbooks with accompanying teachers' guide or using the QCA SoW (QCA, 2000). Adopting a published scheme has many advantages, particularly the ability to cross-reference classroom situations presented in the pupils' book with teaching ideas and guidance in the teachers' guide. However, the sheer volume of information frequently makes it difficult for teachers to pick up on how concepts are developed, making it difficult for them to link related aspects of work. Using the textbook can also stifle teachers' creativity, as it directs them to teach the work as set out on the double-page spread for the lesson. There are always problems with implementing a SoW that has been produced by someone else, mainly in terms of interpretation of the statements, but also in the realisation of the overall aims of the course when they don't readily map onto the ideologies held by members of the science department. The QCA SoW for KS3 is based on the English NC for science, and has been devised so that it builds on pupils' scientific knowledge and understanding from KS2, which also has a published QCA SoW. It has been designed to cater for pupils working between levels 3 and 7. This has been done by providing pupils with a range of stimulating and challenging activities. The underlying philosophy behind the package is based on the constructivist approach, and each unit starts with an exercise that is designed to elicit pupils' understanding and prior learning of the topic. As such, it is in tune with the National KS3 science strategy and has been adopted as the basis for planning improvements in KS3 teaching. In an article reviewing the introduction of the SoW, Henderson (2000) pointed out that it is a well-produced package and that teachers will find it a valuable resource to use as a whole or in part. Monk (2000) is more sceptical about the effect such a SoW will have on teachers and teaching. He points out the possibility that such an established document is likely to influence the way in which questions are set in the KS3 national tests, and is what might be seen as a 'national syllabus' for a 'national test'. Monk goes on to argue that this removal of the element of choice from teachers goes some way to reducing their professionalism.

Bishop and Denley (1997) have provided some guidance for those teachers who wish to plan a SoW from scratch. They propose a five-stage procedure as follows:

1 **Creating an overview.** This can be done by producing a list of concepts involved in the learning of the topic, and possibly linking them together in the form of a concept map. An alternative approach is to use a published science map setting out the key ideas for a topic (Driver *et al.*, 1994).

2 **Identifying a hierarchy of learning outcomes.** It is common practice to identify two to three levels of learning in terms of expected learning outcomes for all students, further learning outcomes for the more able, and another further set of expected outcomes for the most able. Sometimes this might be done in terms of more able pupils completing a larger number of tasks, and on other occasions it might be done by setting tasks for more able pupils that are more complex or require greater conceptual understanding (see page 119). At stage 4 in the preparation of the SoW it will be necessary to relate these expected outcomes to classroom activities, together with suggestions for managing the situation.

3 **Finding learning routes.** This requires teachers to sequence the learning outcomes into an order for teaching. It will involve visiting some learning outcomes more than once, building a curriculum that uses the consolidation of earlier work as a jumping-off point for more demanding learning.

4 **Transformation.** At this stage the learning outcomes are transformed into suitable learning activities. It is useful to keep a check on the different types of task that pupils will be presented with in order to ensure that there is ample variety to cater for individuals' needs. Checks need to be made to ensure that the curriculum will give pupils the opportunity to make progress. This may be done by referring back to the hierarchy of learning outcomes to check that there is an increase in the demand made on pupils. It is worthwhile considering three aspects of the demand: the conceptual demand; the procedural demand and the contextual demand (see Figure 4.1). This process helps to ensure that the SoW caters for pupils as they mature and prepare themselves for key examinations.

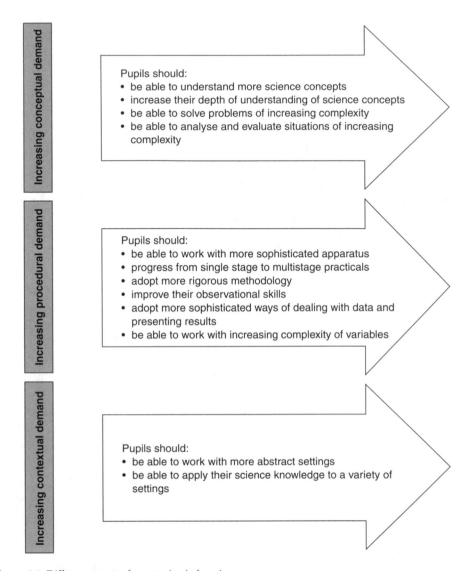

Figure 4.1 *Different aspects of progression in learning*

5 **Identifying assessment opportunities and relating to learning outcomes.** In addition to noting opportunities for key tests, the SoW should also identify when pupils could be involved in self-assessment exercises.

Most schemes of work tend to evolve over years, and teachers may prefer to review and modify an existing scheme rather than start from a blank sheet. Table 4.7 indicates a number of significant areas that need to be considered in the review process.

The question then arises as to who should produce the SoW. The curriculum expert could be sent away to complete the task, but this might lead to the inclusion of items that can only be understood by the 'expert'. A team effort is likely to create a sense of ownership and value and achieve a curriculum that is more readily understood by everyone, with a sound balance of content and activities.

Table 4.7 *Questions that may be posed when modifying a scheme of work*

- Does the SoW provide opportunities for progression in learning?
  Does the SoW for Y7 build on pupils' experiences from KS2?
  Are there opportunities for consolidation without repetition?
  Does the curriculum provide interesting, exciting and worthwhile experiences?
  How does the SoW cater for pupils of different abilities?
- Does the SoW meet the overall aims of the course?
  Do the activities match with what you are trying to achieve with the pupils?
  Are there consistent messages about the nature of science, pupils' learning, pupils' responsibilities, expectations etc.?
  Are there consistent messages about language, e.g. language for learning, scientific vocabulary, units, symbols and abbreviations?
- Is the time allocated for each topic reasonable?
  Do more difficult topics require more time?
  When should each topic be taught?
- Is there overall coherence in each year's course?
  Are there links to related topics?
  Are there links to work carried out in other subject areas within the school?
- Are opportunities for homework clearly identified?
  In what ways do these homework tasks support pupils' learning?
- Are opportunities for the use of ICT clearly identified?
  What ICT skills are required, and how are they going to be taught?
- Is there a reasonable variety of learning activities in order to cater for the different interests of pupils?
  Is the level of detail given in the SoW sufficient for all those teaching the curriculum?
  Can you justify including the activity?
  Is the time spent on each activity about right?
- Are common misconceptions identified?
  What strategies are included in the SoW to help pupils achieve a correct understanding of the science concepts?
- Does the SoW identify areas of work that pupils may find difficult?
  Are there strategies for helping pupils to understand the work?
  Does the SoW identify useful resources?
- Are the learning objectives clear and measurable?
  Is there a policy on how these objectives are conveyed to the pupils?
  Do the objectives cater for different ability groups within a class?
- Are the opportunities for assessment clear?
  Does the assessment match the learning objectives?
  Are opportunities for formative assessment clearly identified?
  Where is the check carried out to determine if both lower-order and higher-order cognitive objectives are assessed?
- Has there been a preliminary appraisal of the safety implications for all the activities?
  Is there sufficient guidance for a science teacher (including non-specialists) to make a full appraisal of the situation?

References

ACCAC (2000) *Implications for Teaching and Learning: Report on the 2000 Tests in Science at Key Stage 3*, Birmingham: Qualifications, Curriculum and Assessment Authority for Wales.

ASE (1999) ASE survey on the effect of the National Literacy Strategy on the teaching of science (available at: http://www.ase.org.uk/natlit1.html).

Asoko, H. (2002) 'Primary Science Review 2001–2: some themes of interest to secondary teachers', *School Science Review*, **84**(306), 111–116.

Barber, B. and Mitchell, M. (1987) *Better Science: Building Primary–Secondary Links: Curriculum Guide 10*, London: Heinemann.

Bishop, K. and Denley, P. (1997) *Effective Learning in Science*, Stafford: Network Educational Press.

Bricheno, P.A. (2001) *Pupil Attitudes: A Longitudinal Study of Children's Attitudes to Science at Transfer from Primary to Secondary School*. Unpublished PhD thesis, University of Greenwich.

Council for Science and Technology (2000) *Science Teachers: A Report on Supporting and Developing the Profession of Science Teaching in Primary and Secondary Schools*, CST (available at: http://www.cst.gov.uk/).

Dawson, R. and Shipstone, D. (1991) 'Liaison in science at the primary/secondary interface', *School Science Review*, **72**(261), 17–25.

DES (Department of Education and Science) (1987) *The National Curriculum 5–16, A Consultation Document*, London: DES publications.

DES and WO (Department of Education and Science and the Welsh Office) (1985) *Science 5–16: A Statement of Policy*, London: HMSO.

DfES (2002a) *Key Stage 3 National Strategy, Framework for Teaching Science: Years 7, 8 and 9*, London: DfES publications.

DfES (2002b) *Key Stage 3 National Strategy, Supporting Transition from Year 6 to Year 7 Science: Course Tutor's Pack*, London: DfES publications.

Doherty, J. and Dawe, J. (1988) 'The relationship between development maturity and attitude to school science', *Educational Studies*, **11**, 93–107.

Driver, R., Squires, A., Rushworth, P. and Wood-Robinson, V. (1994) *Making Sense of Secondary Science: Support Materials for Teachers*, London: Routledge.

Ellis, S.W. (1999) 'National Curriculum testing across the interface at key stage 2/key stage 3: a view from the bridge', *Curriculum*, **20**(1), 38–51.

Estyn, (1999) *Primary and Secondary School Partnership: Improving Learning and Performance*, Cardiff: HM Inspectorate for Education & Training in Wales.

Evans, N. (1998) *Humour, Muse, Inspiration*, Cardiff: Neville Evans.

Ferguson, P.D. and Fraser, B.J. (1998) 'Student gender, school size and changing perceptions of science learning environments during the transition from primary to secondary school', *Research in Science Education*, **28**(4), 387–397.

Galton, M. (2002) 'Continuity and progression in science teaching at key stages 2 and 3', *Cambridge Journal of Education*, **32**(2), 249–265.

Galton, M. and Willcocks, J. (1983) *Moving from the Primary School*, London: Routledge & Kogan Page.

Galton, M., Gray, J. and Ruddock, J. (1999) *The Impact of School Transitions and Transfers on Pupil Progress and Attainment*, London: HMSO (available at http://www.dfes.gov.uk/research/data/uploadfiles/RR131.doc).

Gardner, P.L (1975) 'Attitudes to science', *Studies in Science Education*, **2**, 1–41.

Gorwood, B. (1989) 'Experience of problems relative to curriculum continuity and school transfer in teacher-training courses', in McClelland, V.A. and Varma, V.P. (eds) *Advances in Teacher Education*, London: Routledge.

Gorwood, B. (1991) 'Primary-secondary continuity transfer after the National Curriculum', *School Organisation*, **11**(3), 283–290.

Hargreaves, L. and Galton, M. (2002) *Transfer from Primary to Secondary: 20 Years On*, London: Routledge.

Harlen, W. (1998) 'The last ten years; the next ten years', in Sherrington, R. (ed.) *ASE Guide to Primary Science Education*, Cheltenham: Stanley Thornes.

Harlen, W. and Holroyd, C. (1997) 'Primary teachers' understanding of concepts of science: impact on confidence and teaching', *International Journal of Science Education*, **19**(1), 93–105.

Harris, S. (1996) *Science in Primary Schools*, Slough: NFER.

Hawkey, R. and Clay, J. (1998) 'Expectations of secondary science: realisation and retrospect', *School Science Review*, **79**(289), 81–83.

Henderson, J. (2000) 'QCA key stage 3 science scheme of work – a teacher's view', *School Science Review*, **81**(297), 23–27.

Hendley, D., Parkinson, J., Stables, A. and Tanner, H. (1995) 'Gender differences in pupil attitudes to the national curriculum foundation subjects of English, mathematics, science and technology', *Educational Studies*, **21**(1), 85–97.

Huggins, M. and Knight, P. (1997) 'Curriculum continuity and transfer from primary to secondary school: the case of history', *Educational Studies*, **23**(3), 333–348.

Jarman, R. (1980) *Primary Science, Secondary Science: Some Issues at the Interface. A Discussion Paper*, London: SSCR.

Jarman, R. (1993) 'Real experiments with Bunsen burners: pupils' perceptions of the similarities and differences between primary science and secondary science', *School Science Review*, **74**(268), 19–29.

Jarman, R. (1997) 'Fine in theory: a study of primary-secondary continuity in science, prior and subsequent to the introduction of the Northern Ireland Curriculum', *Educational Research*, **39**(3), 291–310.

Jenkins, E.W. (2000) 'The impact of the national curriculum on secondary school science teaching in England and Wales', *International Journal of Science Education*, **22**(3), 325–336.

Kaur, B. (1998) 'Primary/secondary liaison in science and value added from key stage 2 to 3', *Education in Science*, **179**, 9–11.

Kinder, K., Kendall, S., Halsey, C. and Atkinson, M. (1999) *Disaffection Talks: A Report for the Merseyside Learning Partnership Inter Agency Development Programme*, London: NFER (available at: http://www.nfer.ac.uk/research/papers/HilaryNFERConf2000.doc).

Kruger, C.J., Summers, M.K. and Palacio, D.J. (1990) 'An investigation of some English primary school teachers' understanding of the concepts force and gravity', *British Educational Research Journal*, **16**(4), 383–397.

Lucey, H. and Reay, D. (2000) 'Identities in transition: anxiety and excitement in the move to the secondary school', *Oxford Review of Education*, **26**(2), 191–205.

McCallum, B. (1996) 'The transfer and use of assessment information between primary and secondary school', *British Journal of Curriculum and Assessment*, **6**(3), 10–14.

Monk, M. (2000) 'A critique of the QCA specimen scheme of work for key stage 3 science', *School Science Review*, **81**(297), 29–32.

Murphy, C. and Beggs, J. (2001) 'Pupils' attitudes, perceptions and understanding of primary science: comparisons between Northern Irish and English schools.' Paper presented at the British Educational Research Association conference, University of Leeds (available at http://www.leeds.ac.uk/educol/documents/00001821.htm).

Newton, D.P. and Newton, L.D. (2001) 'Subject content knowledge and teacher talk in the primary classroom', *European Journal of Teacher Education*, **24**(3), 369–379.

Nott, M. and Wellington, J. (1999) 'The state we're in: issues in key stage 3 and 4 science', *School Science Review*, **81**(294), 13–18.

NUT (2001) *Independent Study for NUT – Teacher Workload* (available at http://www.data.teachers.org.uk/pdfs/jto_strb_02.pdf).

Ofsted (1999) *A Review of Primary Schools in England*, London: Office for Standards in Education.

Ofsted, (2000) *Progress in Key Stage 3 Science*, London: Office for Standards in Education.

Ofsted (2002a) *Changing Schools: An Evaluation of the Effectiveness of Transfer Arrangements at Age 11*, London: Office for Standards in Education.

Ofsted (2002b) *Standards and Quality in Education 2000/01: The Annual Report of Her Majesty's Chief Inspector of Schools*, London: Office for Standards in Education.

OHMCI (1999) *Standards for Quality in Primary Schools: Science in Key Stages 1 and 2*, Cardiff: Her Majesty's Inspectorate for Education and Training in Wales.

Osborne, J. (2001) 'Pupils' views of the role and value of the science curriculum: a focus group study', *International Journal of Science Education*, **23**(5), 441–467.

Parkinson, J. and Woodward, C. (1996) 'Promoting primary-secondary links in science during initial teacher training courses', *School Science Review*, **78**(282), 9–16.

Parkinson, J., Hendley, D., Tanner, H. and Stables, A. (1998) 'Pupils' attitudes to science in key stage 3 of the National Curriculum: a study of pupils in South Wales', *Research in Science & Technological Education*, **16**(2), 165–176.

Pell, T. and Jarvis, T. (2001) 'Developing attitude to science scales for use with children of ages five to eleven years', *International Journal of Science Education*, **23**(8), 847–862.

QCA (2000) *Science: A Scheme of Work for Key Stage 3*, London: QCA (available at: http://www.standards.dfee.gov.uk/schemes2/secondary_science/).

Ramsden, J.M. (1998) 'Mission impossible? Can anything be done about attitudes to science?', *International Journal of Science Education*, **20**(2), 125–137.

Reid, K. (1999) *Truancy and Schools*, London: Routledge.

Ryan, M. (2002) 'Tackling key stage 2 to 3 transition problems – a bridging project', *School Science Review*, **84**(306), 69–75.

Schagen, S. and Kerr, D. (1999) *Bridging the Gap? The National Curriculum and Progression from Primary to Secondary School*, Slough: NFER.

Smail, B. and Kelly, A. (1984) 'Sex differences in science and technology among 11 year old school children: II – affective', *Research in Science and Technology Education*, **2**, 87–106.

Speering, W. and Rennie, L. (1996) 'Students' perceptions about science: the impact of transition from primary to secondary school', *Research in Science Education*, **26**(3), 283–298.

TES (2002) 'Teachers "too shy" to pass on paperwork', an article by Helen Ward. TES, 22 March.

Williams, M. and Howley, R. (1989) 'Curriculum discontinuity: a study of a secondary school and its feeder primary schools', *British Educational Research Journal*, **15**(1), 61–76.

Yager, R.E. and Yager, S.O. (1985) 'Changes in perceptions of science for third, seventh and eleventh grade students', *Journal of Research in Science Teaching*, **22**(4), 347–358.

CHAPTER 5

Promoting pupils' learning

A comment made by Albert Einstein:

> Commonsense is the collection of prejudices acquired by the age of 18.
>
> Beale (TES, 2002)

Most of us have very clear ideas about learning, based on our own experiences and particular approaches that have appealed to us over the period of time we have been involved in teaching children. The purpose of this chapter is to revisit some of these ideas and perhaps learn about some new ones in order to help you establish more effective learning situations.

Ideas about learning

Mainly as a result of time pressures to complete courses, some teachers tend to adopt a transmission style of teaching and learning. In theory, the teacher talks to the class and the pupils soak up the information and are able to regurgitate it at the next examination point. In its worst form this is simply learning by rote, and pupils end up having little understanding of the concepts covered. At its best, when the didactic teaching is supplemented by vigorous questioning and productive activities, it can be an effective way of helping pupils to learn. A vital component for effective learning is the active involvement of pupils in some sort of task that leads them to engage with subject matter. The teacher promotes learning by providing motivation and a classroom climate where learning is valued, guides pupils through carefully targeted learning tasks and provides an appropriate level of support.

Learning is a very complex process, and it is doubtful that we will ever understand it completely. However, there are aspects of learning, concerned with the cognitive, social and emotional dimensions, that are well established. An understanding of these learning theories helps a teacher to understand how pupils can learn from particular activities and not from others. At present there are two main strands of learning theory that are drawn on in science education (Leach and Scott, 1999):

1 **Individual perspectives on learning.** This has its origins in the work of Piaget, who suggested that pupils construct meaning through their interaction with their environment. According to Piaget, the process of learning moves from experiences to the known and then to the abstract. Knowledge is seen as something 'inside' an individual's brain, and changes in knowledge are described as 'conceptual change'. Such changes are considered to be brought about primarily through the influence of an individual's 'mental apparatus', and little attention is given to how other individuals might influence the learning process. Constructivism has its origins in this developmental stage model of cognitive growth. While Piaget himself could not be described as being a constructivist, elements of his work (such as his interest in pupils' understanding of natural phenomena) are in accord with the modern constructivist paradigm (Solomon, 1994).

2 **Sociocultural perspectives on learning.** These models of learning extend the developmental theme of Piaget to include the dimension of learning from each other. The initial development of these models was greatly influenced by the work of Bruner (1968) and Vygotsky (1978). Bruner proposed that learning was an active process in which learners construct new concepts based on their present state of understanding. He saw the teacher as someone who engages pupils in active dialogue and fashions the learning activities to suit the learners' current state of understanding. Later, Bruner became influenced by the work of Vygotsky and expanded his theoretical framework to include social and cultural aspects of learning. This led to what has become known as social constructivism, where less emphasis is placed on the individual and more on the learning context and the role of teachers and other pupils in scaffolding the learning.

There have been a number of other areas of research running alongside the development of theories of pupils' learning. Again based on the work of Piaget, Shayer and Adey have developed activities to accelerate pupils' cognitive development and have produced the now well-established CASE materials (Adey *et al.*, 2001a).

In the following sections each of these models of learning will be looked at in more depth, but we will start with a feature that is common to all: motivating the pupils to do the work.

Motivation

In order for learning to take place, there needs to be the desire to learn or the will to be involved in the learning process. If a pupil does not wish to become engaged in the lesson activities, then it is likely that little, if anything, will be learnt. This is particularly worrying when looked at in the light of the decline in pupils' attitudes towards science as they progress through KS3 (page 68). One of the major contributors to our understanding of motivation, Maslow, proposed a hierarchy of basic human needs (Maslow, 1970). He argued that the needs at the bottom of the hierarchy were extremely important to an individual and should be satisfied first. Starting from the lowest level, the needs are as follows:

- physiological needs (e.g. food, drink, shelter)
- safety needs (e.g. physical security, freedom from anxiety)
- emotional needs (e.g. the need to feel that someone cares, the need to feel that one belongs)
- self-esteem (e.g. the need for achievement, the need for status and prestige)
- fulfilling one's own potential.

At its foundation level Maslow placed the need for food and drink and pleasant working environment. Judging from the large number of pupils who appear to need to eat, chew and drink in lessons, it would appear that frequent breaks in the school day to allow them to satisfy these needs could reduce the need for them to bring food into classrooms. Another fundamental need is that of feeling safe and secure in the working environment, free from intimidation and bullying. Teachers need to be very sensitive to this and look out for situations where an initial disagreement or misunderstanding develops into a cruel programme of psychological harassment. One of the most important issues related to pupil learning is the pupil's self-concept. This is related to image (not being seen as a swot or teacher's pet, being 'cool') and to self-esteem (feeling good about the level of personal achievement). Motivating pupils to work by telling them that it is important in terms of passing examinations and gaining employment sometimes works, and sometimes it produces a level of anxiety that results in minimal learning. A longer-term approach involving the development of a positive climate for work is likely to be more successful. This can be achieved through the relationship that the teacher has with the class, and the relationships of groups of pupils within the class. The teacher helps to create a climate where work is valued and enjoyed to the extent that the pupils don't feel as though they are working hard. Pupils know what is expected of them, and they encourage one another to get on with the tasks. Collaborative working in discussion groups or practical tasks improves motivation and enhances pupils' attitudes towards science (Murphy, 1994; Woolnough, 1994). Pupils like to know that the teacher cares about them and will work hard for them in terms of preparing interesting activities and marking their work on time. The relationship between academic achievement and emotional life is taken up further in the discussion on emotional intelligence on page 109.

Pupils' self-perception can be dramatically affected by 'failure' in day to day tasks and tests. Placing pupils in rank order following a test is only likely to motivate those pupils who appear towards the top of the list. Grouping pupils in sets can have a similar effect, making it difficult to generate enthusiasm for work amongst the lower sets. Williams (1997) suggests that teachers can raise pupils' self-esteem by:

- demonstrating that they value each pupil's work
- demonstrating that they value pupils as learners
- actively supporting pupils who experience difficulties
- respecting the individual 'intellectual space' of each pupil by allowing learning in the most personally effective way.

Experienced teachers recognise the importance of giving praise to pupils for trying hard or for producing a good piece of work; however, there are individuals and some classes that certain teachers find it difficult to relate to. These groups frequently experience negative comments, and this leads to a gradual deterioration in pupils' self-perception and the breakdown of teacher–pupil relationships (Glover and Law, 2002). The effect of praise on pupils' approach to future work may not, however, be as simple as might first be believed. Dweck (1986) suggests that the view held by teachers that positive reinforcement leads to desirable behaviour does not tie in with our present understanding of the principles of reinforcement. She points out that frequent praise for short, easy tasks is unlikely to create a desire for long, challenging ones, or to promote persistence in the face of failure. Her research indicates that the willingness to work on different types of tasks depends on pupils' theories of intelligence. Some pupils believe ability is fixed (entity theory) and some believe that hard work will lead to success (incremental theory). These different viewpoints can lead to different orientations towards work, as outlined in Table 5.1. Teachers can only deal with this complex situation when they have a good understanding of their pupils' response to work and are able to mix praise and encouragement judiciously.

Teachers who have been working with a class for a sustained period of time get to know that what works for one child may not work for another. The quiet word of praise to an individual is likely to be far more effective than open comments to the class. The personal approach will help to develop relationships and develop what Kyriacou (1997) calls 'identification'. This is where pupils tend to identify with particular teachers and adopt the values of that teacher to such an extent that it can have a marked effect on the pupil's general behaviour and motivation in that teacher's class.

Some teachers are concerned about the relationship between the curriculum and motivation, and the extent to which compulsory science courses at KS4 meet the needs of all pupils. Donnelly and Jenkins (1999) reported that nearly half of the secondary science teachers questioned in their survey believed that pupils' enjoyment of science teaching has diminished under the influence of the NC, while only 6 per cent thought it has increased. Chapter 12 takes up this point, and provides arguments for changes to the curriculum.

Table 5.1 *The way in which pupils vary in their beliefs about success, motivation and their response to difficult tasks (Dweck, 1986; Watkins et al., 2000)*

	Entity theory	Incremental theory
	Pupils believe that ability leads to success	Pupils believe that effort leads to success
Learning goal	Receive positive comments for work and avoid negative ones	To increase competence
Response to challenge	Satisfaction from doing better than others If confidence in ability is high, then pupils relish challenge and persist in the task until it is completed; if confidence is low, then pupils avoid challenge and do not persist in the task	Preference for challenging tasks

Things to consider

Review the impact of the tasks you give pupils on their level of motivation.

- Can all pupils experience a substantial degree of success in the tasks they are required to do?
- Do you think you have the right balance between presenting the case that 'science is fun' and 'learning science requires hard work'?
- Do the tasks challenge the pupils sufficiently? Do the pupils feel that it has been a worthwhile activity?
- Do you see any relationship between the expectations you have of individuals or groups and the extent to which they learn? (Pupils' performance tends to fall in line with the teachers' expectancies (Rosenthal and Jacobson, 1968))

Review your use of praise and its affect on motivating pupils by considering:

- the range of pupils you praise (Do some pupils receive a great deal of praise and others none at all? Do you think that some pupils resent the way in which you distribute praise within a class?)
- the extent to which you praise (Do you only give praise for exceptional effort or work, or do you shower pupils with praise for all sorts of reasons?)

Piaget's contribution to our understanding of learning

A great deal of what we now know about learning is based on the work of Piaget and therefore, in order to understand constructivism and CASE, it is important to be aware of Piagetian ideas. The major aspect of Piaget's theory of learning is that of pupils developing in stages. Each stage is characterised by a group of cognitive abilities, which increase in complexity and abstraction as pupils move from one stage to the next (Table 5.2). Pupils pass through each of the stages as they get older, but there is no clear transition between one stage and the next and there will be a period when pupils show characteristics of more than one stage. The determination of a pupil's stage of cognitive development can be achieved by using Piagetian Reasoning Tasks (PRTs),[1] which take the form of a structured demonstration and the pupils completing a worksheet when directed by the teacher. In a large-scale analysis of pupils' cognitive development, Adey and Shayer determined that 'fewer than 30 per cent of 16 year-olds were showing the use of even early formal operations' (Adey and Shayer, 1994: 31). In addition, their results indicated that the spread of cognitive levels in any one age group was much wider than previously expected. A Curriculum Analysis Taxonomy was

Table 5.2 *Stages of pupils' mental development according to Piaget*

Piagetian stage	Approximate mental age	Characteristics
1 Pre-operational	5–7 years	Thinking is dominated by what a child observes at a particular moment. Observations may be inconsistent. Contradictory explanations do not bother the child
2A Early concrete operational 2B Mature concrete operational	8–14 years	Thinking becomes increasingly consistent and logical when applied to things that the child can see or imagine. The child is able to classify objects and place them into groups. The child can communicate ideas about science in concrete terms but is unable to explain observations that require abstract concepts
3A Early formal operational 3B Mature formal operational	15+ years	The pupil can explain things in abstract terms, e.g. use science models and can generate hypotheses and design experiments to test them

devised in order to compare pupils' cognitive abilities with the level of difficulty of the science curriculum they were required to study (Shayer and Adey, 1981). When this was applied to the science curriculum used in the 1970s, it was found that the demand was considerably higher than the Piagetian stage of development attained by most pupils. This result led to changes in the science curriculum and to the development of materials to accelerate pupils' learning through the stages.

Constructivism – individual perspectives on learning

Constructivism is a very well established theory of learning. Its origins probably lie in the work of Kelly in the 1950s, and his theory of 'personal constructs', and Ausubel's principle (1960s) that the most important factor in learning is 'what the learner already knows' (Bennett, 2003).[2] The theory made considerable advances in status and acceptance following the publication of a paper by Driver and Easley where they argued that: 'achievement in science depends to a greater extent upon specific abilities and prior experience than cognitive functioning' (Driver and Easley, 1978: 66). Solomon (1994) suggests that this paper provided the impetus for new research into constructivism by providing a new 'language' (e.g. 'informal learning in small groups', 'the essential individuality of learning'), which enabled the constructivist approach to be used by others.

The constructivist view of learning is based on the view that learning is the product of interactions between existing understanding and new experiences. The characteristics have been clearly summarised by Driver and Bell (1986: 453) as follows:

1 **Learning outcomes depend not only on the learning environment but also on the knowledge of the learner** (i.e. students don't always see a situation in the same way as the teacher sees it. Their previous experiences and prior understanding is likely to influence what they see as important).

2 **Learning involves the construction of meanings. Meanings constructed by stu-dents from what they see or hear may or may not be those intended. Construction of meaning is influenced to a large extent by our existing knowledge** (i.e. students' understanding of phenomena is determined from prior learning and everyday experiences. They tend to explain things based on intuition rather than using scientific principles. Meaning is constructed by creating links between existing knowledge and the new topic being studied).

3 **The construction of meaning is a continuous and active process** (i.e. students are constantly checking out their understanding by thinking things through themselves or by talking with others).

4 **Meanings, once constructed, are evaluated and can be accepted or rejected** (i.e. sometimes pupils accept the meanings given by the teacher at the time of the lesson and they may be able to reproduce this meaning at appropriate times in the future, e.g. during question and answer sessions and tests, but they may not actually believe it, particularly if the scientific explanation is counter-intuitive. Some ideas tend to be very resistant to change. For example, some students find it difficult to believe that wood has been formed from carbon dioxide and water, although they may be perfectly able to recite the equation for photosynthesis. Intuition tells them that a solid such as wood should be made, at least in part, from something substantial – soil).

5 **Learners have the final responsibility for their learning** (i.e. students learn by con-structing meaning for themselves by drawing on their present knowledge and information from their new experiences. Sometimes pupils don't have time to assim-ilate the new ideas before the teacher gives them the 'right answer').

6 **There are patterns in the types of meanings students construct due to the shared experiences with the physical world and through natural language** (i.e. in many cases there are common patterns of pupils' misunderstandings. These are frequently referred to as 'misconceptions' or 'alternative frameworks', but other terms have also been used in the research literature).

These ideas are consistent with the views held by Piaget, who believed that knowledge is constructed through the interaction between the learner and the environment. Piaget used the terms 'assimilation' to describe how new learning experiences are created within existing mental frameworks, and 'accommodation' to indicate how existing thinking is modified in the light of new experiences. Where Piaget differs from the con-structivists is in the different perspectives each takes on learning. Piaget's work was concerned with the way in which children's cognitive abilities develop, whereas con-structivists are interested in the building up of understanding within a particular area of knowledge. According to Driver and Easley (1978: 66), pupils' learning in science may proceed by the making of imaginative leaps followed later by critical reflection. They coined the term 'paradigm shift' to label the change in learning that the pupils would have to overcome, linking it to the work of Kuhn and the development of scientific theories (see page 170). In her book *The Pupil as Scientist?*, Driver (1983) explained how children make sense of the world by making observations, looking for patterns and drawing conclusions from their personal set of data. Unfortunately, a common-sense understanding is not always in agreement with a scientific understanding. Driver found that pupils' alternative conceptions[3] tended to influence the way they related to experiments in science lessons. If the results did not match their preconceptions, then they would say that there was something wrong with the experiment and only record results that fitted in with their previous patterns of thinking. Some ideas are very secure and are resistant to change by teaching, but others are less strongly held and can be readily turned into 'correct science'. Resistance to change is likely to be greatest when a pupil's understanding is based around a whole framework of ideas, many of which turn out to be misconceptions. Some pupils distinguish what they see and learn in science lessons from what goes on in the real world. Once they have been taught a science topic they may be able to give correct answers to questions on the topic, providing they are presented in a scientific context. If the questions are set in an everyday context, pupil's may draw on information from their alternative frameworks to compose the answer (Taber, 2002). The vast majority, if not all, pupils hold alternative frameworks of one sort or another. More able pupils may be able to mask their misunderstandings through their ability to recognise what is important in science and apply their scientific learning in all school and examination contexts. However, in a study of pupils following the Salters' Advanced Chemistry course (a course known for its ability to motivate pupils), Barker and Miller (1999) found that while the majority of pupils understood the key concepts, there was a significant minority who appeared to retain their misconceptions. In particular, these groups of pupils appeared to have difficulties in understanding conservation of mass during a reaction and ideas about dissolving, ions and ionic compounds.

The research into alternative frameworks is vast, and has covered most of the scientific topics in the school curriculum. Different age groups of pupils have been studied and, for some topics, changes in understanding have been monitored as the pupils have progressed through school. In addition there have been comparative studies between countries, and research into the misconceptions held by teachers. Summaries of research findings into alternative frameworks are published from time to time, for example:

- *Making Sense of Secondary Science* (Driver *et al.*, 1994a, 1994b) – covers most topics in KS3 and KS4
- *Beyond Appearances: Students' Misconceptions about Basic Chemical Ideas* (Barker, 2000).

The main focus of constructivism research has been the understanding of pupils' alternative frameworks and how pupils learn about scientific concepts. The amount of research into teaching strategies based on a constructivist view of learning is very small, and has not produced any significant results. However, a number of teaching strategies have been proposed that tie in with other approaches to teaching. The original teaching model derived from the Children's Learning in Science (CLIS) Project is shown on the left-hand side of Table 5.3, and is matched with a four-phase lesson approach suggested by the proponents of accelerated learning. There are some common features between the two approaches, but two key features of the CLIS approach (elicitation and cognitive conflict) are not featured in the accelerated learning

Table 5.3 *Sequences in learning activities: a comparison between a constructivist approach and a multiple intelligences/accelerated learning approach*

Key phases in teaching from a constructivist standpoint (adapted from Needham, 1987)	Key phases in teaching from a multiple intelligence standpoint (adapted from Smith, 2001)
Orientation • use of stimulus material, e.g. newspaper items, demonstrations, discussion of everyday event • preparatory homework, e.g. asking pupils to write down what they already know about the topic, carrying out an experiment or survey at home <div align="center">↓</div>	**Stimulation** • stimulate the brain by exercises and activities that require listing, sorting, observing and describing, demonstrating and showing
Elicitation of ideas • whole-class and/or group discussion followed by reporting back (e.g. based on: card-sorting exercises, sorting of pupil statements, commenting on given scenarios) • ideas compiled on the board, OHP or flip chart (in a place where they can be kept for referral later on) • practical activity followed by class discussion <div align="center">↓</div>	<div align="center">↓</div>
Restructuring of ideas a process of clarifying ideas through group and class discussion <div align="center">↓</div> getting pupils to question their original ideas by exposing them to cognitive conflict situations, e.g. through teacher demonstrations, personal experiments, worksheets <div align="center">↓</div> constructing new ideas through activities such as: teacher input, reading, discussion <div align="center">↓</div> testing out the newly constructed ideas through activities such as: practical work, teacher demonstration <div align="center">↓</div>	**Amplification** • pupils use a variety of learning tools that allow them to expand, deepen and nurture a stimulated intelligence, e.g. group work, thought experiments, flow charts, memory maps, practical tasks <div align="center">↓</div>
Application of ideas • opportunities to use the ideas in problem solving situations • writing about the science in their own words • carrying out experiments and interpreting them <div align="center">↓</div>	**Learning and understanding** • the developing intelligence is refined through problem solving tasks and structure learning • the pupil is presented with challenging tasks and develops a more autonomous approach to learning as he or she gains in confidence <div align="center">↓</div>
Review • preparing posters summarising the key points • personal writing • discussion sessions	**Transferring and effecting** • pupils apply the skills or knowledge to new situations • the goal of this strategy is 'mastery' to the extent that it becomes part of the learner's cognitive, affective and sensory life.

scheme. Elicitation of pupils' original ideas is seen as the cornerstone of constructivist teaching. It is where the teacher finds out about pupils' prior understanding of the topic through brainstorming activities, group discussion, short practical tasks or a completed written homework exercise. The principle has been adopted in some of the QCA SoWs, e.g. in the Y7 unit on forces (sci7k), and it could be argued that many of the starter activities of the KS3 strategy provide opportunities for pupils to consider their prior learning. The CLIS teaching approach recommends that pupils' ideas are recorded in some sort of way so that they can be revisited at the end of the topic in order that pupils can check on the extent of their learning. Does the evidence from the practical work and other activities indicate that their prior understanding was correct or false? In the past, flip charts and posters have been the means of recording this information, but with the advent of electronic whiteboards it becomes much easier to store the information and retrieve it at key points in the teaching sequence.

Things to consider

Asking pupils to explain familiar situations using their knowledge of science can often give an indication of the nature of their understanding and may help to identify misconceptions. The questions provided in Table 5.4 could be used as the basis for starter activities, or some time after the topic has been taught to check on the retention of understanding. The multiple-choice element of many of the questions provides teachers with the opportunity to ask groups of pupils to get together and explain the reasoning behind their choice.

Social constructivism – sociocultural perspectives on learning

Constructivist research has produced, and continues to produce, valuable information about pupils' alternative frameworks. The research has also been useful in identifying the way that certain misconceptions persist in children's minds even when they have been taught the correct science. Constructivist theory has a good record of informing teachers about the nature of learning problems, but it has been less successful in providing guidance for teachers to overcome the problems. Millar (1989) was one of the first to level criticism and pointed out that the 'process of eliciting, clarification and construction of new ideas takes place internally, within the learner's own head. This occurs whenever any successful learning takes place and is independent of the form of instruction' (Millar, 1989: 589). Matthews (1994, 1998) has criticised the way in which constructivism articulates the construction of knowledge. He states that from a constructivist standpoint, the way in which an individual constructs personal understanding is akin to building scientific understanding. He argues that this does not represent reality, and that 'real' scientific understanding is a much more complex process involv-

Table 5.4 *Examples of questions that could be used to determine the nature of pupils' understanding of key science concepts (simple diagrams often accompany the questions, to act as a stimulus or help pupils visualise the situation)*

Topic	Diagnostic question
Particle theory	After many experiments, scientists think that: • all things are made of small particles • these particles move in all directions • temperature affects the speed they move at • they exert forces on each other. Use any of these ideas to answer the following question: A football is pumped up hard during the day when it is warm. In the evening when the temperature falls, the football does not feel so hard. How does this happen? (Assume the football does not leak.) (Brook *et al.*, 1983)
Energy	A girl has a dynamo on her bicycle to light her lamps. She notices that when the dynamo is being used it is harder to pedal at the same speed. She is told that this is because energy cannot be created or destroyed, only changed from one form to another. How does this explain what she has noticed? (Brook and Driver, 1984)
Heat	A cook put two saucepans of potatoes on a stove to boil. When they were both boiling, she turned the gas under one down so low that the water was just kept boiling. She left the other on high. She thought the one on high would cook the potatoes faster. A friend said that it would make no difference to the cooking time of the potatoes. Which person do you think is correct? Give your reason. (Brook *et al.*, 1984)
Conservation of mass	When 2 g of zinc and 1 g of sulphur are heated together, practically no zinc or sulphur remain after the compound zinc sulphide is formed. What would happen if 2 g of zinc were heated with 2 g of sulphur? (Choose one letter) A. Zinc sulphide containing twice as much sulphur will be formed. B. Twice as much zinc sulphide will be formed. C. The same amount of zinc sulphide will be formed as before, and some sulphur will not react. D. The same amount of zinc sulphide will be formed as before, and some zinc will not react. Give the reason for your choice. (Briggs and Holding, 1986)
Plant nutrition	A small tree was planted in a meadow. After 20 years it had grown into a big tree, weighing 250 kg more than when it was planted. Where does the extra 250 kg come from? Explain your answer as fully as you can. (Bell and Brook, 1984)

ing a range of issues such as objectivity, scientific decision-making and methodology. It would be a considerable oversimplification to say that personal understanding is the same as scientific understanding.

The early constructivist's lack of attention to teaching was prevalent until the early 1990s, and there was then a shift in opinion from an emphasis on the individual making sense of his or her personal experiences to individuals learning with the help of others. The term 'social constructivism' was adopted to indicate the importance of learning through the social interactions with another, whether a teacher or a more able peer. The development in the theory was largely based on the work of the Russian psychologist Vygotsky (Hodson and Hodson, 1998a).

Vygotsky made great play of the role of language and its function in sharing information and enabling an individual to think things through and organise learning. Unlike Piaget, whose studies were centred on the development of concepts that arose spontaneously, Vygotsky was concerned about learning in school. There are many similarities between the work of the two psychologists, and while there are differences, they tend to be merely a matter of degree or emphasis (Howe, 1996). The exception to this is that Vygotsky suggested that Piaget's view of children functioning at particular operational levels was not entirely true. Children who are deemed to be working, for example, at Piagetian level 1B may be able to solve problems with a higher cognitive demand with the guidance of an adult or in collaboration with more able peers (Vygotsky, 1978). Vygotsky proposed a model of learning involving two 'layers'; an inner layer consisting of the learning that an individual can achieve independently, and an outer layer that requires the help of adults or more capable peers. He called the distance between these two layers the 'Zone of Proximal Development' (ZPD). Intelligence, he argued, is determined not only by a capacity to learn but also by a capacity for being taught. Bruner took Vygotsky's ideas further, and introduced the concept of 'scaffolding'. This involves the teacher setting up a support structure to help the learner keep on the right track and avoid too many pitfalls. The teacher's job is to stimulate and support learning, leading pupils to new levels of conceptual understanding by interacting with and talking to them. Pupils are guided into tackling problems that would 'normally' be seen as only achievable by the more able. The process involves the teacher not only in presenting pupils with challenging activities but also in providing situations where the

---

Things to consider

Consider the extent to which you incorporate scaffolding mechanisms into your teaching. Scaffolding has a number of distinctive features:

- **Recruitment.** Motivating pupils to carry out the task.
- **Reduction of degrees of freedom.** Simplifying the task by reducing the number of steps needed to arrive at a solution – breaking it down into manageable chunks. (There may be time when the use of a computer can promote this aspect of scaffolding; Kennewell *et al.*, 2000.)
- **Direction maintenance.** Keeping pupils motivated – maintaining the drive to get an answer to the problem.
- **Marking critical features.** Highlighting key points on the road to a successful solution in order to help pupils judge the correctness of their work.
- **Demonstration.** The teacher models how to solve part of the problem, or shows how similar problems can be solved.

(Wood *et al.*, 1976)

learning process is modelled. In this way, pupils are gradually led into the culture of learning. As enculturation is established, the learner is able to take greater responsibility for his or her own learning and the scaffolding can be removed.

Hodson and Hodson (1998b) propose a three-phase scaffolding strategy. In the first phase, teachers determine pupils' prior understanding of the work and create links between old knowledge and the new study. The teacher is involved in the process of revitalising stored information and setting up a situation where the pupils appreciate that there is more to learn. From the initial question and answer session and classroom discussion the teacher has a clear idea of the depth of understanding held by different groups of pupils, and this enables him or her to make decisions about the level of cognitive demand of the new learning tasks. The second phase involves working within the ZPD, breaking down the learning into manageable chunks. In some cases the teacher might lead the pupil through the learning, while at the same time explaining his or her thought processes; on some occasions pupils are left to work things through themselves; and on others pupils work things out together with the teacher or with a group of pupils. In the third phase, the pupil has to check his or her personal understanding of the topic. Learners have the final responsibility for their own learning, and must be prepared to ask questions of others. One way of accomplishing this is to provide pupils with exercises where they are given the opportunity to apply their knowledge to new situations. As they test things out they may come across gaps in their understanding, which can hopefully be filled by asking others.

Vygotskian theory has moved constructivism into a new era, where the role of teaching is enhanced. The job of the teacher is to provide support and promote pupil independence through activity, questioning, explanation and discussion. Constructivism is likely to grow and branch into new categories of learning theory as we develop our understanding of teaching and learning, and as new technologies are incorporated into classrooms. One such embryonic theory is that of communal constructivism, which is concerned with the way in which ICT can influence a learning environment. It refers to the way that pupils learn together at a computer, constructing knowledge for their community – i.e. beyond their immediate group (Leask and Younie, 2001).

Things to consider

How do you see the process of enculturation taking place?

It is likely to involve situations where knowledge is co-constructed, where the learning process is made explicit. Classroom dialogue may contain phrases such as 'let's think about this', 'what would happen if...' and 'how do we know that to be true?'.

It is also likely to involve work on the nature of science as a discipline, looking at how scientists solve problems, how they interpret data, the strength of evidence etc. Pupils will need opportunities to examine critically how the scientific knowledge is constructed and how it is represented to the public (Roth, 2001).

Thinking skills and metacognition

Teaching thinking skills enables pupils to understand **how** they learn as distinct from **what** they learn. Although the term 'thinking skill' is commonly used in education circles, the processes involved go way beyond what might be simply described as 'skills' (Wilson, 2000). Thinking skills include 'higher-level' activities such as critical and creative thinking. McGuinness (1999) points out that different researchers have produced different taxonomies of thinking, but most include some, or all, of the following:

- collecting information
- sequencing and sorting information
- analysing information
- drawing conclusions, giving reasons for the conclusions
- 'brainstorming' new ideas
- problem-solving
- determining cause and effect
- evaluating options, determining bias, the reliability of evidence
- planning and setting goals
- monitoring progress
- decision-making, weighing up pros and cons
- reflecting on one's own progress.

These are activities that all teachers will use from time to time, but they may neglect to give sufficient emphasis to the processes involved. Advocates of thinking skills recommend that pupils need to be taught how to think things through. This can be achieved by making the thinking process explicit through techniques such as 'thinking diagrams' (where the sequence of steps are written down) or 'think aloud methods' (where individuals explain how they reason through an argument). Pupils need time and the opportunity to talk about thinking processes, and support to enable them to reflect on their own strategies. It is likely to be more effective if the school as a whole develops a learning community ethos and encourages the use of thinking strategies across the whole school. McGuinness (1999) identifies three approaches to teaching thinking skills used in schools:

1 Specifically designed programmes that are additional to the normal curriculum, e.g. Somerset Thinking Skills (Blagg *et al.*, 1995)
2 Teaching infused across the curriculum, e.g. Philosophy for children (Lipman *et al.*, 1980)
3 Teaching embedded in a particular subject e.g. CASE (Adey *et al.*, 2001a).

According to McGuinness (1999: 3), 'acquiring and using metacognitive skills has emerged as a powerful idea for promoting a thinking skills curriculum'. Metacognition is a high-level activity concerned with knowledge about cognition/knowing. It requires learners to develop:

- an awareness of their own knowledge, their strengths and weaknesses

- the ability to reflect on their own ways of acquiring an understanding of the nature of the subject
- the ability to regulate their own actions in the application of that.

In metacognitive classrooms, learners are expected to ask questions about where they went wrong and to tell the teacher when they don't understand. White and Mitchell (1994) emphasise the need for consistency in approach across the science curriculum and across all science teachers in a school in order to ensure that pupils appreciate that in science lessons they will exhibit good learning behaviours (Table 5.5) and be required to think. Some pupils will reject the idea, particularly if they have managed to succeed in school using shallow learning techniques such as rote learning and have never consciously adopted metacognitive strategies (Thomas and McRobbie, 2001). It is likely to take a great deal of time and effort on behalf of both teachers and pupils for metacognitive practices to become part of the routine of science teaching and learning. Activities such as getting pupils to write 'Thinking Diaries', or homeworks where pupils write about what they learnt, what was difficult, what was easy and why, all help to promote metacognition (Adey *et al.*, 2001a).

Table 5.5 *Examples of good and poor learning behaviours (White and Mitchell, 1994)*

Poor learning behaviours	Good learning behaviours
Pupils rarely make contributions of their own ideas in lessons	Pupils tell the teacher when they don't understand
Pupils expect to be told what to do; they do not want to try to work things out for themselves	Pupils ask a teacher why they went wrong
Pupils accept everything they read or hear without question	Pupils refer to previous work before asking the teacher
Pupils repeat the same mistakes time and again	Pupils think things through before offering an opinion, and are therefore able to justify what is said
Pupils fail to make links with other lessons	Pupils look for links with other subjects

Things to consider

Concept mapping is seen as an activity where pupils are given the opportunity to make their understanding of science explicit (see page 244). Consider using the principle of concept mapping to elucidate science teachers' views about the relationships between teaching and learning. Covering all aspects of teaching and learning is too much to consider at any one time, and so it will be more workable to study one aspect of learning and its relationship with the common methods of teaching used. This may start with a brainstorming activity, leading to a list of teaching techniques and notions about pupils' learning. The map may then be constructed showing links between the ideas. To what extent do the teaching activities generally used by staff foster quality learning?

Cognitive Acceleration in Science Education (CASE)

> We are convinced that some 80 per cent of the school population currently perform academically well below their potential, yet by means of suitable intervention virtually all can function at levels where presently only the top 20 per cent lie.
>
> (Shayer and Adey, 2002: 1)

As mentioned above, in the mid 1970s Shayer and his colleagues carried out a large-scale study of pupils' stages of cognitive development and matched this to the cognitive demand of one of the popular O-level syllabuses at the time, the Nuffield scheme (Shayer and Adey, 1981).[4] This research, combined with other research, led to the production of the *Thinking Science* CASE materials in 1984 and Inset materials in 1993 (Adey, 1993). CASE is based on the principle that it is possible to develop intelligence by presenting pupils with challenging activities. Pupils are encouraged to make their thinking explicit and to co-construct knowledge with their peers in small group situations.

At present there are three different CASE programmes:

1 The original CASE at KS3 using the *Thinking Science* publication (Adey *et al.*, 2001a). This was written for use with Y7 and Y8 pupils and contains 30 activities, each lasting a typical science lesson. At this age pupils are beginning to use formal thinking, stage 3A, and the materials are designed to nurture this growth.
2 CASE at KS1 using the *Let's Think* publication (Adey *et al.*, 2001b). This was written for use with Y1 and Y2 pupils and contains 30 activities, each lasting about 30 minutes. The materials are designed to benefit from the growth in thinking as pupils enter the concrete operations stage, 1A.
3 CASE at KS2 using *Let's Think Through Science* publication (Adey *et al.*, 2003). This was designed for use with Y3 and Y4 pupils and contains 15 activities, each lasting about 40 minutes, linked to the QCA SoW for science. There is no rationale based on Piagetian levels for using the materials with pupils of this age.

In addition there are related programmes in mathematics (CAME, Adhami *et al.*, 1998), and technology (CATE, Hamaker *et al.*, 1997), and a similar scheme in geography, *Thinking Through Geography* (Leat, 1989).

The activities in the *Thinking Science* (TS) book each have a special focus for promoting logical thinking. These are:

• Control and exclusion of irrelevant variables (lessons 1–5 and 16 for variables; lessons 26, 27, 29 for compound variables)
• Classification (lessons 6 and 7)
• Ratio and proportionality (lessons 8 and 9)
• Inverse proportionality and equilibrium (lessons 10–12 for inverse proportionality and 28 and 30 for equilibrium)

- Probability and correlation (lessons 13, 14, 17, 18, 21, 22 for probability and 19 and 20 for correlation)
- The use of abstract models to explain and predict (lessons 23–25).

There are well defined lines of progression through the activities, and teachers are advised to stick to the sequence of lessons given in the book and to keep them separate from 'normal' science lessons. The TS lessons can be given once a fortnight, spread over the first two years of secondary school. Each lesson contains a number of core features:

1 **Concrete preparation.** This is about introducing and explaining the problem to be solved.
2 **Cognitive conflict.** This is the term used 'to describe an event or observation which the pupil finds puzzling and discordant with previous experience or understanding' (Adey and Shayer, 1994: 62). Pupils need to think about a range of possible explanations for causes and effects that may interact in complex ways with each other. For example, one lesson involves pupils blowing over the tops of tubes and listening to the note produced. Pupils consider the variables of length, width and material. The conflict is about which variable is the key factor.
3 **Social construction.** This is where pupils work together, clarifying factors and checking understanding. Teachers contribute by asking questions or providing guidance. Here, pupils are working in Vygotsky's ZPD.
4 **Metacognition.** The teacher will promote this by asking questions such as: 'How did you solve that? Please explain to the others in your group why you think that' (Adey *et al.*, 2001a: 12).

Another important feature is the creation of links between concepts. It is hoped that after a number of lessons looking at controlling variables pupils will be able to transfer their learning to a new situation and make correct decisions. This is referred to as 'near-transfer'. A more ambitious goal is for pupils who have understood about controlling variables to apply their reasoning skills to another context, say proportionality, and be able to solve problems where this is involved. This type of reasoning is called 'far-transfer', and it is something that happens infrequently. Another aspect of linking concepts is where the teacher helps the pupils to link the type of thinking developed in each TS lesson to other TS lessons, to 'normal' lessons and to 'real life'. This is called 'bridging'. In TS lessons, it occurs when the teacher reminds pupils of connections between what they are doing and reasoning patterns they have experienced previously. At the end of the lesson, the teacher identifies how the work relates to work they are going to do in other lessons. Shayer and Gamble (2001) suggest that bridging should play an important role in all lessons and they have produced a series of outline plans for normal lessons, for both KS3 and KS4 topics, each with a strong CASE influence and an emphasis on the creation of links. Once a teacher has become accustomed to the CASE approach it is likely that he or she will take the CASE principles and activities and adapt them to suit individual situations. Moran and Vaughan (2000) have done just that and have used the CASE approach to teach atomic structure and bonding to KS4 pupils. In order to generate cognitive conflict, the authors produced 'check and challenge' cards requiring pupils to make decisions and justify their decisions. Jones and Gott (1998) go one step further, and argue for a curriculum that incorporates CASE methods and other activities that promote pupils' procedural understanding in order to present a more coherent picture of science.

It has been shown that CASE training impacts on teaching practices beyond the use of the materials in CASE lessons. Research carried out by McGregor and Gunter (2001) has shown that CASE-trained teachers:

- spent more time discussing pedagogy
- changed their questioning techniques
- provided more opportunities for pupils to predict outcomes
- were more proactive in grouping pupils.

CASE has been used with pupils of all abilities. Simon (2002) has shown how CASE can be used with pupils with learning difficulties by careful control of the language used and consideration of the pupils' capability to operate within their ZPD. Teachers need to resist the temptation to tell them what to do and try to help pupils gradually to recognise what is involved through the use of questions and advice. *Philosophy in the Classroom* (Lipman *et al.*, 1980), has been found to be effective with primary school pupils and also less able secondary school pupils (Adey and Shayer, 1994). Pupils are presented with problems based on familiar situations and asked to reason things through. This reasoning must be made clear to others in the group and thus it provides individuals with the opportunity to think about their own thinking – i.e. act metacognitively.

There are gender differences in the extent in which CASE improves the pupils' performance. This may be due to the earlier maturation of girls, or it may be due to the way in which Y7 classes are organised. Whitelegg (1996) reports that boys' groups who started the intervention at age 13 and girls' groups who started at 12 showed significant improvements in their GCSE grades, after individual pre-test results were taken into account. However, girls who started at 13 and boys who started at 12 showed no improvement in performance.

There have been a number of studies of the effectiveness of using the CASE materials reported in the literature (for example, see the review in Adey and Shayer, 1994). The results indicate that the use of an educational intervention programme can have long-term positive effects on pupils' academic achievement. A more recent study (Shayer, 2000) looked at achievement from a value-added approach. Baseline data were taken from the results from PRTs taken by pupils soon after they had started the school in Y7, and the outgoing data consisted of the GCSE results in science, maths and English. One group, comprising of 11 schools, used CASE with their KS3 classes; the other group of 16 schools, the control group, did not use CASE at the time but were planning to do so in the near future. The assumption was made that both cohorts of schools contained teachers who were equally enthusiastic for innovation. Also, in the control schools the data on Y7 PRTs and GCSE results was not for the same pupils. The researchers made the additional assumption that the intake of pupils for any one school would remain roughly constant from year to year, which is statistically justifiable over a large number of pupils and schools. The results showed that CASE pupils generally achieve higher grades at GCSE, not only in science but also in maths and English (see Table 5.6), and it was reported that, if the results were repeated nationally, the percentage of pupils gaining a C grade or above would rise from the present 50.8 per cent to 77.2 per cent. For the first time, the data reported the effect of CASE for more able pupils. It was shown that, contrary to the views held by some teachers, CASE was particularly effective in improving this group's GCSE grades.

Endler and Bond (2000) investigated the effectiveness of using CASE materials in a school in Australia by comparing the progress of a group of pupils who had followed the intervention programme with a group who had not received any CASE lessons. The pupils' cognitive development was determined using a short multiple-choice test devised and validated by one of the authors. The researchers found that there was increased cognitive development between Y8 and Y10 for most of the pupils who had followed the CASE programme in comparison to those who had not experienced CASE activities. They were surprised at the wide variation in metal growth within the CASE group, and the fact that rapid gains were made by pupils from a wide range of starting levels. They found that although boys were more advanced in cognitive development than girls in Y8 and Y10, there was no difference in the rate of cognitive change based on sex up to Y10. However, in the following two years girls showed additional cognitive gains that were not shown in boys.

Table 5.6 *Some of the benefits of using CASE (see article by Sebba and Viner at http://www.aaia.org.uk/ mikeviner.htm; DfEE KS3 Strategy website www.aaia.org.uk)*

The impact of using CASE on pupils' achievement
Comparing CASE schools to control schools:

- Nineteen per cent more pupils obtained A*–C in science
- Fifteen per cent more pupils obtained A*–C in mathematics
- Sixteen per cent more pupils obtained A*–C in English
- The percentage of pupils gaining level 6 at KS3 was double the percentage in the control schools
- CASE schools raised pupils' grades in GCSE English, mathematics and science by an average of one grade

---

Things to consider

Are pupils receiving consistent messages about thinking skills from all members of the science team? How does the work in cognitive acceleration in science relate to work done in other curriculum subjects?

Learning styles

In the same way that human beings have preferences for the way in which they carry out many everyday activities (e.g. the way they do their hair, the mannerisms they display), they also have an 'in-built' preference for a particular type of learning. An individual's preferred learning style is determined partially by nature and partially by nurture. Some researchers consider that learning styles change as a person matures, but others believe that it tends to be fixed from an early age and cannot be changed significantly. What appears to be certain is that at any one time a pupil will have a preferred learning style and will apply it to every lesson, irrespective of the subject or topic (Adey *et al.*, 1999). There are several approaches to determining and classifying learning styles reported in the research literature, and most of them feature characteristics that are at opposite ends of a scale. The most commonly accepted scale is that of wholist–analyst. Here, a person who likes to see the complete situation first rather than examine the constituent parts is described as a wholist, while someone who prefers to look at the detail of what is being learnt and to consider it bit by bit is described as an analyst. A second dimension has been identified as verbaliser–imager; however, the evidence for the scale is not as strong as for the wholist–analyst component. A verbaliser prefers to learn through spoken or written words, whereas an imager prefers to learn through a pictorial or diagrammatic format. Individuals will have characteristics of both these dimensions, and their preferred learning style will be situated on the grid, such as person 'A' in Figure 5.1. A person's position

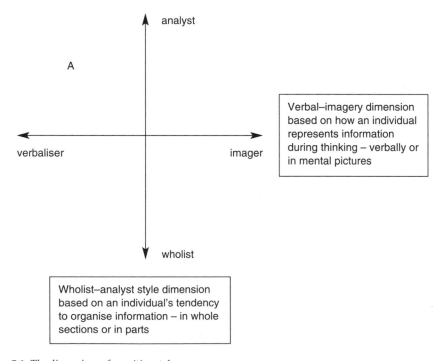

Figure 5.1 *The dimensions of cognitive style*

on the grid can be determined using a Cognitive Style Analysis (CSA), which is made up of three sets of tests that can be completed in about 10 minutes either in pen and paper format or on a computer (Riding and Raynor, 1998). The CSA has been used successfully with pupils as young as 10, and with pupils from different ethnic backgrounds.

Advocates of accelerated learning tend to base their arguments on a learning style model based on three distinct communication and learning preferences: visual, auditory and kinaesthetic (Smith, 2001). Research of this model indicates that the preferred learning styles of the population tend to be distributed as follows:

- **Visual.** About 29 per cent prefer to learn through graphs, pictures, diagrams and visual artefacts.
- **Auditory.** About 34 per cent prefer to learn through the spoken word.
- **Kinaesthetic.** About 37 per cent prefer to learn by engaging with the experience physically.

The VAK approach to learning has proved to be very popular in some schools, possibly because it appears to match the pupils being taught and it has a common-sense feel to it. In addition, it fits in neatly with Gardner's classification of intelligence (see page 106). However, some researchers would say that the evidence for VAK as distinct learning styles (in the sense of deep personally-linked constructs) is weak (Adey *et al.*, 1999).

Things to consider

An appreciation of different learning styles strengthens the argument for providing pupils with a variety of activities. Some pupils may prefer to receive information in bullet-point format, whereas others may be able to follow the argument more clearly if it is written in a paragraph, and a further group of pupils may find it easier if the information is presented diagrammatically.

Carry out a review of textbooks and worksheets to check that pupils' preferred learning styles are catered for. Consider including exercises that require pupils to change information from one format to another (e.g. text to diagram).

Multiple intelligences

> And so it becomes necessary to say there is not, and there can never be, a single universally accepted list of human intelligences. There will never be a master list of three, seven or three hundred intelligences that can be endorsed by all investigators.
>
> (Gardner, 1993: 59)

Gardner and his followers suggest that there is evidence for at last eight different types of intelligence, broadly grouped into three categories, as follows:

1 **Personal-related**
   - Interpersonal
   - Intrapersonal
2 **Language-related**
   - Linguistic
   - Musical
3 **Object-related**
   - Mathematical and logical
   - Visual and spatial
   - Kinaesthetic
   - Naturalist

Pupils will possess each of the intelligences, but some will be more dominant than the others. Smith (2001) has produced a self-perception questionnaire to enable individuals determine the balance of their intelligence profile, where respondents are invited to express their views to 40 statements using a scale of 0–5. The scores for groups of statements are then totalled and the values plotted on a chart. Not surprisingly, in any one class there will be pupils whose intelligence strengths lie in each of the areas. The implication of this for teaching is that if we are to promote learning for every child, we need to provide pupils with activities that stimulate their dominant intelligences. Table 5.7 indicates some of the typical characteristics found in pupils possessing each of the intelligences. Experienced teachers, who are aware of this perspective on learning, are able to correlate teaching activities that match different intelligences. For example, pupils who show a dominance in interpersonal intelligence will learn well in group activities, whereas a linguistically intelligent person will benefit from using DART-type exercises (Parkinson, 2002). Teachers who prescribe to this approach will try to access and develop each type of intelligence as often as possible, and certainly aim to structure their work to ensure that all the intelligences are called into play within a small group of lessons.

Smith (2001) incorporates the principle of multiple intelligences in his accelerated learning approach to teaching. He proposes a seven-stage cycle of learning, starting with an important pre-stage involving the building up of a positive learning climate:

Table 5.7 *Characteristics of pupils showing different intelligences after Gardner (adapted from* The Learners' Co-operative, *1998 and Smith, 2001)*

Intelligence	Typical characteristics
Interpersonal	• relate well to others • see issues from different perspectives • are at ease in groups • are prepared to take on the role of team leader
Intrapersonal	• often enjoy working alone • are self-motivated • value personal growth and development • are metacognitive learners
Kinaesthetic	• are good at sport, good hand–eye co-ordination • show dexterity in fine and gross motor movement • can be restless if required to sit still for long periods • learn by doing and clearly remember what was done rather than what was said or seen • benefit from frequent physical breaks
Linguistic	• enjoy communicating, sometimes through writing and talking and sometimes just through one method • are good at spelling • have a good vocabulary
Mathematical and logical	• are familiar with the concepts of time, space, quantity, number, cause and effect • see patterns easily • construct hypotheses and test them, collect data, formulate models • are organised in their approach to work • measure things accurately • adopt a problem-solving approach to tasks
Musical	• enjoy listening to, and sometimes playing, music • have a good appreciation of rhythm and movement • appreciate that word and sound groupings can often lead to change in mood and feeling
Visual and spatial	• learn through seeing and observing • interpret and construct graphs, maps and other visual media • have artistic talent • are able easily to visualise things in three dimensions • can easily find their way around text
Naturalist	• show awareness of the interrelatedness of environment, change and time • demonstrate a concern about the impact of human intervention on the natural environment • understands the significance of environment and social balance and have a sense of fairness

Pre-stage: Create the supportive learning environment

Pupils are made to feel good about themselves and their ability to learn the topic; they are made to appreciate that they will need to work hard and do their best

Stage 1: Connect the learning

The teacher talks about the links to previously learnt work and may show how the work they are about to do fits into position on a learning map

Stage 2: The big picture | The teacher explains the outline of the lesson, indicating what they are going to do and why they are going to do it. Pupils will need to know what sort of questions they should be asking themselves, i.e. metacognition is promoted

Stage 3: Describe the outcomes | The learning outcomes are explained in terms that make sense to the pupils; pupils consider their personal learning targets for the lesson

Stage 4: Input | The teacher provides information for the pupils using techniques that they will find interesting and that will appeal to the different learning VAK styles. Activities and questioning should be interspersed with the teacher input to check on pupils' understanding

Stage 5: Activity | The activities are varied and designed to access the multiple intelligences. They are interspersed with longer activities that contain opportunities for pupils to externalise their learning, e.g. by group discussion or short writing exercises. The pupils are given the opportunity to reflect on what they have learnt

Stage 6: Demonstrate | Pupils carry out an activity to show what they have learnt, e.g. short talk to the rest of the class, production of a poster or piece of written work

Stage 7: Review for recall and retention | The teacher reviews the key points with the pupils, referring back to the big picture, and focuses on memory techniques for future recall. Pupils review their learning in their groups

Smith's approach to teaching incorporates a number of tried and tested methods, but it also includes relatively new ideas concerned with catering for different groups of pupils and giving greater emphasis to an individual's responsibility for his or her own learning. In an accelerated learning classroom, pupils tend to be very busy concentrating on the task in hand – so much so that Smith suggests that they need learning breaks from time to time. He also supports the use of music to create different moods in learning, e.g. *The Four Seasons* (Vivaldi) for energising pupils, *Claire de Lune* (Debussy) for relaxing, *Tubular Bells* (Mike Oldfield) as ambient music to manage noise levels.

As mentioned on page 86, Maslow's work on motivation stresses the importance of paying attention to pupils' emotional needs. Goleman (1996) has taken this one step further and suggests that pupils' thinking and, therefore, academic success is determined in part by what he calls 'emotional intelligence'. This is the extent to which a pupil has control and understanding over his or her feelings or emotions.

Rockett and Percival (2002) suggest that teachers should help pupils to develop a number of skills that support emotional intelligence:

1 Self talk and self awareness – tackling the problem with a positive attitude
2 Recognising the reactions of others – understanding the clues that can be given through non-verbal behaviours (e.g. eye contact, gestures) and verbal behaviours (e.g. listening, positive responses)
3 Problem-solving/decision-making applied to feelings – one aspect of this could be discussions about the emotional experiences of scientists when they make discoveries that have significant influence on the lives of everyone (e.g. J. Robert Oppenheimer and his work on the atomic bomb)
4 Understanding other perspectives – recognising that everyone has something to offer (possibly linked to the idea of multiple intelligences and/or ideas and evidence).

The use of multiple intelligences and accelerated learning appears to be an increasingly popular approach. It encourages teachers to use a variety of activities and to pay attention to pupils' learning. However, it needs to be borne in mind that the research evidence for multiple intelligences is thin. According to Adey (2000: 164):

> I believe that it is only because this is an idea very comforting to liberal-thinking teachers that the idea of multiple intelligences has been so widely accepted. In a book devoted to 'what research says' to the science teacher, we are bound to look critically at the evidence, and the evidence of the existence of abilities in different intellectual areas which are quite independent of one another is not good.

Things to consider

Some teachers subscribe to the multiple-intelligences approach and design their curriculum in such a way that each of the intelligences is called into play in most lessons. Frequently these lessons are interesting and exciting because of the variety of tasks employed, but there will always be pupils who, for one reason or another, do not become engaged in the learning process. Whatever stance you take on learning, it is worthwhile taking one step back from time to time and evaluating the effectiveness of your teaching by considering pupils' attitudes towards science and their academic achievement, perhaps in comparison with other subjects.

References

Adey, P.S. (1993) *Thinking Science INSET (The King's-BP CASE inset pack)*, London: BP Educational Services.

Adey, P.S. (2000) 'Science teaching and the development of intelligence', in Monk, M. and Osborne, J. (eds) *Good Practice in Science Teaching: What Research has to Say*, Buckingham: Open University Press.

Adey, P.S. and Shayer, M. (1994) *Really Raising Standards: Cognitive Intervention and Academic Achievement*, London: Routledge.

Adey, P., Fairbrother, R. and William, D., with Johnson, B. and Jones, C. (1999) *Learning Styles & Strategies: A Review of Research*, London: Kings College London.

Adey, P.S., Shayer, M. and Yates, C. (2001a) *Thinking Science: The Curriculum Materials of the Cognitive Acceleration through Science (CASE) Project*, 3rd edn, Cheltenham: Nelson Thornes.

Adey, P., Robertson, A. and Venville, G. (2001b) *Let's Think! A Programme for Developing Thinking Skills in Five and Six Year Olds*, Windsor: NFER-Nelson.

Adey, P., Robertson, A., Wilson, N., Nagy, F. and Wadsworth, P. (2003) *Let's Think Through Science! Developing Thinking Skills in Seven and Eight Year Olds*, Windsor: NFER-Nelson.

Adhami, M., Johnson, D.C. and Shayer, M. (1998) *Thinking Maths the Programme for Accelerated Learning in Mathematics*, Oxford: Heinemann Educational Books.

Barker, V. (2000) *Beyond Appearances: Students' Misconceptions about Basic Chemical Ideas*, London: RSC (available at: http://www.chemsoc.org/networks/learnnet/miscon.htm).

Barker, V. and Millar, R. (1999) 'Students' reasoning about chemical reactions: what changes occur during a context-based post-16 chemistry course', *International Journal of Science Education*, **21**(6), 645–665.

Beale, M. (2002) *TES Teacher*, 4 October, 18.

Bennett, J. (2003) *Teaching and Learning Science: A Guide to Recent Research and its Applications*, London: Continuum.

Bell, B.F. and Brook, A. (1984) *Aspects of Secondary Students' Understanding of Plant Nutrition: Full Report*, Children's Learning in Science Project, Leeds: University of Leeds.

Blagg, N., Ballinger, M. and Gardner, R. (1995) *Somerset Thinking Skills Course: Handbook*, Oxford: Basil Blackwell.

Briggs, H. and Holding, B. (1986) *Aspects of Secondary Students' Understanding of Elementary Ideas in Chemistry: Full Report*, Children's Learning in Science Project, Leeds: University of Leeds.

Brook, A. and Driver, R. (1984) *Aspects of Secondary Students' Understanding of Energy: Full Report*, Children's Learning in Science Project, Leeds: University of Leeds.

Brook, A., Briggs, H. and Driver, R. (1983) *Aspects of Secondary Students' Understanding of the Particulate Nature of Matter: Full Report*, Children's Learning in Science Project, Leeds: University of Leeds.

Brook, A., Briggs, H., Bell, B. and Driver, R. (1984) *Aspects of Secondary Students' Understanding of Heat: Full Report*, Children's Learning in Science Project, Leeds: University of Leeds.

Bruner, J. (1968) *Towards a Theory of Instruction*, New York: W.W. Norton.

Donnelly, J.F. and Jenkins, E.W. (1999) *Science Under the National Curriculum*, Leeds: Centre for Studies in Science and Mathematics Education/Centre for Policy Studies in Education.

Driver, R. (1983) *The Pupil as Scientist?*, Milton Keynes: Open University Press.

Driver, R. and Bell, B. (1986) 'Students' thinking and the learning of science: a constructivist view', *School Science Review*, **67**(240), 443–456.

Driver, R. and Easley, J. (1978) 'Pupils and paradigms: a review of literature related to concept development in adolescent science students', *Studies in Science Education*, **5**, 61–84.

Driver, R., Squires, A., Rushworth, P. and Wood-Robinson, V. (1994a) *Making Sense of Secondary Science: Support Materials for Teachers*, London: Routledge.

Driver, R., Squires, A., Rushworth, P. and Wood-Robinson, V. (1994b) *Making Sense of Secondary Science: Research into Children's Ideas*, London: Routledge.

Dweck, C.S. (1986) 'Motivational processes affecting learning', *American Psychologist*, **41**, 1040–1046 (available in Pollard, A. (ed.) (2002) *Readings for Reflective Teaching*, London: Continuum).

Endler, L.C. and Bond, T. (2000) 'Cognitive development in a secondary science setting', *Research in Science Education*, 2000, **30**(4), 403–416.

Gardner, H. (1993) *Frames of Mind: The Theory of Multiple Intelligences*, London: Fontana.

Glover, D. and Law, S. (2002) *Improving Learning: Professional Practice in Secondary Schools*, Buckingham: Open University Press.

Goleman, D. (1996) *Emotional Intelligence – Why Can it Matter More than IQ*, London: Bloomsbury.

Hamaker, A., Jordan, P. and Blackwell, J. (1997) 'An evaluation of a two year cognitive intervention for Key Stage 4 students in the UK', *Journal of Design & Technology Education*, **3**(1), 26–33.

Hodson, D. and Hodson, J. (1998a) 'From constructivism to social constructivism: a Vygotskian perspective on teaching and learning science', *School Science Review*, **79**(289), 33–41.

Hodson, D. and Hodson, J. (1998b) 'Science education as enculturation: some implications for practice', *School Science Review*, **80**(290), 17–24.

Howe, A.C. (1996) 'Development of science concepts with a Vygotskian framework', *Science Education*, **80**(1), 35–51.

Jones, M. and Gott, R. (1998) 'Cognitive acceleration through science education: alternative perspectives', *International Journal of Science Education*, **20**(7), 755–768.

Kennewell, S., Parkinson, J. and Tanner, H. (2000) *Developing the ICT Capable School*, London: RoutledgeFalmer.

Kyriacou, C. (1997) *Effective Teaching in Schools: Theory and Practice*, Cheltenham: Stanley Thornes.

Leach, J. and Scott, P. (1999) 'Teaching and learning science: linking individual and sociocultural perspectives', paper presented at the *European Association for Research in Learning and Instruction*, Göteborg, Sweden.

Leask, M. and Younie, S. (2001) 'Communal constructivist theory: information and communications technology pedagogy and internalisation of the curriculum', *Journal of Information Technology for Teacher Education*, **10**(1 & 2), 117–134.

Leat, D. (1998) *Thinking Through Geography*, Cambridge: ChrisKington Publishing.

Lipman, M., Sharp, M. and Oscanyan, F. (1980) *Philosophy in the Classroom*, Philadelphia: Temple University Press.

McGregor, D. and Gunter, B. (2001) 'Changing pedagogy of secondary science teachers: the impact of a two year professional development programme', *Teacher Development*, **5**(1), 59–74.

McGuinness, C. (1999) *From Thinking Skills to Thinking Classrooms: A Review and Evaluation of Approaches for Developing Pupils' Thinking*, Nottingham: DfEE.

Maslow, A.H. (1970) *Motivation and Personality*, New York: Harper & Rowe.

Matthews, M.R. (1994) 'Discontent with constructivism', *Studies in Science Education*, **24**, 165–172.

Matthews, M.R. (1998) 'In defence of modest goals when teaching about the nature of science', *Journal of Research in Science Teaching*, **35**(2), 161–174.

Millar, R. (1989) 'Constructive criticisms', *International Journal of Science Education*, **11**(5), 587–596.

Moran, J. and Vaughan, S. (2000) 'Introducing CASE at key stage 4: an example of bridging', *School Science Review*, **82**(299), 47–55.

Murphy, P. (1994) 'Gender differences in pupils' reactions to practical work', in Levinson, R. (ed.) *Teaching Science*, London: Routledge.

Needham R. (1987) *Teaching Strategies for Developing Understanding in Science*, Leeds: CLIS.

Parkinson, J. (2002) *Reflective Teaching of Science 11–18*, London: Continuum.

Riding, R. and Rayner, S. (1998) *Cognitive Styles and Learning Strategies: Understanding Style Differences in Learning and Behaviour*, London: David Fulton.

Rockett, M. and Percival, S. (2002) *Thinking for Learning*, Stafford: Network Educational Press.

Rosenthal, R. and Jacobson, L. (1968) *Pygmalion in the Classroom*, New York: Holt, Rinehart & Winston.

Roth, W.-M. (2001) 'Enculturation: acquisition of conceptual blind spots and epistemological prejudices', *British Educational Research Journal*, **27**(1), 5–27.

Shayer, M. (2000) *GCSE 1999: Added-Value from Schools Adopting the CASE Intervention*, London: Kings College London.

Shayer, M. and Adey, P. (1981) *Towards a Science of Science Teaching: Cognitive Development and Curriculum Demand*, London: Heinemann.

Shayer, M. and Adey, P. (eds) (2002) *Learning Intelligence: Cognitive Acceleration Across the Curriculum*, Buckingham: Open University Press.

Shayer, M. and Gamble, R. (2001) *Bridging from CASE to Core Science*, Hatfield: ASE.

Simon, S. (2002) 'The CASE approach for pupils with learning difficulties', *School Science Review*, **83**(305), 73–79.

Smith, A. (2001) *Accelerated Learning in Practice*, Stafford: Network Educational Press.

Solomon, J. (1994) 'The rise and fall of constructivism', *Studies in Science Education*, **23**, 1–19.

Taber, K. (2002) *Chemical Misconceptions – Prevention, Diagnosis and Cure, Volume 1: Theoretical Background*, London: The Royal Society of Chemistry.

Thomas, G.P. and McRobbie, C. (2001) 'Using a metaphor for learning to improve students' metacognition in the chemistry classroom', *Journal of Research in Science Teaching*, **38**(2), 222–259.

Vygotsky, L. (1978) *Mind in Society: The Development of Higher Psychological Processes*, Cambridge, MA: Harvard University Press.

Watts, M. and Bentley, D. (1991) 'Constructivism in the curriculum. Can we close the gap between the strong theoretical version and the weak version of theory-in-practice?', *The Curriculum Journal*, **2**(2), 171–182.

White, R.T. and Mitchell, I.J. (1994) 'Metacognition and the quality of learning', *Studies in Science Education*, **23**, 21–37.

Whitelegg, E. (1996) 'Gender effects in science classrooms', in Welford, G., Osborne, J. and Scott, P. (eds) *Research in Science Education in Europe*, London: Falmer Press.

Williams, C. (1997) 'Managing motivation', *Managing Schools Today*, **6**(9), 28–30.

Wilson, V. (2000) *Can Thinking Skills be Taught? A Paper for Discussion*, Scottish Council for Research in Education (available at: http://www.scre.ac.uk/scot-research/thinking/index.html).

Woods, D., Bruner, J.S. and Ross, G. (1976) 'The role of tutoring in problem solving', *Journal of Child Psychology and Psychiatry*, **17**, 89–100.

Woolnough, B. (1994) *Effective Science Teaching*, Buckingham: Open University Press.

CHAPTER 6

Dealing with differences

Schools with a majority of white pupils are not tackling racism...
Many teachers have little or no idea of what defines an ethnic minority, what racism is or how to teach about it...
Openly racist attitudes among pupils are often ignored by staff...
Most teachers at the schools admitted their pupils left ill prepared for life in a multicultural society.

(TES, 1999a: 1)

This chapter covers a number of very difficult issues for which there are no ready-made solutions. Critics will say that each topic covered here deserves a book on its own and, while that is true, I feel that at the end of such a book you would still be left wondering how to cope with such important aspects of your work. Individuals' reactions to each of the issues is governed, to a very large extent, by their own personality and outlook on life, and, for some, no amount of rhetoric will make them change their point of view. Much of what is written about here is concerned with creating a more equitable and tolerant society. It is about attitudes and relationships, all of which lurk in the background and form part of the hidden curriculum that is an important facet of school life.

In this chapter I have attempted to highlight important aspects of research into each of the issues and have considered how current thinking could influence teaching for the better. Where appropriate, I have summarised areas of research into a series of bullet points in order to give a general overview of current understanding about the topic. The danger of carrying out this sort of reduction is that it might lead to the belief that success can be achieved by following a few easy steps. Far from it: each point may represent the initial stage in a range of practices linked to an extended programme of staff development.

Differences in ability

Rapidly following the introduction of comprehensive education in the 1970s came the restructuring of classroom organisation from setting and streaming to mixed-ability teaching. Science teachers, as usual, were always keen to be involved in new developments, but found the changes very difficult to deal with at the time:

But while science teachers, in the last fifteen years, have often been at the fore-front of subject-based educational development, accelerating comprehensivisation and the introduction of non-streaming in many schools has produced entirely new situations to be dealt with.

(George, 1976: 1)

Working groups were organised throughout the country by LEAs and the Association for Science Education. Many changes were made to teaching styles, particularly in the ways teachers communicated with pupils. There was a move to a less formal approach, as teachers considered the effect of their language on pupils' learning and attitude towards the subject. There was a revolution in the way subject matter was presented to pupils as more and more teachers rejected the dull and impersonal style of textbooks and moved towards producing their own worksheets. Teachers were concerned about the effect of assessment on the morale of low-ability pupils, who would always be at the bottom of the list. In order to alleviate the problem, there was a move towards more teacher-based continual assessment and a greater emphasis on rewarding effort in addition to attainment. Much of the pioneering work that went on at this time has stayed with us and has become the typical practice of science teaching today. Until fairly recently, pupils were taught in mixed-ability settings almost exclusively in state schools. However, recently there has been a shift to pupils being taught in sets (Ofsted, 2002a). The reasons for this are not 100 per cent clear, but are likely to be associated with pressure from the government, which has given its support to this method of grouping pupils in two significant publications – *Excellence in Schools* (DfEE, 1997) and *Schools Building on Success* (DfEE, 2001).

It [*mixed ability*] requires excellent teaching and in some schools it has worked well. But in too many cases it has failed to stretch the brightest and to respond to the needs of those who have fallen behind. Setting, particularly in science, maths and languages, is proving effective in many schools. We do not believe that any single model of grouping should be imposed on secondary schools, but unless a school can demonstrate that it is getting better than expected results through a different approach, we do make the assumption that setting should be the norm in secondary schools.

(DfEE, 1997: 38)

Ofsted appears to be a little more cautious about backing any one particular way of grouping pupils. In a report on good practice, it said: '...the best subject departments identify and respond in their plans to the needs of all pupils' (Ofsted, 2002b: 63), without ever describing how this can be done. The Welsh inspectorate has expressed concern about placing pupils in sets in KS3, as this could result in a high proportion of girls being assigned to top sets. This could, they warn, establish a pattern of under-achievement by boys from an early stage of their secondary education (OHMCI, 1997). Inspectors recognise that teaching mixed-ability classes, is difficult, and requires departments to have a clear policy on differentiation together with teachers who are committed to work hard to make it a success. In the Chief Inspector's Annual Report for 1997–1998, concerns were raised that setting was not always accompanied by high-quality teaching and that pupils in middle groups were often insufficiently challenged (Ofsted, 1999).

It is very difficult for a science department to make a decision about how pupils should be grouped. There are bound to be critics, no matter which method is chosen. A strong argument for setting is that it is the government's preferred approach. This is presumably based on the premise that it is far easier to target pupils' learning needs using this method. It seems obvious that teachers can provide pupils with appropriately challenging work dependent on their set. Using such a system, it might be argued, very able pupils could complete KS3 work by the end of Y8 and GCSE work by the end of Y10. Teachers would be able to plan an appropriate curriculum over the three years of KS3 for the less able. Classroom management and teaching tend to be easier when pupils are grouped in sets (Ireson *et al.*, 1999); however, teaching the lower-ability sets can sometimes be very demanding in terms of maintaining pupil motivation and good behaviour. In theory pupils who do well in the lower sets can be promoted to a higher set, but in practice little movement takes place (Troyna, 1991; Taylor, 1993). The research carried out by Ireson *et al.* (1999) mainly studied the effects of different grouping arrangements on pupils' achievement and self-concept. The study examined a large sample of KS3 pupils from 45 secondary comprehensive schools in England. The schools were selected to give 15 in each of three groups: schools that were predominantly mixed ability for all subjects; schools where there was a gradual increase in setting; and schools with streaming, banding or setting throughout KS3. Achievement was determined by comparing KS2 and KS3 national test results for each pupil, and self-concept and attitudes were determined by the self-completion of questionnaires. Setting did not appear to have any effect on pupils' attainment in science. In general, higher-attaining pupils had higher self-esteem, but self-esteem was highest in the partially set schools. In science, boys tended to have more positive views of themselves than girls. This research supported much of the previous research in this area, indicating that for science, at least, there is no advantage in placing pupils in sets to improve academic results.

Having looked at this evidence, there will still be teachers who have a strong conviction about setting pupils by ability. The following criteria were used to allocate pupils to ability groups in the sample of schools studied by Ireson *et al.* (2002):

- Pupils' scores in various types of assessment. Internal tests and examinations were most frequently used, followed by KS2 test results. A smaller percentage of schools used cognitive ability tests (CATs) or information from partner primary schools.
- In English and maths, and to a much lesser extent in science, teachers considered pupils' attitudes, motivation and self-esteem when forming the groups.
- Social considerations, such as friendship groups and the distribution of potentially disruptive pupils, were utilised more by science teachers than by English or maths teachers.
- Gender balance was also considered in some schools.

When all the tweaking has been taken into account, it is highly likely that each set will consist of pupils with a broad range of attainment and there is a danger that teachers may fail to appreciate that the group is not homogeneous. Some schools are particularly good at providing appropriate teaching and resources for pupils in different ability-level groups. However, there is a worry that lower sets tend to contain a high proportion of boys, pupils from ethnic minorities and pupils from low socio-economic groups (Sukhnandan and Lee, 1998; Ofsted, 1999).

Things to consider

It is worth spending some time reflecting on the arguments used when the decision was made to introduce the present system of pupil grouping in science. You may find it useful to refer to the list of advantages and disadvantages of grouping pupils by ability given in Table 6.1.

In a department where pupils are placed in ability sets, it should be possible to move pupils into different sets should their performance improve or deteriorate. In a department where pupils are placed in mixed-ability groups, it may be necessary to move pupils from one group to another for social or behavioural reasons. What is the department's policy on pupil movement? What records are kept on pupils that are moved in terms of monitoring their progress in order that the system can be evaluated?

Table 6.1 *The advantages and disadvantages of grouping pupils by ability (setting) as established by international research (Hallam and Toutounji, 1997: 63)*

Advantages	Disadvantages
• Pupils can progress commensurate with their abilities • Techniques of instruction can be adapted to the needs of the group • The number of school failures is reduced • Interest and motivation are maintained because higher-ability pupils are not held back by those of lesser ability • Slower pupils participate more when not eclipsed by those who are much brighter • Teaching is easier • Individual or small-group instruction for the less able becomes possible	• Less able pupils need the presence of more advanced pupils to stimulate and encourage them • A stigma is attached to being in the low set or stream, and this has a negative effect on motivation • Most teachers do not like teaching the bottom sets • Ability grouping discriminates against pupils from ethnic minorities and lower socio-economic groups • Pupils in the lower streams or sets tend to receive instruction at a slower pace and of a lesser quality than pupils in higher streams • Accurately and fairly placing children into ability groups is difficult • Once ability groups are established, movement between groups is limited • Ability grouping plays down the importance of pupil, teacher and parental effort

Differentiation

Differentiation refers to the ways that teachers cater for the needs of individual pupils, usually in a mixed-ability situation. It is a term that is often used but is perhaps not well understood. It can take the form of providing pupils with different types of resources, or it can be the way the teacher speaks to different groups of pupils. A useful definition is provided by Revell (1995: 6):

> Differentiation is the management of pupils' learning through the use of appropriate teaching methods and resources to meet the different needs and abilities of individuals in a group as well as possible.

One of the principles for differentiation given by O'Brien and Guiney (2001: 13) that I think is particularly important is that 'progress will be expected, recognised and rewarded'. It is about recognising pupils' needs and identifying ways of helping them to learn. Clearly this cannot be done through traditional whole-class teaching, where a common strategy used by teachers is to direct the lesson to the middle of the ability range. Experienced teachers will recognise that there are three main approaches to differentiation (Harrison, 1997):

1 Differentiation by task
2 Differentiation by outcome
3 Differentiation by support.

Differentiation may take place in any lesson given by an experienced teacher, but is likely to be most effective when it is planned for and built into the normal practice of the science department (Piggott, 2002). Opportunities for specific activities that provide differentiation should be outlined in the schemes of work, but care needs to be taken to ensure that members of the department don't assume that it is sufficient to simply follow the guidelines set out in this document. On a similar level, providing teachers with a resource such as differentiated textbooks does not necessarily result in effective teaching. In addition to planning and preparing resources, departments need to consider what sort of approach to teaching is likely to get the best out of different groups of pupils.

Differentiation by task

Teachers have experimented with various strategies to differentiate by task. The general rule is: complex procedures tend to fail; simple procedures tend to work. Possibly the simplest of all is the use of particular types of oral questions to different groups of pupils. It is common practice for teachers to direct questions to pupils who they think will be able to answer them.

One of the early methods of differentiation by task was resourced-based learning, which was used in some schools during the 1980s. It was based on a system involving the use of task cards to direct pupils to resources such as books, worksheets, small practical tasks or video clips. The teacher would direct groups of pupils to particular tasks based on a knowledge of their capabilities. Once the task was completed, the pupils either carried out a self-assessment or took their work to the teacher for checking. Pupils were then directed to the next task and so on until the topic was completed. Other schemes have been produced for other subjects and different age ranges. A slight variation of this approach, called supported self-study, involved groups of pupils working together on a topic over a number of lessons. The class was divided into groups of about five pupils, with the main criterion used for selecting pupils for a group being that they must be able to get on with one another. Tasks were initiated through tutorials with the teacher, who was able to guide pupils towards suitable learning resources and goals dependent on their ability and aptitude. A learning contract was struck with the group, and the period of work began. The main emphasis of the process was the support the pupils received at all stages of their work through tutorial contact with the teacher. The level to which the teacher chose to direct their studies varied from a simple flow of learning objectives to a detailed guide to resources materials. Pupils were encouraged periodically to assess their own level of understanding of the topic. The learning cycle (Figure 6.1) was repeated as often as thought necessary, but with each group receiving at least one tutorial per lesson. In a study of using this approach Calder and Parkinson (1994) found that pupils responded well to the demands made on them and worked well through their designated tasks. Those pupils who tended not to work well in a whole-class situation blossomed when given responsibility for their own learning.

There may be elements of these methods still in use today, but teachers have largely abandoned them and I suspect their reasons for doing so are mainly related to the substantial amount of effort required to plan and prepare the resources. The resource-based learning method was difficult to manage, and required the teacher to keep

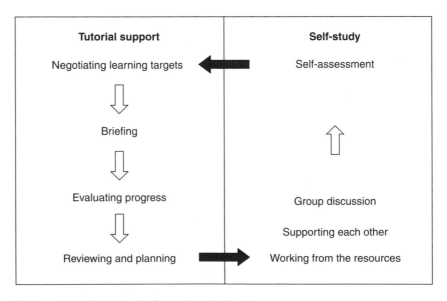

Figure 6.1 *Supported self-study cycle of tutorial and self-review*

complex records of which pupils were doing which tasks. Looking at it from the pupils' point of view, if they are asked to work independently for a prolonged period of time topic after topic, then they are likely to lose interest in the same way that they do when any teaching technique is used repeatedly.

Hall (1997) describes an attempt to differentiate by task through the use of colour-coded workcards. The school concerned, in an inner-city area, advocated mixed-ability teaching throughout the curriculum. In the first attempt to introduce the new practice, pupils were given a card based on the teacher's perception of the pupil's ability. This meant that in some cases different pupils in a group had different coloured cards. This approach failed because some pupils who received the middle-ability or low-ability cards felt hurt and upset by being labelled as less able. In a second attempt with another class, cards of a single colour were allocated to tables – with the result that although most members of the group received cards that matched their ability, there were cases where high-ability pupils received low-ability cards. This new strategy was partially successful in reducing intra-group conflict, but a greater amount of inter-group conflict arose out of derogatory comments made to groups with both high- and low-ability cards. Hall concludes that labelling in this sort of way damages self-esteem and demotivates pupils to such an extent that their academic performance is adversely affected.

Teachers want their pupils to leave the lesson being proud of what they have achieved, the 'feel good' factor is so important in maintaining motivation and interest in the subject. Giving pupils differentiated tasks has to be done very sensitively, and it requires a very good working relationship between the teacher and pupils. There are, of course, subtle ways of doing it when different groups of pupils are working on different aspects of the work the results of which are going to be presented to some sort of plenary at the end of the lesson, as shown in the following two examples:

1 When the mode of working is based on a jigsaw activity (page 240), the teacher can direct less-able pupils to easier aspects of the topic
2 Worksheets have a core section, which everyone completes, followed by a series of options. The teacher directs individuals to complete appropriate parts of the option section.

Computer-based learning can help considerably when it come to giving pupils different tasks to do, and may even be able to help with managing a sequence of activities related to the learning needs of different ability groups. Working on the computer is generally a solitary activity; other pupils may occasionally look at their neighbour's screen, but on the whole they restrict their interactions to their own computer. This gives teachers the opportunity to give pupils different versions of instructions and exercises dependent on their ability without having the problems described by Hall (1997).

Differentiation by outcome

Some may argue that differentiation by outcome is of less merit, in that it evades the principle of providing all pupils with work that matches their capabilities. Others will say that it is less limiting than differentiation by task, and it has the advantage of providing all pupils with the opportunity to extend their knowledge. There are a number of ways of setting a common task that ensures that pupils of different abilities are suitably challenged, including:

1 **Graded exercises.** Pupils work through as much of the exercise as they possibly can. The early parts are short and simple to ensure that all pupils achieve success and gain confidence. Later tasks might involve the pupils using other resources, and some should be more intellectually demanding. Getting the balance right is not easy, and ensuring that pupils don't give up too soon may require some encouragement from the teacher.
2 **Concept mapping.** Producing a concept map gives the pupil, and the teacher, a clear indication of how much of the work is understood. The teacher can then direct the pupil to resources that will help him or her to make progress.
3 **Writing tasks.** When a writing task is set, the teacher can indicate what is expected from everyone and then go on to indicate what additional information would make it a better piece of work. More able pupils should rise to the challenge, but they may need a little encouragement from the teacher.

Differentiation by support

Differentiation by support is something that every teacher does when talking to pupils. One way of doing this, suggested by Naylor and Keogh (1995), is to target certain pupils or groups for extra attention at certain times. Teachers commonly give alternative explanations or present things in a different way to help clarify situations. Another approach is when teachers ask questions to get pupils to think about what they are doing: those all-important 'why?' questions. Differentiation by support is about keeping up the pressure to get pupils to learn and 'being there' when they need some help. This is the process described as 'scaffolding' (page 96), where the teacher provides a supporting structure to help the learner explore the new concepts and make them part of his or her framework of understanding.

Things to consider

Review the extent to which differentiation is used at different stages of the science course by:

- examining a section of the SoW and highlighting how differentiation is planned for
- reviewing the teaching resources used and looking for agreement with the SoW
- carrying out a self-review to determine the extent to which differentiation is used in practice.

What additional information would you need to improve differentiation?

Gender differences

Table 6.2 shows the performance of boys and girls in GCSE science examinations from 2000 to 2002. Over this period, girls significantly outperformed boys in single and double science. The differences in the separate sciences are not so marked, but boys appear to do slightly better in physics and girls in chemistry. However, it is interesting to note that, nationally, about 8000 more boys than girls choose to do the separate sciences. This might go some way to explaining the underperformance of boys in the double award examination. The more able male pupils may opt to study the separate sciences, leaving a depleted cohort to study for the double award.

In an analysis of pupils' performance in the Nuffield Co-ordinated Science Double Award examination papers for 1997, Bell (2001) found that male candidates obtained slightly better results than female candidates. When the mark distributions were analysed for the different attainment targets, the following was revealed:

- Candidates tended to get higher grades with Sc1 compared to the other attainment targets
- Females significantly outperformed males in Sc1
- There was a small gender difference in favour of boys for Sc2
- There were no gender differences for Sc3
- Males significantly outperformed females in Sc4.

In a detailed study of pupils' attainment in Wales at each level or grade from KS1 to A-level for the period 1992–1997, Gorard *et al.* (2001) found that:

- at KS3 there were no large differences in attainment between boys and girls at any level

Table 6.2 *GCSE results for 15-year-old boys (B) and girls (G) for 2000 to 2002 (source: Autumn Packages for each year, DfEE)*

			Single science	Double science	Physics	Chemistry	Biological sciences
2000	Attempted GCSE	B	25	221	23	22	23
	(in thousands)	G	24	224	15	15	16
	Percentage achieved	B	15	49	90	89	89
	A*–C	G	21	52	89	91	89
2001	Attempted GCSE	B	25	231	23	23	23
	(in thousands)	G	24	234	15	16	17
	Percentage achieved	B	15	50	90	89	90
	A*–C	G	21	53	89	91	90
2002	Attempted GCSE	B	26	232	23	23	23
	(in thousands)	G	26	234	15	16	17
	Percentage achieved	B	15	50	90	89	90
	A*–C	G	20	53	89	91	91

- in the early 1990s a higher percentage of boys than girls obtained A*–B grades, but this gap narrowed and by 1997 it was almost gender-neutral
- at A-level the achievement gap reduced over the period of study, and was more or less gender-neutral by 1997.

The authors suggest that the standard view of the gender gap is questionable or exaggerated, and place the blame for this on the lack of reliable data sets. They go on to argue that 'standard' data does not take into account changes in the examination system, and may be contaminated by data from a range of age cohorts. As a result of this analysis, the authors conclude that there were few significant gender differences for science across the whole range of schooling for the period studied.

There has been a tremendous amount of research into gender differences. In some ways this type of research is relatively straightforward, as there are two distinct cohorts to compare; however, much of the research fails to give due significance to the range of differences within both girls' and boys' groups. There is a tendency to make generalisations, which are helpful to a certain extent but will always lack the detail required for individual class situations. There is more variance to be found within groups of boys and girls (e.g. related to ethnic group and/or social class) than there is between boys and girls as a whole (MacDonald *et al.*, 1999). While there may well be an argument that the overall statistics are not as informative as would be hoped for, and that the gender problem might not be as acute in science as it is in other subjects, there is still a strong case for carrying out improvements. I see these as lying in two areas: first I would argue that we need to target boys' under-achievement in science, particularly in the area of mid- to low attainers; and second I believe that there is an urgent need to encourage girls to go on to study science post-16 and to address the imbalance in physics.

In a review of the literature on assessment and motivation, Harlen and Crick (2002: 4) were able to draw the following conclusions:

- After the introduction of the National Curriculum Tests in England, low-achieving pupils had lower self-esteem than higher-achieving pupils, whilst beforehand there was no correlation between self-esteem and achievement.
- When passing tests is 'high stakes', teachers adopt a teaching style which emphasises transmission teaching of knowledge, thereby favouring those students who prefer to learn in this way and disadvantaging and lowering the self-esteem of those who prefer more active and creative learning experiences.
- Repeated practice tests reinforce the low self-image of the lower-achieving students.

Many reasons have been suggested for boys' under-achievement, and countless teachers can recall instances of loud boys pushing and shoving one another and generally exhibiting what has become known as 'laddish' behaviour. Some boys find it difficult to sit still and pay attention. Boys readily succumb to peer pressure, and they monitor each other's behaviour and attention to work (Holland, 1998). Because of the difficulties they cause, these are the pupils that tend to stick in teachers' minds. However, a substantial number of boys do conform and work hard. The question is, how can we tame this 'macho' image and improve the pattern of behaviour? Much of this needs to be done on a whole-school level in terms of making schooling more attractive to boys so that they are not always kicking against the system. Pupils need a comfortable and welcoming environment in which to work, where the teachers are approachable and are seen as being fair. Boys in particular are influenced by the human relationships aspects of teaching, and rate fairness, friendliness and firmness as key attributes of an effective teacher (Pickering, 1997). The attitude of the teacher to the pupils plays a key role in changing the way 'macho' boys behave. The teacher needs to create a classroom climate where boys' masculinity is not dependent on physical toughness but is more associated with success and achievement. There is no magic formula for doing this; it simply involves giving private praise and encouragement to individuals, along with some reasonable advice for improvement. The use of praise is likely to generate a more positive response if it is given as close to the event as possible to enable the learner to make the link between the two. Constantly telling pupils off for poor behaviour is unlikely to produce any long-term solutions. Pickering (1997) reported that girls noticed that teachers tend to reprimand boys disproportionately, given the levels of disruption by boys and girls. This may of course be due to the fact that boys tend to disrupt loudly, whereas girls often quietly chat to one another.

Boys tend to bluster their way through some aspects of their learning with the attitude that it will all be 'all right in the end'. This bravado can lead to positive outcomes when pupils believe in themselves and take the approach that they can achieve. In a large-scale piece of research carried out in 1993–1994, when asked to assess their own ability, more boys than girls thought they were able and fewer boys than girls thought they were below average (Barber, 1994). Boys overall, in comparison with girls, have higher levels of self-esteem and optimism and are more optimistic about the way they explain and accredit academic success and failure (Mitchell and Hirom, 2002). This overall confidence in themselves might go some way to explaining why more boys than girls opt to do separate sciences rather than the double award. Alternatively, it may be that by the time it gets to decide on GCSE courses the girls have decided that science is not one of their favourite subjects and therefore they choose to do as little of it as possible.

There are extensive data on pupils' preferred subjects, collected over many years. For example, prior to the introduction of the NC pupils were allowed to choose which, if any, science subjects they wished to study for the GCE Ordinary level exam. The data for 1982–1983, in Table 6.3 are typical of the choices made by pupils at this time, and show that girls preferred to study biological sciences and that many girls chose not to study science at all. According to research carried out by Stark and Gray (1999),

Table 6.3 *Percentage of leavers attempting GCE O-level science subjects in 1982–1983 (source: DES Statistical Bulletin 11/84, October 1984)*

	Boys	Girls
Biological sciences	17	29
Chemistry	20	14
Physics	29	12

biological science is still the girls' favourite. In contrast, boys tend to hold a more even distribution of favourites across all topics. The study went on to look at pupils' enjoyment of learning activities, and found that there was little difference between the responses from girls and boys. Worryingly, the results showed that much of what went on in the science classrooms was not particularly attractive to either boys or girls.

Girls tend to achieve because of the way they work and the way they respond to the assessment procedures currently used. However, if pupils are allowed to select the subjects they study, science tends to be an unpopular choice for girls. This has been a problem for many years, and has been particularly persistent and significant for physics (Stewart, 1998), with very few students going on to study the subject at degree level.

> All sciences except for biological science are dominated by men, whereas all the arts are dominated by women.
>
> (EOC, 1998: 3)

Many reasons have been put forward for girls' dislike of physics at school (see, for example, Solomon, 1997), including:

- the perception that it is a boys' subject (linked with engineering, remoteness of concern with living beings)
- the perception that girls who do physics are less feminine and, perhaps, not 'one of the crowd'
- the style of teaching that is often used in physics lessons (questioning and challenging) may not appeal to girls.

Some teachers are likely to place some of the blame on the content of the curriculum, saying that there are far too few topics that are of interest to girls. Perhaps some blame might be pointed at the nature of the subject itself, but I suspect that a large proportion can be attributed to the nature of society itself and, in particular, to youth culture. Physics is simply not seen as a girls' subject, partly due to the lack of role models in teaching, but also because of the messages that are passed on from one generation to another. Who wants to go on to university and be stuck in a dusty room with an array of electronic equipment when you could be sitting with a group of other students, mainly girls, discussing the works of a famous author? In a study carried out in Canadian universities, Erwin and Maurutto (1998), found that one of the reasons why girls were put off studying physics was because of social and psychological issues and a generally unwelcoming climate. In an account of the complexities of gender issues in science, Kenway and Gough (1998) suggest that the under-achievement of boys has clouded the problem of girls' participation in science. They argue for greater involvement of girls in science for reasons of personal fulfilment and for the future of society as a whole. Plummer (2000) points to the problems experienced by girls from working-class backgrounds, where frequently there are low expectations of education and little parental support.

When all the evidence is looked at dispassionately, it can be concluded that we need to consider ways of raising the achievement of both boys and girls. In addition, we need to look at ways of improving pupils' attitudes to science and getting girls to question existing stereotypical views of physical scientists. It is easy to say that nothing can be done, or 'it's not my job', but if we are to break the mould of the under-representation of girls in physics, the issue must be tackled at every level.

Things to consider

- How does the science department implement the school's equal opportunities policy?
- Analyse classroom groupings for effective arrangements that ensure that boys listen and encourage girls to participate.
- Consider the benefits of structured mixed groups or single-sex groups to encourage girls' and boys' participation in different activities.
- Consider how you can avoid stereotypical attitudes and behaviour, by being alert to differences in attitudes and maturity between boys and girls (EOC Wales, 1999).
- Most schools use some type of baseline data to monitor pupils' achievement. Does the system let you know about under-achievement early enough? Keep a record of pupils' achievement in science, noting results by gender for each level at KS3 and each grade at KS4. Are there significant differences at any of the points? Does an analysis by teacher lead to any useful conclusions?
- What mechanisms are in place to help under-achievers?

Strategies to improve achievement

Everyday strategies

As a result of a long-term study of pupils' learning at a comprehensive school in Oxfordshire, Postlethwaite and Haggarty (2002) produced a list of eight suggestions that teachers should consider when planning for improvement. In summary, these are:

1 **The attribution of success or failure.** Pupils will attribute the extent of their learning to either external factors (e.g. the teacher, parents) or internal factors (e.g. willingness to work hard, good behaviour). Teachers need to make pupils aware that individuals have at least some responsibility for, and scope for influence over, the situation in which they are participants. Teachers may need to make this clear to pupils and suggest that they must move away from any attitude that blames others for failure.

2 **Explaining teachers' actions.** Pupils can sometimes get the wrong end of the stick and come to the conclusion that the teacher is being unfair. Being explicit about what teachers do will help pupils to understand the wide range of actions that pupils are exposed to.

3 **Raising pupils' awareness of the different ways of looking at a situation.** Frequently pupils see a particular situation from their point of view only and adopt an attitude that they are right and the teacher is wrong. Outside of a conflict situation, they need to be made aware that there are different perspectives to every situation. Pupils need to be made aware that teachers have to make judgements based on how they see things and what they see as important, e.g. restoring behaviour quickly. Pupils need to be willing to question their own explanations of situations.

4 **Providing a supportive classroom atmosphere.** Pupils must be encouraged to try, knowing that they will not be put down for partial or incorrect answers.

5 **Providing tools for metacognition.** One way of achieving this is by sharing ideas about how some pupils were able to complete a task – e.g. what strategies did they use, what did they do when they got stuck. This opening up of the learning process helps the lower achievers to think about ways that they can structure their own learning.

6 **Ensuring good communication.** Pupils need to be made aware that the teacher wants to hear about any problems that they may have with their learning. The teacher is there to listen and respond.

7 **Rewarding effort.** By giving praise to pupils for making an effort, they begin to develop a notion that effort leads to success.

8 **Targeting under-achievement early.** Many under-achieving pupils will begin to appreciate that their motivation for doing work is not as good as it should be at some stage during KS3. Teachers need to encourage pupils to judge their own efforts and to make the necessary adjustments to improve their learning. The teacher will of course provide the support, but it is only the pupil who can make the difference.

Teaching boys and girls separately

A number of co-educational comprehensive schools have experimented with the idea of teaching boys and girls separately for some subjects, usually maths and science. By doing this it was thought that the needs of each sex could be more easily met – for example, girls might become more confident and willing to answer oral questions once the noisy boys, who shout out answers, had been removed. Alternatively, time could be set aside in boys-only lessons to develop their scientific writing. It was also thought that behaviour would be improved in single-sex environments, particularly that associated with boys showing off. The research in this area mainly points to gains for girls, although there are signs that it can improve boys' work in English (Sukhnandan *et al.*, 2000). Following a three-year study in a comprehensive school, Gillibrand *et al.* (1999) found that girls gained in confidence and achievement when taught physics in single-sex classes during their GCSE course. These girls also showed an increased likelihood of studying A-level physics. The authors reported:

Freed from the dominating and competitive behaviour of the boys and their perception of not being up to the boys' standard, girls felt free to participate in classrooms. Engaging proactively in learning and gaining encouragement from each other and from the teacher, they grew in confidence and entered a 'virtuous cycle' of positive feedback.

(Gillibrand *et al.*, 1999: 360)

In a study carried out by Jackson (2002) into the use of single-sex teaching in mathematics, she found that girls-only classes had a positive effect for the girls. There were no similar gains for the boys-only classes; in fact, boys' behaviour actually got worse and their work performance and relationships with the teachers deteriorated. Some studies have shown that boys and girls benefit from having their own working space (e.g. Price and Talbot, 1984; Younger and Warrington, 2002) and feel more relaxed and comfortable than in mixed classes. Perhaps the secret to success is to adjust the teaching style to match the group of pupils. In the study carried out by Younger and Warrington (2002), the researchers noted that only a few teachers adjusted their teaching styles when teaching boys' classes or girls' classes. They propose that single-sex teaching has the potential to raise achievement, but that this potential will only be maximised when differential teaching approaches are systematically planned and explicitly implemented, monitored and evaluated. Parker and Rennie (2002) have been investigating the use of gender-inclusive strategies for teaching science in a sample of schools in Western Australia. In order to provide a gender-inclusive science curriculum, they suggest that teachers need to:

* provide a supportive learning environment that emphasises communication, interpersonal communication, interpersonal negotiation, interaction amongst all participants, harassment-free discussion, and participation by all pupils
* use real-life contexts
* provide school-based informal assessment procedures with relatively open-ended tasks drawing on contexts that are familiar to both boys and girls
* raise pupils' self-awareness of the extent to which their education-related decisions and experiences are socially constructed.

The researchers found that teachers were able to implement gender-inclusive strategies more readily and effectively in single-sex settings. In addition, a period of single-sex teaching heightened teachers' awareness of some problems that they tended to ignore in mixed-sex classes, such as:

* using the influence of girls to manage boys' behaviour
* boys' poor oral communication skills
* boys not completing very much written work, both in class and for homework
* not providing girls with risk-taking and open-ended problem-solving activities.

Reducing the amount of whole-class teaching

In some schools it is common practice for science lessons to involve a significant amount of whole-class teaching (see page 64). This approach tends to treat all pupils in the same way, and can provide opportunities for some reluctant learners to 'hide'. Myhill (2002) has studied patterns of classroom interaction of boys and girls from a sample of classes ranging from Y1 to Y10. Her results show that under-achievers of either gender are the least likely to interact positively in the classroom and the most likely to be engaged in off-task interactions. The research questions the extent to which whole-class teaching is benefiting the learning experiences of under-achievers. In a longitudinal study tracking Y7 pupils, Reiss (2000) found that towards the start of the year girls tended to contribute to class discussions more than boys, but this declined throughout the year to a point where girls' interactions with the teacher were significantly less than boys'. Similar findings have been recorded by the Welsh inspectorate, which has reported that boys tend to dominate class discussions and shout out answers without thinking whereas girls tend to undervalue their contributions to oral work (OHMCI, 1997).

These are very strong arguments for reducing the amount of whole-class discussion work and for adopting a strategy of asking pupils questions by name rather than using hands up or, worse still, allowing pupils to shout out the answers. Holland's case study of boys' under-achievement (Holland, 1998) found that boys showed a strong liking for lessons that included a range of activities, such as personal research, using books and computers, group work, discussions and debates. This goes against the belief held by some teachers that boys don't like reading, writing and talking tasks. To a large extent it depends on what the task is and whether the pupil recognises that it has a purpose. For example, Bray *et al.* (1997) reported that boys enjoyed reading factual accounts. While boys are not keen to do meaningless tasks such as copying, they are more motivated to write something that is useful. Providing the group work has a clear focus, boys are more than willing to participate in a discussion and, as mentioned below, the quality of the discussion is often better in mixed groups:

> Overall, boy-only groups and pairs within classes were generally less effective than mixed-sex groups and pairs in terms of output, their contribution to the lesson and the complexity of the language they used.
>
> (OHMCI, 1997: 3)

Mentoring

Mentoring appears to be growing in popularity, particularly with borderline C–D grade pupils in years 10 and 11. Some schools also use it in Y8, and the numbers are likely to increase as schools adopt the KS3 National Strategy for science, where it is one of the key features in Y8. In a study of mentoring across eight secondary schools, Sukhnandan *et al.* (2000: 5) found that mentors and pupils considered it to be a useful process and reported improvements in:

- pupils' organisation and study skills
- confidence, self-esteem, motivation and attitudes among pupils
- attitudes to school and learning among boys
- quality of analysis of post-16 choices among both boys and girls
- levels of achievement among boys and girls.

The Welsh inspectorate has identified the benefits of mentoring for boys:

> Most schools identify, and support through 'mentoring' systems, those pupils who are underachieving and who could achieve a C grade or above at GCSE. In most cases significantly more boys than girls have been identified in this way. Such approaches have a positive effect on boys' general attitudes to school life as well as improvement in examination performance.
>
> (OHMCI, 1997: 4)

Mentoring is generally carried out by one of three groups of people. Form tutors (or sometimes members of the SMT) mentor all the pupils in a form, usually through a series of regular interviews. The second option is peer mentoring, which may be seen as being useful for the personal development of the pupil mentor as well as valuable for the pupil being mentored. There are benefits in terms of the subject relating to the peer mentor, but he or she requires appropriate training and should know when it is time to seek help from a teacher. The third approach is to use people from the local business partnership. This can be particularly useful when it comes to talking to pupils about the world of work and getting a job, but such people may not be able to give advice on study skills (Noble *et al.*, 2001). They will, of course, need to be cleared by the Criminal Records Bureau.

According to Sukhnandan *et al.* (2000), mentoring sessions typically take about 15–30 minutes. It is helpful if the mentor has some background information on the pupil, such as records of marks, in order to be able to identify quickly where the problem areas are. Noble *et al.* (2001) suggest that the sessions should start with some general questions, such as those listed in Bradford (1996): 'How are things going at the moment? Are you enjoying schoolwork more or less than last year?' This may be followed by questions that focus on identifying the causes of the problems and looking for possible solutions. The discussion might be centred on the following:

- what to do if you don't understand
- where to look for help and guidance
- support from home (e.g. somewhere to work quietly)
- methods of learning and revising for exams
- organising time for work and relaxation
- presentation of work
- meeting deadlines
- planning for the next stage (e.g. options at KS4 or AS subjects, career).

Things to consider

- Are pupils selected to be mentored, or are they willing volunteers? Is it best to have an adult who knows the pupil to act as mentor, or is it best to use someone who has no preformed ideas about the pupil's approach to work?
- Mentoring is very expensive in terms of teacher time. Would it be better to arrange the timetable so that teachers have more time to talk to pupils in their science lessons?

Including more social issues in science

Most pupils are interested in the applications of science and the impact scientific development has on their lives. Young people often hold very strong opinions about what is right and what is wrong about many socio-scientific topics. The science-technology–society movement, mainly through the SATIS project in the UK, has produced useful resources for teachers knitting together scientific knowledge with industrial, medical or environmental situations. The Salters' curriculum projects have taken this one step further by developing GCSE and A-level courses where each topic has its origins in aspects of everyday life. The courses have attracted a great deal of interest and have continued to expand. Salters' A-level chemistry was introduced in the early 1990s, followed by Salters' Horners A-level physics, and in 2002 Salters-Nuffield A-level biology was piloted. These courses have the potential to improve pupils' interest in science and to improve gender inclusivity in science. Hughes (2000) points out that this potential may not be realised due to the marginalisation of the social context in most examination specifications. Some pupils, mainly boys, perceive the contextual approach as peripheral to learning about the 'real' science. Hughes argues that what is needed is a clear signal from curriculum developers that a thorough understanding about debates and issues involving science in society is essential for all pupils.

Summary of classroom strategies

If you think your school has a problem with under-achievement, investigate the situation thoroughly before taking action. Based on case studies on performance, the TES (1999b) has suggested the following classroom strategies to help under-achievers, particularly boys:

- Sit under-achievers with high achievers (research evidence suggests that boys are more affected by peer pressure and need to be placed in a situation in which they have no choice but to work)

- Offer clear targets for each lesson
- Give more information in bite-sized chunks
- Organise tasks step by step
- Build in challenge rather than completion as a goal
- Provide opportunities for group work, active involvement, practical work
- Offer more discussion, role play, story writing
- Provide models and frameworks to support different kinds of writing (boys may need to be helped/taught to organise their work)
- Don't single out individuals for praise or criticism in front of peers – do it privately (boys will not respond well to being told that girls are doing much better than they are; it is much better to give advice on improvement to individuals)
- Make homework tasks focussed and brief, mark work and return it quickly
- Use homework for extension and enrichment of classwork
- Take in and mark extended coursework in sections.

The key strategy is to have the highest expectations and demand the highest standards from both boys and girls.[1]

Differences in 'race'

> Almost all pupils, in most parts of the country, have considerable levels of confusion, misunderstanding and ignorance about 'race'. Many have high levels of prejudice and hostility.
>
> When faced with the consequences of racial hostility people often say the answer, and a better future lies in education.
>
> (Gaine, 1987: 17)

Equality of opportunity is an important issue that affects us all. The United Kingdom, along with many other countries worldwide, is a multicultural society, and our social and economic well-being depends on nurturing this developing society in order that we can all benefit from the vast array of expertise present throughout the country. As from May 2002, all schools are required by law to have a written race equality policy containing details such as the school's commitment to tackling racial discrimination and promoting equality of opportunity. There may still be some schools with a mainly White school population who feel that such legislation is not relevant to them. According to a report published in 1999, many teachers have little or no idea of what defines an ethnic minority, what racism is, or how to teach about it. The study goes on to report that openly racist attitudes are often ignored by staff (Hamilton, 1999). The 'no problem here' syndrome described by Gaine (1987, 1995) still exists in a few schools. If we are to develop a society where people are not judged on the colour of their skin, the way they talk or what they look like, it is up to all schools to raise pupils' awareness of racial issues. Race is just as important an issue in the mainly White areas of Devon and Cornwall as it is in the multicultural environments of London and Birmingham. There are promising signs that racism is on the decline amongst young people. In a study of

13–14-year-old pupils it was found that about three-quarters of the White pupils surveyed showed no prejudice against ethnic minorities (Bath and Farrell, 1996). The authors speculate that the greater prominence given to multicultural issues in school has made a significant impact on pupils' attitudes. The NC curriculum for citizenship will ensure that in future all schools in England will address the issue through units such as 'Britain – a diverse society?' at KS3 and 'Challenging racism and discrimination' at KS4 (units 4 and 3 of the QCA SoW).

There are two issues that will briefly be discussed in this section: first, the particular problems of Black Caribbean pupils concerned with their behaviour and academic achievement and second, how science teachers could help pupils to understand about race and contribute to the wider goals of the school in the creation of a more tolerant society.

Problems of behaviour and achievement

More than four times as many boys than girls were excluded from schools in England in 1996. Black pupils were far more likely to be excluded than white or Asian pupils, possibly due to the different interpretations placed on their behaviour by teaching staff.

(EOC, 1998: 3)

In an investigation into reasons for the high exclusion rate for Black pupils, carried out by Sewell (1997), it was suggested that some blame should be attributed to the teachers and some to the pupils. Some teachers were irritated by the Black youth sub-culture and found it difficult to cope with the language and attitude from some pupils. The most difficult pupils, described as Black nationalists, believed that White teachers and the Eurocentric curriculum were working against their interests.

Sewell makes the following suggestions to avoid confrontation:

- avoid negative comments on cultural style
- respect pupils' personal space
- use friendly gestures, not aggressive ones
- use the pupil's preferred name
- get on pupils' level physically
- ask questions rather than make accusations
- deal with problem behaviour in private
- listen carefully when pupils speak to you.

Black pupils tend to create very strong bonds with one another, and develop what Sewell (2000) describes as a kinship culture where group values are considered to be more important than individual interests. This fusion of minds can be a very powerful and persuasive force, and individual Black pupils have to negotiate carefully between the demands of the kinship group and the individualistic demands of the school.

In a report written by Blair and Bourne (1998), a headteacher reported on the deteriorating situation in her school where African-Caribbean males in particular were experiencing a high level of alienation and exclusion. The head and the staff worked together to create a new ethos where staff listened carefully to the concerns of the pupils, and involved parents in drawing up an anti-racist policy. Systematic effort was also made to raise achievement by changing pupils' attitudes through strategies such as the use of mentoring sessions to support the more vulnerable pupils who were likely to be influenced by gangs outside school. Majors (2001) has also suggested that part of the problem may be the way that teachers misinterpret Black culture and are too quick to exclude Black boys for trivial offences such as having dreadlocks or walking arrogantly.

Gillborn and Mirza (2000) challenge the stereotypical view that Black pupils lack motivation and are alienated and disenchanted with school. They argue that research evidence, comparing White peers of the same sex and social background, indicates that Black pupils tend to display higher levels of motivation and commitment to education. Social class has been shown to be a crucial factor in determining whether a child does well or badly at school (TES, 1998). Stereotypical views held by teachers could lead to lower teacher expectations, and the report suggests that schools should do more to identify pupils' abilities and plan to ensure that pupils from different ethnic and social class backgrounds make the most of their potential.

Data on pupils' achievement according to ethnic origin are not readily available, and are, perhaps, not 100 per cent reliable. However, there are some trends that are clear. Within each of the principle minority ethnic groups girls tend to outperform boys, but there are consistent and significant inequalities of attainment between ethnic groups regardless of gender. The well-publicised improvement in GCSE results year on year has not been applicable to African-Caribbean and Pakistani pupils. When comparing like with like, in terms of gender, class and ethnic origin, consistent and significant ethnic inequalities of attainment remain clear (Gillborn and Mirza, 2000). There is some evidence to suggest that the progress made by African-Caribbean boys drops during their time at secondary school (Richardson and Wood, 1999; Samaraweera, 2002; Ofsted, 2002c). Figure 6.2 illustrates some data for the schools served by Birmingham City Council. The data give a general picture, looking at pupils who were examined in 2000. The size of each of the groups varies considerably (e.g. 40 Chinese and 1749 Pakistani pupils at GCSE level). Taking KS2 results in English and maths as the baseline, it can be seen that African-Caribbean

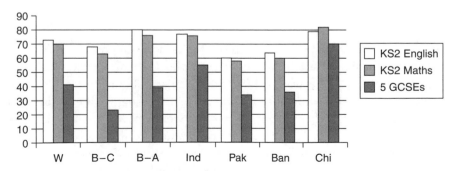

Figure 6.2 *Comparison of KS2 results (percentage of pupils achieving level 4 or above) in English and Maths with percentage of pupils gaining 5 or more GCSEs A*–C for White (W), Black – Caribbean heritage (B–C), Black – African heritage (B–A), Indian (Ind), Pakistani (Pak), Bangladeshi (Ban) and Chinese (Chi) pupils for 1999–2000 for Birmingham (Samaraweera, 2002)*

pupils do not perform well in the secondary school whereas Indian and Chinese pupils perform very well. The main group of under-achievers in this country is of Black males from poor families.

Ofsted (1998) also points to the problem of the lack of data, and goes on to suggest some strategies to help ethnic minority groups:

> The pattern of achievement of pupils from ethnic minority groups remains very complex. Identification of trends is hindered by the lack of detailed and accurate data produced for, or by, schools and LEAs. In general, pupils of African Caribbean heritage, and particularly boys, continue to underachieve. Some schools, however, have successfully tackled the underachievement of specific ethnic minority groups by well-targeted initiatives. These include additional tutorial time for monitoring pupils' academic progress, setting specific targets for pupils, and homework clubs at lunchtime and after school, sometimes with Section 11 teachers as the driving force. These initiatives have improved attendance and behaviour and increased parental involvement, and in a small number of cases the pupils' examination results have improved. Pupils for whom **ENGLISH IS AN ADDITIONAL LANGUAGE** often make good progress, especially where they receive continued support to refine their knowledge and use of language as they become more competent
>
> (Ofsted, 1998: para. 102)

Rasekoala (1997) draws our attention to the fact that very few Black students go on to study any of the sciences at university. She suggests that while other groups of students are expected and encouraged to achieve in science, Black students are expected to achieve in other areas of the curriculum. Rasekoala has been involved in setting up the African Caribbean Network for Science and Technology, which is a network that provides a nationwide service committed to enhancing the public understanding of science in the Black community (see http://www.dti.gov.uk/ost/ostbusiness/puset/sciconn/p03.htm).

Teaching considerations

A study carried out by Ofsted (2002c) showed that schools can make a difference. The performance of the Black Caribbean boys in a sample of schools visited was better than the national average. There was nothing extraordinary about the teaching methods used, and the curriculum differed little from what was being offered in most secondary schools. Like all other schools, there were well-behaved classes and those that were not so well behaved. The distinguishing features of these schools were rather hard to identify, but there were two clear classroom features that were important. The first was concerned with the tone of the classroom, which was always positive towards pupils' potential for achievement. This encouraging atmosphere was further strengthened by the sense of belonging to a community that cared. The second feature, stemming from this, was the support offered by the teachers by listening to what the pupils had to say and providing extra help when required. On a whole-school basis, the strengths of the sample of good schools were:

- communication with parents
- informing young people about an ethnically diverse world
- the use of a data analysis system that monitored all aspects of attainment by ethnicity and gender
- a robust anti-racist policy.

The main issue for science teachers is the same as for teachers of all other subjects, that of combating racism by stamping on any racist comments or actions, no matter what section of the community they come from. In addition there are a number of activities and strategies that can be used in science lessons, such as:

- explaining to pupils that 'race' is not a valid science concept. The opportunity to discuss the notion of 'race' arises during the teaching of genetics at KS4. Pupils need to be made aware that race is purely a sociological construction, and there is no genetic way of separating definitively and completely any two populations or 'races'. Every person on Earth shares 99.99 per cent of the same genetic code, and the differences within racial groups are often greater than those between people of different colours. People who are African or who are of recent African descent are closer to Caucasians than they are to other Africans (Sykes, 2001).
- using examples of non-western scientists. Pupils need to see examples of adults who have succeeded in the scientific world. If you restrict this to pictures of famous scientists involved in NC science, they will be predominantly White males, and therefore you need to look for more modern examples.[2] Our textbooks give the impression that White males have dominated science in the past, and they tend to ignore scientists from other cultures. Examples of scientists from other cultures, and ideas about teaching multicultural issues in science, have been documented by Thorp *et al.* (1995).
- using examples of food, clothing etc. used by people from different cultures living in this country. Opportunities arise throughout the secondary curriculum – e.g. food tests, variation, diet, early ideas about the movement of the Earth, Moon and Sun, materials for clothes.
- viewing technology as a response to human needs and demonstrating the validity of technology in particular cultural contexts. Sustainability and other environmental issues are of great interest to pupils. There are plenty of opportunities to challenge the 'West is best' attitude and young people's obsession with materialism.
- being part of a global community of science learners. There are many opportunities through the Internet and international organisations to link up with pupils in other countries to exchange ideas and information about science – e.g. Science Across the World from the ASE. This helps to create a global awareness of issues, and can have plenty of spin-off benefits.
- using oral work. According to Sewell (2000), Black children tend to come from a culture where oral communication is dominant and therefore they tend to retain

more information when it is spoken rather than written. Pupils with EAL may find this beneficial in terms of developing their language through listening and making contributions in a less threatening environment.

• adopting a view that sees cultural diversity as a positive advantage, so that use can be made of the varied experiences of young people from different cultural backgrounds.

Hodson (1993) warns against a tokenistic approach. It is not a matter of doing an occasional session with a multicultural slant to satisfy the powers that be that the issue has been covered. Pupils are clearly going to see through this. It has got to arise naturally from the lesson when the opportunity presents itself.

Things to consider

Review the work of the science department in terms of its contribution to anti-racism. For teachers who work in a predominantly White school: to what extent do you prepare your pupils to live in a multicultural society?

References

Barber, M. (1994) *Young People and their Attitudes to School*, Keele: Keele University.

Bath, L. and Farrell, P. (1996) 'The attitudes of white secondary school students towards ethnic minorities', *Educational & Child Psychology*, **13**(3), 5–13.

Bell, J.F. (2001) 'Investigating gender differences in the science performance of 16-year-old pupils in the UK', *International Journal of Science Education*, **23**(5), 469–486.

Blair, M. and Bourne, J. (1998) *Making the Difference: Teaching and Learning Strategies in Successful Multi-ethnic Schools*, London: DfEE (available at http://www.gtce.org.uk/pdfs/differencestudy.pdf).

Bradford, W. (1996) *Raising Boys' Achievement*, Kirklees: Kirklees Advisory Service.

Bray, R., Downes, P., Gardner, C., and Parsons, N. (1997) *Can Boys do Better?*, Bristol: SHA.

Calder, G. and Parkinson, J. (1994) 'Using supported self-study to teach a modular GCSE science course: a case study', *School Science Review*, **76**(275), 112–114.

DfEE (1997) *Excellence in Schools*, London: The Stationery Office.

DfEE (2001) *Schools Building on Success*, London: The Stationery Office.

EOC (1998) 'Gender and differential achievement in education and training: a research review', Equal Opportunities Commission, UK (available at: http://www.eoc.org.uk/EOCeng/EOCcs/Research/gender_and_differential_achievement_findings.pdf).

EOC Wales (1999) *Different But Equal*, Cardiff: Equal Opportunities Commission.

Erwin, L. and Muarutto, P. (1998) 'Beyond access: considering gender deficits in science education', *Gender & Education*, **10**(1), 51–69.

Gaine, C. (1987) *No Problem Here: A Practical Approach to Education and 'Race' in White Schools*, London: Hutchinson.

Gaine, C. (1995) *Still No Problem Here*, Stoke-on-Trent: Trentham Books.

George, C. (ed.) (1976) *Non-streamed Science: Organisation and Practice*, Hatfield: ASE.

Gillborn, D. and Mirza, H.S. (2000) *Educational Inequality. Mapping Race Class and Gender: A Synthesis of Research Evidence*, London: Ofsted.

Gillibrand, E., Robinson, P., Brawn, R. and Osborn, A. (1999) 'Girls' participation in physics in single sex classes in mixed schools in relation to confidence and achievement', *International Journal of Science Education*, **21**(4), 349–362.

Gorard, S., Rees, G. and Salisbury, J. (2001) 'Investigating the patterns of differential attainment of boys and girls at school', *British Educational Research Journal*, **27**(2), 123–139.

Hall, S. (1997) 'The problem with differentiation', *School Science Review*, **78**(284), 95–98.

Hallam, S. and Toutounji, I. (1997) 'What do we know about grouping pupils by ability?', *Education Review*, **10**(2), 62–69.

Hamilton, C. (1999) *Racism and Race Relations in Predominantly White Schools: Preparing Pupils for Life in a Diverse Multi-Cultural Society*, London: The Children's Legal Centre (available at http://www2.essex.ac.uk/clc/hi/press/text/press003.htm).

Harlen, W. and Crick, R.D. (2002) *A Systematic Review of the Impact of Summative Assessment and Tests on Students' Motivation for Learning*, London: Evidence for Policy and Practice Information and Co-ordinating Centre (EPPI) (available at: http://eppi.ioe.ac.uk/EPPIWebContent/reel/review_groups/assessment/ass_rv1/ass_rv1.pdf).

Harrison, C. (1997) 'Differentiation in theory and practice', in Dillon, J. and Maguire, M. (eds) *Becoming a Teacher: Issues in Secondary Teaching*, Buckingham: Open University Press.

Hodson, D. (1993) 'In search of a rationale for multicultural science', *Science Education*, **77**(6), 685–711.

Holland, V. (1998) 'Underachieving boys: problems and solutions', *Support for Learning*, **13**(4), 174–178.

Hughes, G. (2000) 'Salters' curriculum projects and gender inclusivity in science', *School Science Review*, **80**(296), 85–89.

Ireson, J., Hallam, S., Mortimore, P., Hack, S., Clark, H. and Plewis, I. (1999) 'Ability grouping in the secondary school: the effects on academic achievement and pupils' self-esteem'. Paper presented at the British Educational Research Association Annual Conference (available at: http://www.leeds.ac.uk/educol/documents/00001359.htm).

Ireson, J., Clark, H. and Hallam, S. (2002) 'Constructing ability groups in the secondary schools: issues in practice', *School Leadership & Management*, **22**(2), 163–176.

Jackson, C. (2002) 'Can single-sex classes in co-educational schools enhance the learning experiences of girls and/or boys? An exploration of pupils' perceptions', *British Educational Research Journal*, **28**(1), 37–48.

Kenway, J. and Gough, A. (1998) 'Gender and science education in schools: a review "with attitude"', *Studies in Science Education*, **31**, 1–30.

MacDonald, A., Saunders, L. and Benefield, P. (1999) *Boys' Achievement, Progress, Motivation and Participation: Issues Raised by the Recent Literature*, Slough: NFER.

Majors, R. (2001) *Our Black Children*, London: Routledge.

Mitchell, G. and Hirom, K. (2002) 'The role of exploratory style in the academic underperformance of boys', Lisbon: European Conference on Educational Research (available at: http://www.leeds.ac.uk/educol/documents/00002146.htm).

Myhill, D. (2002) 'Bad boys and good girls? Patterns of interaction and response in whole class teaching', *British Educational Research Journal*, **28**(3), 339–352.

Naylor, S. and Keogh, B. (1995) 'Making differentiation manageable', *School Science Review*, **77**(279), 106–110.

Noble, C., Brown, J. and Murphy, J. (2001) *How to Raise Boys' Achievement*, London: David Fulton Publishers.

O'Brien, T. and Guiney, D. (2001) *Differentiation in Teaching and Learning: Principles and Practice*, London: Continuum.

Ofsted (1998) *The Annual Report of Her Majesty's Chief Inspector of Schools: Standards and Quality in Education 1996/97*, London: Office for Standards in Education.

Ofsted, (1999) *Annual Report of Her Majesty's Chief Inspector of Schools: Standards and Quality in Education 1997/98*, London: Office for Standards in Education.

Ofsted (2002a) *Annual Report of Her Majesty's Chief Inspector of Schools: Standards and Quality in Education 2000/01*, London: Office for Standards in Education.

Ofsted (2002b) *Good Teaching, Effective Departments*, London: Office for Standards in Education.

Ofsted (2002c) *Achievement of Black Caribbean Pupils: Good Practice in Secondary Schools*, London: Office for Standards in Education.

OHMCI (1997) *Standards and Quality in Secondary School: The Relative Performance of Boys and Girls*, Cardiff: OHMCI.

Parker, L.H. and Rennie, L.J. (2002) 'Teachers' implementation of gender-inclusive instructional strategies in single-sex and mixed-sex science classrooms', *International Journal of Science Education*, **24**(9), 881–897.

Pickering, J. (1997) *Raising Boys' Achievement*, Stafford: Network Educational Press.

Piggott, A. (2002) 'Putting differentiation into practice in secondary science lessons', *School Science Review*, **83**(305), 65–71.

Plummer, G. (2000) *Failing Working Class Girls*, Stoke-on-Trent: Trentham Books.

Postlethwaite, K. and Haggarty, L. (2002) 'Towards the improvement of learning in secondary school: students' views, their links to theories of motivation and to issues of under- and over-achievement', *Research Papers in Education*, **17**(2), 185–209.

Price, J. and Talbot, B. (1984) 'Girls and physical science at Ellis Guildford School', *School Science Review*, **66**(234), 7–11.

Rasekoala, E. (1997) 'Ethnic minorities and achievement: the black hole in science ranks part 2: post-16 education', *Multicultural Teaching*, **16**(1), 12–15.

Reiss, M.J. (2000) 'Gender issues in science lessons as revealed by a longitudinal study'. Paper presented at the British Educational Research Association Annual Conference (available at: http://www.leeds.ac.uk/educol/documents/00001599.htm).

Revell, M. (ed.) (1995) *The Differentiation Book*, Northampton: The Science Centre NIAS (Northampton Inspection and Advisory Service).

Richardson, R. and Wood, A. (1999) *Inclusive Schools, Inclusive Society*, Stoke-on-Trent: Trentham Books.

Samaraweera, Y. (2002) *Scrutiny Report to the City Council*, Birmingham: Birmingham City Council (available on the Birmingham city website at http://www.birmingham.gov.uk/).

Sewell, T. (1997) *Black Masculinities and Schooling: How Black Boys Survive Modern Schooling*, Stoke-on-Trent: Trentham Books.

Sewell, T. (2000) 'Beyond institutional racism: tackling the real problems of Black underachievement', *Multicultural Teaching*, **18**(2), 27–33.

Solomon, J. (1997) 'Girls' science education: choice, solidarity and culture', *International Journal of Science Education*, **19**(4), 407–417.

Stark, R. and Gray, D. (1999) 'Gender preferences in learning science', *International Journal of Science Education*, **21**(6), 633–643.

Stewart, M. (1998) 'Gender issues in physics', *Educational Research*, **40**(3), 283–293.

Sukhnandan, L. and Lee, B. (1998) *Streaming, Setting and Grouping by Ability: A Review of the Literature*, Slough: NFER (available at: http://www.nfer.ac.uk/htmldocs/Outcome_SSG.doc).

Sukhnandan, L., Lee, B. and Kelleher, S. (2000) *An Investigation into Gender Differences in Achievement, Phase 2: School and Classroom Strategies*, Slough: NFER (available at: http://195.194.2.100/htmldocs/Outcome_BUP.doc).

Sykes, B. (2001) *The Astonishing Story that Reveals How Each of Us Can Trace Our Genetic Ancestors*, London: Bantam Press.

Taylor, N. (1993) 'Ability grouping and its effect on pupil behaviour: a case study of a Midlands comprehensive school', *Education Today*, **43**(2), 14–17.

TES (1998) '5,000 pupils prove social class matters', *Times Educational Supplement*, 25 September, 3.

TES (1999a) 'Schools ignore issues of racism', article by Nadine Ghouri, *Times Educational Supplement*, 26 February.

TES (1999b) 'Everything you need to know about anything', *Times Educational Supplement*, 4 June, 30.

Thorp, S., Deshpande, P. and Edwards, C. (1994) *Race, Equality and Science Teaching: A Handbook for Teachers and Educators*, Hatfield: ASE.

Troyna, B. (1991) 'Underachievers or underrated? The experiences of pupils of South African origin in a secondary school', *British Educational Research Journal*, **17**(4), 361–376.

Younger, M. and Warrington, M. (2002) 'Single-sex teaching in a co-educational comprehensive school in England: an evaluation based upon students' performance and classroom interactions', *British Educational Research Journal*, **28**(3), 353–374.

CHAPTER 7

Making use of information from assessment

Instead of giving the children a task and measuring how well they do or how badly they fail, one can give the children the task and observe how much and what kind of help they need in order to complete the task successfully.

(Newman *et al.*, 1989: 77)

Teachers spend a considerable amount of time on assessment matters, from marking pupils' work to agonising over comments to be written on reports. In order to help pupils do their best in external examinations teachers scrutinise every aspect of the specification (syllabus), check on question types, read examiners' reports and provide considerable support for pupils in helping them to complete their coursework. On top of this, teachers are expected to use baseline data to monitor pupils' progress and set targets for improvement. A teacher can quickly accumulate a vast amount of numerical data on each pupil. Teachers are then faced with two problems: what does it all mean, and how can it be used efficiently and effectively?

This chapter will review the research on day to day assessment and its relationship to pupils' learning. It will suggest that some current practices are not as helpful to pupils as might initially be expected, and that what is needed is a change in the way we approach assessment.

What is formative assessment?

Formative assessment appears to have been one of the most neglected areas of classroom practice, and has always been the poor relation to the 'all important' summative assessment. Until recently, teachers have been content at putting short remarks on pupils work, such as 'Well done', 'Be careful about your spelling' and 'see me', at the end of a piece of work. This is not surprising considering the large volume of work to be marked and the time that it would take to write copious comments on each pupil's book.

Formative assessment (or assessment for learning, as it is sometimes called) is simply giving feedback to pupils that will support and assist them in their learning of science. It goes beyond telling pupils that they have got this or that wrong to telling them why they have got it wrong and how they could get it right next time round.

The introduction of formative assessment into teachers' regular practice will require some radical changes to current classroom pedagogy (Black and Wiliam, 1998a). Giving feedback of this nature to pupils does take up time, and teachers will argue that there is no time available in an already overcrowded curriculum. Teachers feel that they are under pressure to get through the specification, make sure everything is covered and give pupils plenty of examples of past questions. They might argue that practise at examination questions is the key to good examination results and, in the present educational climate, teachers are judged on the number of A*–C grades gained. Examination results are of paramount importance, and in some situations it doesn't seem to matter how you achieve them.

Black and Wiliam have carried out an extensive review of the literature on formative assessment, and have shown that there is firm evidence that the use of certain techniques concerned with strengthening feedback given to pupils about their learning yields results in significant improvements in understanding (Black and Wiliam, 1998a: 7; 1998b: 61):

> The research reported here shows conclusively that formative assessment does improve learning. The gains in achievement appear to be quite considerable, and as noted earlier, amongst the largest ever reported for educational interventions.

A synopsis of the review together with additional implications has been produced and published by the Assessment Reform Group (1998), and a paper has been written targeted specifically at science teachers (Black, 1998). The research literature indicates that there are five assessment factors that lead to improved learning. These are:

1 The provision of effective feedback to pupils
2 The active involvement of pupils in their own learning
3 Adjusting teaching to take account of the results of assessment
4 A recognition of the profound influence assessment has on the motivation and self-esteem of pupils, both of which are crucial influences on learning
5 The need for pupils to assess themselves and understand how to improve.

(Assessment Reform Group, 1998: 4)

The study resulted in the production of a research project (Black *et al.*, 2002) looking at how these principles could be implemented in science classrooms, and many of the results are included in the sections below.

Overall, there is strong evidence to suggest that good use of formative assessment will:

- lead to improved results in examinations (even though by spending time on formative assessment teachers might not have time to 'cover' all the GCSE specification)
- help raise the standards of the 'low-attainers' more than the rest, reducing the spread of attainment (Black, 1998)
- 'wake up' those pupils who are getting by on the minimum of work and simply cruising along

- help to highlight those things that are important to learn
- help pupils learn how to learn (by influencing the choice of learning strategies; by inculcating self-monitoring skills; by developing the ability to retain and apply knowledge, skills and understanding in different contexts) (James and Gipps, 1998)
- help pupils to learn how to judge the effectiveness of their learning
- promote deep rather than shallow learning
- raise pupils' self-esteem and improve attitudes towards learning.

These are hardly things that can be dismissed lightly and you may now be wondering, if it is such a good idea, why haven't we been doing it already. I think the answer to that is twofold. First, we haven't had all this evidence together in one place before; it has been scattered across the education research journals, and they have a limited readership. Second, teachers have had their lives dominated by government initiatives in recent years, and have been reluctant to take on something new as it may not match with the 'approved' way of doing things.

Of course, formative assessment is being used in schools today. Teachers are constantly giving feedback to pupils. As they go round the classroom they are listening to what pupils say and giving advice and support. Teachers go over things that pupils haven't understood properly, they correct things in books and provide helpful comments. All this is excellent, but what the research indicates is that by planning for formative assessment we can make our teaching far more effective.

Teachers who adopt a socio-constructivist methodology, however, will be no strangers to formative assessment. A central part of this teaching is to be involved in a dialogue with pupils to clarify their existing ideas about a science concept and to help them construct the scientifically accepted view. Helping pupils to modify their thinking in this way is a good example of the value of formative assessment.

Weaknesses in current practice

There has been an increased emphasis on testing pupils on a regular basis in recent years – short tests to keep them on their toes, and longer tests to check they can answer questions appropriate to the part of the curriculum they are currently studying. This tradition for teaching for tests and examinations often encourages rote learning. Pupils may become very efficient at this form of memorisation, but in the long term the information fades (James and Gipps, 1998). Also, science teachers need to consider what sort of message this is giving to pupils about the nature of science. Is science a list of facts that have to be memorised? Rote learning gives rise to what James and Gipps call surface (or shallow) learning, where pupils have a passive acceptance of the ideas and information and a lack of recognition of the guiding principles or patterns. Other problems with current practice are as follows:

- The lack of review of assessment questions and the test overall. Schools use past paper questions, questions from commercially produced teachers' guides and their own ideas to produce in-house tests. However, they have little time for analysis of these questions in terms of the types being asked and the extent to which they are testing higher-order skills (in terms of Bloom's taxonomy, i.e. synthesis, analysis and evaluation).[1]

- Teachers continue the traditional practice of giving grades or marks when sometimes the meaning behind these is not clear to the pupil (Henry, 2001). Errors are highlighted, but the practice gives little (or no) indication to the pupils as how to improve the work. The practice can be demotivating, particularly to the less able child who may have put in a great deal of effort into the production of a piece of work although the outcome may look poor in comparison with other pupils' work.

- In spite of a move towards criterion-referenced assessment, there is still a tendency for teachers to use a normative approach. There is an assumption that healthy competition will help those pupils who are at the bottom of the mark distribution profile and encourage them to 'get their act together'. However, what tends to happen is that these pupils become demotivated and lose their confidence in their own capacity to learn (Black and Wiliam, 1998b).

Things to consider

Review the science department's assessment policy, and consider:

- how it relates to the overall school assessment policy
- the quality of the guidance it gives to members of the department in terms of formative assessment
- the extent to which guidance is given on the assessment of skills (e.g. numeracy, practical skills, information technology, presentational skills) and processes (e.g. processing information, modelling, interpreting, evaluating, predicting)
- how it promotes a range of formative feedback strategies
- how it ensures that higher-order as well as lower-order cognitive demands are assessed
- the quality of guidance given on testing
- what quality assurance procedures are in place to ensure that procedures are implemented consistently and that common standards are applied throughout the department (moderation)
- the extent to which the policy is put into practice and how often it is reviewed.

Characteristics of formative assessment

In a review of formative assessment in science teaching in New Zealand, Bell and Cowie (2001) identified a number of features of formative assessment. The problem is that many of the facets of this type of teacher activity are ephemeral and in order to improve teachers' practice they need to be made more visible and explicit. Among the characteristics recognised are:

1 **Responsiveness.** A teacher notices, recognises and responds to a pupil's learning. Frequently this is unplanned and sometimes, therefore, involves the teacher in risk-taking. Planned formative assessment is often used at the beginning of a unit to elicit prior knowledge.
2 **Sources of information and evidence.** Formative assessment relies on non-verbal (facial expressions, body language) as well as verbal information.
3 **A tacit process.** Teachers frequently comment that they are not always conscious of carrying out formative assessment.
4 **Making judgements.** Teachers use their professional knowledge to make judgements as to which information to act upon and which to ignore.

Ways of carrying out formative assessment

Black and Wiliam (1998b) have identified a number of strategies that can be used to promote formative assessment. These can be summarised under the following headings:

* Setting appropriate tasks
* Classroom discourse
* Oral questioning
* Written work
* Self and peer-assessment.

In planning for formative assessment, teachers need to bear in mind that the purpose is to help the individual pupil. It is not concerned with ranking pupils in order of achievement or putting down pupils because of what they don't know. Low-achieving pupils can be very easily demotivated and turned off learning science if they are constantly faced with a culture of comparative achievement. Formative assessment provides pupils with solutions to specific problems with their work, and promotes a culture of success and the raising of self-esteem. There are many ways of giving feedback to pupils and setting targets. McCallum (2001) stresses the point of giving pupils clear information about which aspects of their work are correct and which are incorrect, and goes on to identify other factors that should be present in good quality feedback and target setting:

* Describing why an answer is correct
* Telling pupils what they have or have not achieved
* Specifying or implying a better way of doing something
* Getting pupils to suggest ways in which they can improve.

Setting appropriate tasks

Pupils respond well to being presented with a variety of activities in lessons. It helps to maintain interest and motivation, and goes some way to assuring that the different types of learners in any one class have their needs catered for. However, in planning for these activities the teacher must not lose sight of the opportunities for assessment and how this can be introduced into different tasks. Some will be of relatively low cognitive demand, and the teacher will need to consider how to ensure that pupils are appropriately challenged. An effective way of doing this is through comments and questions to small groups of pupils or individuals that prompt them to think more deeply about the work they are doing, followed by some feedback on their work.

Sometimes pupils can get lost in the wilderness of lessons; they don't know what they are doing this period, and certainly find it difficult to relate it to what they have done before. Pupils need a guide to remind them of past learning and to show them what they are aiming for today. For example, pupils can get very confused when doing a practical activity. They may be able to follow the routine procedures, but are not sure about why they are doing it. It is as though the busyness, or the 'noise', of the practical clouds pupils' perspectives of what is actually going on (see page 192).

A textbook frequently acts as reminder of where the lesson fits in to the grand scheme of things, but pupils will still need help in linking the new work with previous work and, where possible, with work done in other subjects. Teachers also need to share with them the objectives for the current lesson. The KS3 National Strategy for science suggests that clarifying the objectives and explaining the purpose of the lesson should be part of the starter activities for each lesson (DfES, 2002). There are a number of ways of communicating the objectives to the pupils, such as:

- writing the objectives on the board or on an overhead transparency (using an electronic whiteboard enables the teacher to retrieve the objectives at key points during the lesson and show pupils how they have been achieved)
- photocopying them onto a (small) piece of paper so that pupils can stick them in their book
- talking to the pupils about what they are going to learn about today.

Having the learning goals of the work in front of the pupils throughout lesson serves as a useful reminder of what everyone is working towards. However, clearly the goals must be stated in terms that the pupils can fully understand. They should serve as a reminder to pupils throughout the lesson and the teacher could come back to them when any refocussing is required.

Teachers need to make the learning explicit and force pupils to think about what they have learnt during the lesson. Clearly this cannot be a repetitive 'what have we learnt today class' approach, which, at best, would only result in the pupils regurgitating some of the key phrases heard during the lesson. A process of drip feed, where different types of questions are asked to different groups of children, is likely to be more effective. Teachers may ask questions and make comments such as:

- What have you learnt by doing that?
- How do you know that?
- What does that tell you?
- Write down two things your teacher wants you to learn from doing this investigation
- How do you know what your teacher wants you to learn?
- Why do you think that has happened?
- Explain that to me in terms of what you know about how the particles are moving.
- I want you to use what you have learnt to do this next activity.

Some pupils find science hard to learn because they see it as a mass of isolated facts to be remembered. Teachers need to emphasise the patterns, the consistencies and the logic in science to help pupils see the big picture. Unfortunately we sometimes give conflicting messages to pupils by doing something one way in this lesson and then doing a similar task in an entirely different way in another lesson. For example, on one occasion we may be very concerned about using accurate measurements, ensuring that all the fair test criteria are met, etc., and then in another lesson have no concern for these factors. Although there may be a perfectly valid reason for doing things differently, we don't always relate this to the pupils.

Over a period of time, a classroom climate could be established where there is an expectation that:

- the teacher will ask pupils to work things out for themselves
- pupils will be given challenging work
- pupils will be required to find things out for themselves
- there will be a variety of learning activities to suit the needs of the different types of learners within the class
- pupils will be responsible for their own learning and will ask if they don't understand.

It is worthwhile considering the value of the current fashion of providing pupils with merits and prizes, and the extent to which this motivates different groups of pupils. Such a scheme may motivate high achievers, but it is likely to have the opposite effect on low achievers. A system that uses written feedback rather than rewards is likely to benefit everyone in terms of achievement, motivation and the raising of self-esteem (Black *et al.*, 2002).

Classroom discourse

Teachers are constantly looking for ways to get pupils to talk about science, to make explicit their understanding and identify those things that they don't understand. Whole-class discussions and question-and-answer sessions can help to identify patterns in understanding and can act as a catalyst for remedial action or further work, but there is a danger that key gaps in learning may be overlooked.

Things to consider

Table 7.1 illustrates the sort of proforma that could be used to analyse a lesson in terms of the learning opportunities offered to the pupils. By asking yourself a series of questions directly focussed on pupils' learning, you should be able to filter out much of the other activity that goes on in the classroom. The comment column is there for you to clarify what exactly happened in the lesson and the evaluation column is there for you to make suggestions for personal improvement.

It is useful to ask a colleague to observe a lesson and comment on a number of the aspects listed in Table 7.1, particularly the extent to which pupils are appropriately challenged.

Table 7.1 *Task analysis*

Questions	Comments	Evaluation
• How were the lesson objectives conveyed to the pupils? • How did you monitor pupils' understanding of the concepts taught? • How do these relate to the learning activities used in the preceding 10 lessons with this class? • What were the learning activities carried out in the lesson? • How did the learning in this lesson build on: previous knowledge? previously acquired skills (practical, communication, ICT etc.)? • Did all pupils experience some degree of success? • Were you happy that pupils were sufficiently challenged?		

Properly focussed group discussions (see page 235) place pupils in a situation where they are forced to examine their own understanding. Two examples of these types of tasks are:

1 Asking pupils to prepare questions on the topic
2 Asking pupils to construct a concept map.

Sometimes teachers can get a very good indication about the level of pupils' learning by analysing the types of questions that pupils ask. Woodward (1992: 146) makes the point that:

> Questions asked by children can lead teachers towards making appropriate assessments of children's understanding or alternatively their misconceptions.

Unfortunately pupils don't always ask questions and teachers are left pondering 'do they all understand because they had no questions to ask, or did they not understand it sufficiently well to be able to ask questions?'. The real reason for them not asking is often going to lie somewhere in the region of them not wanting to spoil their super-cool image and needing to get out of the door as soon as the bell goes.

One way of getting over this problem is to ask pupils to write down questions asking about anything they haven't understood or what they would like to know more about. This can be done either as an individual activity or in groups, as a class exercise or for homework. Some pupils will enjoy it when you give them a 'reverse test' by supplying them with a list of answers and asking them to supply the questions. Over a period of time it is likely that such activities will give rise to a climate where it is more acceptable to ask questions in public. Watts *et al.* (1997) have studied the types of questions pupils ask, with a view to diagnosing particular periods of conceptual change exhibited by pupils, and have identified three broad categories:

1 Consolidation – where pupils are attempting to say what they think, clarify the rationale for classroom tasks, confirm explanations and consolidate new under-standing
2 Exploration – where pupils seek to expand knowledge and test constructs that they have formed
3 Elaboration – where pupils lack conviction about either their own frameworks of understanding or those on offer to them. They are examining claims and counter-claims, elaborating on and challenging both their previous knowledge and experience.

As with all of these techniques, getting pupils to ask questions is a process that needs to be taught. Van Zee *et al.* (2001) have shown that once it has been taught it can become part of the way of that pupils work – e.g. they ask questions of one another, they adopt ways of speaking to one another based on the model used in whole-class discussions.

Concept mapping (see page 244) can provide an excellent focus for pupils to discuss their understanding of concepts and the nature of the links between them. In this context concept maps need to be seen as a means to an end, and not as objects that have to look neat and tidy. In practical terms it may be a good idea to have the key concepts on paper with re-usable adhesive on the back, or to use an electronic concept map so that things can be changed as the learning develops. One way of using concept maps to help pupils monitor their learning is by asking them to con-struct a map at the start of a topic to identify their prior understanding of the subject, and then to modify it and add to it lesson by lesson. A group of teachers from Stafford-shire, working on methods of formative assessment, have come up with the idea of asking pupils to explain the links between concepts. Pupils are presented with a com-pleted simple concept map containing speech bubbles coming from each of the link phrases. In each speech bubble is a question that directs pupils to explain the nature of the link.[2]

Any type of group work will provide pupils with the opportunity to put their understanding of science into their own words.

> Meaning is also central to formative assessment. For formative assessment to occur students and teachers have to disclose to each other, on an ongoing basis, the meanings that they are making in the lesson.
>
> (Bell, 2000: 54)

We are bedevilled in science by the complex meanings that we give to words, some of which are at variance to their everyday meaning (see page 233). Pupils will need reminding of this from time to time, and will need to be given the opportunity to use the language in a scientific context.

Oral questioning

Carrying out a question-and-answer session with a class is one of the most difficult things that teachers do. Not only does it require the teacher to provide suitable questions, it also involves listening very carefully to pupils' answers and making the appropriate follow-on statement. When answering questions pupils often rush to give an answer, sometimes shouting out the words that they have recently heard or they know are connected to the topic. In some instances it can boil down to a 'guess what is in my mind quiz', particularly when the teacher doesn't articulate the question well and the pupils are left to guess the meaning. Quick-fire questioning encourages pupils to guess rather than think things through. If a more reasoned response is required, then the teacher has to set the scene and help pupils to make the connections between concepts and pieces of information. Black *et al.* (2002) also point to the importance of providing pupils with valuable follow-up activities, which enable pupils to extend their understanding.

Asking questions is not just about finding out what pupils remember from previous lessons, indeed it will never give a clear picture of this for all pupils. It is a learning activity. Kerry (1998) identifies the following reasons for asking questions:

- to provide pupils with the opportunity to talk constructively on task
- to provide pupils with the opportunity to express their views
- to encourage a problem-solving approach to thinking
- to help pupils externalise and verbalise knowledge
- to encourage thinking aloud
- to help pupils learn from, and respect, one another
- to monitor the extent and deficiencies of pupils' learning
- to deepen thinking levels and improve conceptualisation.

The trick is to ask questions that stimulate pupils into talking about science. Conversations are going to be very limited if the questioning is restricted to closed questions requiring one- or two-word answers. Torrance and Pryor (2001) refer to this as convergent assessment, where the aim of the assessment is to discover *if* the learner knows, understands or can do a predetermined thing. This is in contrast to divergent assessment, which aims to discover *what* the learner knows, understands or can do, and is typified with open questioning. They go on to argue that each type of assessment has its theoretical origins based in different learning theories. Convergent assessment could be said to be derived from behaviourist theory, whereas divergent assessment is linked to a socio-constructivist view of learning. In a divergent mode, the teacher works in the proximal zone of development and promotes scaffolding of the metacognitive activity of the pupils (see page 96).

Experienced teachers are capable of thinking of the questions as a lesson evolves, but if you are thinking about improving your questioning technique then you will find it valuable to spend some time thinking through the key questions you are going to ask and how you want things to develop. In their research looking at the different types of questions used by science teachers, Koufetta and Scaife (2000) found that questions requiring high-order mental operations were not used very frequently. This may be due to teachers feeling insecure and worried about losing the focus of the lesson in situations where they are confronted with a wide range of views. However, it doesn't require a great deal of experience to predict the broad nature of pupils' responses and consider how they can be dealt with. Using Table 7.2 as a reminder of the different types of questions, you could work out how and when you are going to use certain questions. A key factor in determining the success of a question-and-answer session is the relationship between teacher and pupils. Pupils must feel confident that that they won't be put down or ridiculed for saying the wrong thing. Body language plays an important role in helping to read the situation. The teacher's facial expressions and intonation of speech can tell the pupil if he or she is on the right lines and provide encouragement to carry on. Teachers, quite naturally, tend to praise pupils for their responses in order to increase motivation. However, teachers need to be careful about excessive use of praise, as this can be ineffective in terms of pupils' learning (Brophy, 1981). Tables 7.3 and 7.4 provide some suggestions for different approaches to questioning and managing the situation.

To improve the effectiveness of question-and-answer sessions, teachers may have to

Table 7.2 *Types of questions (for further examples, see Carr, 1998)*

Closed questions
Used to check on pupils' retention of information (recall of knowledge)
Can sometimes be given in quick succession to keep pupils on their toes or help to focus pupils' attention on a particular aspect of the work
Persistent use of this type of question can give pupils the impression that science consists of a list of facts to be remembered

Open questions
These ask pupils for their opinions or views, or they may ask a pupil to describe and/or explain a phenomenon. There may be a variety of acceptable responses. Some sub-categories of open questions are given below

Probing questions These test higher-order thinking, requiring the pupil to give an opinion based on scientific understanding or to proffer an explanation	**Reflective questions** These questions provide pupils with the opportunity to check on their understanding of work, e.g. 'Are you sure?' type questions
Hypothetical questions These allow pupils to apply their understanding of science to new situations. They frequently contain the phrase 'what if?'	**Prompting pupils into action** These require no immediate response, but require the pupil to carry out some sort of task in order to be able to answer them

Table 7.3 *Questioning technique*

Distribution around the class
- Remember to ask pupils who are not in your immediate arc of vision
- Consider matching pupil with question, based on ability of pupil and level of difficulty of question

Hands up
- Insistence on not shouting out the answer is essential
- What does the teacher learn by looking at the numbers of pupils who have not got their hands up?
- Choose different pupils to answer, including those who have not put up their hands

No hands up
The aim of this technique is to give pupils more time to think about the answers
- The question is asked to the whole class, but nobody is permitted to answer straight away
- There is a period of 'wait time' with no hands up
- The teacher selects a pupil to answer and other pupils to elaborate on the answer
(Black and Harrison, 2001)

Three coloured cards approach
- Each member of the class is issued with three coloured cards (e.g. red, green, orange)
- Each card has a specific meaning when used to answer a question, e.g.

Type	Red	Green	Orange
Yes/no	No	Yes	Not sure
True/false	False	True	Maybe
Multiple choice	A	B	C

- All members of the class respond
- Individuals are asked to expand on their responses

Loop questions*
- Pupils are given a card containing a question on one side and an answer on the other
- The teacher starts by reading the question on his or her card, and the pupil with the answer to the question stands up and reads out the answer followed by his or her question
- This goes on round the class until everyone has had a turn
Takes time to prepare, fun activity to do (especially for younger age groups), limited in the type of question that can be asked

Group responses
- Pupils work in groups on responses to a small number of 'in-depth' questions
- Group representative gives group's answer to the rest of the class
- Without saying if the group is right or wrong, other groups are invited to comment, offer alternative answers or ask the first group for further explanation
- The teacher needs to anticipate pupils' responses and consider how they can be followed up
(based on Selley, 2000; Black *et al.*, 2002)

Write down the answer
- For one or two key questions in a QA session, ask all the pupils to write down an answer on a piece of paper
- Ask pupils to read out their answers, without comment
- After three or four set of answers, ask the pupils to identify things that are common and things that are different
- Tease out a correct response and, if appropriate, discuss why pupils were saying things that were wrong

I'll come back to you
- The first pupil doesn't know the answer to the question and so the teacher says 'Don't worry I'll come back to you later'
- Other pupils are asked the question and the teacher makes no comment on their answers
- The teacher comes back to the first pupil and says 'Now you've heard a number of different answers, which one do you think is right and why?'

Dealing with responses
- Praise for trying and for correct responses
- Look to others to expand on the answer or give a different point of view
- Emphasise the key points by repeating them and/or writing them on the board
- Coming back to answers given earlier on in the session to see what has been remembered

*Examples available at: http://www.sycd.co.uk/can_we_should_we/explore/fun_size.htm

Table 7.4 *Managing the questioning session*

Classroom arrangement	Use of blackboard
• Consider bringing pupils together at a focal point in the room to create an atmosphere suitable for class discussion • Eye contact with pupils is important • Watch pupils' body language • If moving the pupils is difficult, consider how you could move throughout the room	• To provide some visual stimulus for questions • To record key points obtained from the QA session • Consider using a flip chart (overhead transparency or electronic whiteboard) so that points raised in one lesson can be revisited at a later date
Timing	**Linking**
• Allow time for pupils to think about the answers • Don't let the whole session go on for too long (10 minutes at the most, otherwise pupils' attention wanes)	• Consider how you are going to show the pupils how valuable the QA session was, e.g. by referring back to what certain individuals said, asking 'why did I ask that question?' • Consider following up some of the questions as a homework activity

rethink their current practice and identify opportunities for pupils to work together on solving open-ended questions or problem-solving tasks. The teacher's role then shifts from being a presenter of content to a leader of an exploration in which all pupils are involved in the development of ideas (Black *et al.*, 2002).

Written work

It is common practice to provide pupils with frequent tests in the period building up to an external examination. The questions posed are usually similar in nature to those in the forthcoming external examination, and give pupils practise in answering specific types of questions. Not unexpectedly, research has shown that frequent testing of this type leads to improved learning so long as the frequency doesn't get too high (Black and Wiliam, 1998a, 1998b). Teachers could consider reducing the number of tests given to pupils but increasing the quality of the feedback given. This might initially involve relatively simple issues, such as explaining the language and the question require-ments to pupils. Pupils frequently get confused by words such as describe, discuss, evaluate and explain. Feedback could then move on to looking at improving the struc-ture of answers and composing arguments.

The idea of providing extensive feedback on pupils' written work is more con-tentious. Teachers do not have the time to provide detailed feedback to pupils on every piece of work that they do, and so for the most part they give either a grade or a mark with a short comment. There is evidence to suggest that this approach might not be particularly helpful. Pupils are sometimes confused about the meaning of grades and marks, particularly when one is allocated for attainment and the other for effort.[3] They can feel offended if the comment indicates that they haven't made a great deal of effort when they have tried very hard but not been able to put a great deal down on paper. The comment needs to tell the pupil how to improve his or her work, using language that the pupil can understand and act on. Phrases such as 'include more detail' may seem clear in the mind of the teacher, but the pupil may not understand what 'detail' is required. One way of solving this problem is to make it clear from the outset as to what is required, and the criteria for the assessment of their work. Butler (1988) has examined the effect of different types of feedback on pupils' motivation, by comparing three groups of pupils who were all taught the same work. One group received feedback in the form of marks, another group received comments, and the third group received both marks and comments. Their achievement and interest was monitored over a number of sessions. Table 7.5 summarises the outcomes, showing that simply providing comments is the best way of giving feedback.

To make the task manageable, it is worthwhile considering giving different types of feedback to different types of work. Some work can be described as fairly routine, such as completing a close procedure exercise, answering a few short questions. This might be marked with a tick or similar symbol to indicate work done correctly, and work not done or done incorrectly. It may be that, for routine work, the pupils could mark their own tasks or swap with another member of the class. Periodically there could be key pieces of work for pupils to do, requiring pupils to use some of the science they have been taught over a few lessons. Pupils would need to be made aware that these items are important in so much that they will show both the pupil and the teacher how much has been learnt. It may be that you would want to mark this initial attempt in pencil and provide guidance to the pupils as to how the work could be improved. Many teachers use this sort of approach with pupils' investigations for GCSE. Black *et al.* (2002: 9) suggest that teachers should consider devoting some lesson time to rewriting selected pieces of work, **so that emphasis can be put on feed back for improvement within a supportive environment**. Freed from the drudgery of marking everyday or straightforward activities, teachers would be able to find the time to devote to giving quality feedback to a limited number of longer pieces of written work. This should go a long way to combating the strong criticism levelled at teachers by Ofsted (1998: 14):

> Routine marking of pupils' work in key stage 3 science is rarely of good quality. The majority of work set, such as descriptions of experiments, copying notes from a textbook and completing the blanks in worksheets requires minimal marking. Even in such cases, however, much marking is negligent, rewarding gaps and scientific errors with ticks. Annotation is more concerned with presentation and points of English than with science. Where, more rarely, extended work is set that requires pupils to seek and analyse information, their responses do not get the level of feedback that they deserve.

Table 7.5 *Consequences of different types of feedback (Butler, 1988)*

Type of feedback given	Achievement gain	Change in interest in the work
Marks only	None	High achievers – increase in interest Low achievers – decrease in interest
Comments only	Scores increased by one-third	All pupils – increase in interest
Marks and comments	None	High achievers – increase in interest Low achievers – decrease in interest

Self- and peer assessment

Self-assessment is not used widely as a strategy to support pupils' learning. In most cases it is used mechanically to mark pieces of work such as a test, and even then teachers take in the work to check that pupils have marked it accurately. Teachers have tended to shy away from self-assessment because of concerns about cheating and have tended not to regard it in high esteem, but more as a way of getting things marked quickly and saving time for more important things. The research indicates that these concerns are generally unfounded:

> ... the main problem that those developing self-assessment encounter is not the problem of reliability and trustworthiness: it is found that pupils are generally honest and reliable in assessing both themselves and one another, and can be too hard on themselves as often as they are too kind. The main problem is different – it is that pupils can only assess themselves when they have a sufficiently clear picture of the targets that their learning is meant to attain.
>
> (Black and Wiliam, 1998a: 9)

What appears to be more important if pupils are to develop as independent learners is that they must be able to know how to carry out assessment of their own work. In order for them to be able to do this, it is vital that:

- the teachers share the learning objectives with the pupils
- the pupils are trained in the ways of making judgements on their work.

Methods of presenting objectives were mentioned earlier on in this chapter, but I would like to take this one step further at this point and consider how the teacher can share constructed meanings with pupils. When asking pupils to carry out self-assessment there must be no ambiguity; the pupils must have a clear understanding of what must be learnt (Bell, 2000). Classroom discussion will give the pupils the opportunity to express the objectives in their own words and allow the teacher to check on understanding. The whole process improves the communication and under-standing between the teacher and the pupils.

Learning about self-assessment can start in the primary school, with pupils becom-ing used to using sets of criteria to judge the quality of their work (Dann, 2002). Pupils can continue to use these principles through the exercises provided in some KS3 science textbooks (e.g. the self-tests in the *World of Science* books published by Oxford University Press). It is a gradual process of developing situations where pupils have to think about the quality of the work so that, over time, there becomes an ethos where pupils see it as the natural thing to do.

> Increasingly, schools are encouraging pupils to analyse their own strengths and weaknesses through the use of self-assessment forms. In one school, when a test paper is returned to pupils they are asked to identify, from a list of suggestions, the reasons why they lost marks. In the light of their analysis, they write a target

for themselves (e.g. I shall read the questions more carefully and check all my calculations) and set a target mark for the next test. The self-assessment form is taken home to be counter-signed by parents, who are thus kept informed of their children's progress.

(Estyn, 2001: 23)

Self-assessment forms are sometimes used in practical work to guide pupils into carrying out and writing down all the relevant information (see Table 7.6). This checklist type of approach can be used in any writing activity, and can help pupils to focus in on what is important.

A strategy suggested by Clarke (1998) involves teachers preparing a poster that can be displayed in the classroom, providing pupils with a group of questions that will help them reflect on their learning. She suggests the following:

- Do you remember the learning intention of the lesson?
- What did you find difficult?
- Did anyone or anything help you move on to learn something new? (friend, equipment, resources, teacher)
- What do you need more help with?
- What are you most pleased with?
- Did you learn anything new?

Another technique that is useful in helping pupils to identify errors and appreciate the importance of including all the steps in an argument is to ask them to correct a piece of work written by you under a pseudonym. Pupils could then be asked to identify:

- What is scientifically incorrect?
- What is missing?
- How the structure could be improved.

A variation on this theme is to supply pupils with a list of answers for a test on the topic they have just been taught and then ask them to write the questions. Black *et al.* (2002) suggest that, from time to time, pupils should be given the opportunity to produce a mark scheme for a test. This exercise will help them to focus their attention on the requirements for a good answer.

Much of what has been described above can be done on an individual basis or in groups, where it can be described as peer assessment. Being assessed by one's peers can conjure up images of threatening behaviour from those who want to do well but who don't want to work hard. Peer assessment needs to be open and carried out in a constructive manner. For example, groups of pupils may be asked to identify criteria for assessment, indicating what sorts of things should be included in the piece of work and the feedback given to others would then be in terms of 'you forgot to include' or 'you didn't quite get this right'. As you will appreciate, conversations at this level help everyone to understand the topic.

Table 7.6 *An example of a self-assessment checklist for the planning component of an investigation on the resistance of a wire*

Name: ....   Date: ....

Mark	Checklist for Investigating the Resistance of a Wire	Pupil	Teacher
Planning			
6a	Have you explained what current and resistance are? Have you identified the key factors affecting the resistance of a wire? Have you used scientific knowledge and understanding to decide what apparatus to use in the investigation and how you are going to use it? Have you made a prediction (preferably quantitative) and used scientific knowledge and understanding to explain it?		
4b	Have you drawn a clear circuit diagram using correct circuit symbols? Look at your apparatus. Have you listed *everything*, including the crocodile clips and scales on the ammeter and voltmeter?		
2a	Is your method clear and detailed? Remember, your granny should be able to carry out the experiment following your write-up. Have you included safety? It must refer to the experiment.		
4a	Have you described the fair testing? Don't say, 'I kept everything the same'. Say *exactly* what you kept the same.		
6b	Have you drawn a table of results? This will show that you intended to take sufficient, systematic readings and repeat them.		
8b	Have you given your preliminary results? Have you included everything you tried, i.e. all currents and voltages for the different lengths of wire at all the rheostat settings. Say why you chose the ones you did and rejected the others.		

Things to consider

Review the department's system of record keeping in terms of:

- the reliability of the data
- the use made of KS2 national test and teacher assessment results
- the transfer of data from one teacher to another (e.g. to monitor progress across the sciences in any one year when the pupil is taught by different teachers, to monitor progression over the key stages)
- how the system provides teachers with information about pupils' ability to communicate science, numerical and graphical skills, practical skills, understanding of science etc.
- the information it gives in terms of identification of strengths and weaknesses of individual pupils, problematic areas in the assessment process, weaknesses in the teaching, common misconceptions held by pupils
- how the data can be used to improve teaching and learning and provide information for parents.

Summative assessment

This section looks at the influence that end of topic, end of year and external examinations have on teaching, and how teachers can use summative assessment information to plan for improvement. Test results play an important role in teachers' statutory duties, as they form a basis for the teacher assessment judgements at the end of KS3 alongside aggregates of marks from homework/classwork and recording of written, oral and practical work (Swain, 1996). We collect a tremendous amount of data on pupils as they go through school, almost to the extent that we are drowning in numbers. What we sometimes forget is the meaning behind the numbers.

According to Ofsted (1998), science departments are over-reliant on the use of end of unit and end of year tests at KS3, and they recommend that pupils receive regular feedback on their work with a clear indication as to what they need to do to improve. It may be the case that a department, using a published scheme for KS3, feels secure and comfortable using the tests provided in the teachers' guide, and uses them without considering the quality of the questions and how they cater for different abilities. A department may find it useful to review not only its methods of ongoing assessment, but also the quality of its periodic tests.

A major problem faced by science teachers is the fact that the subject is perceived as difficult by the pupils, and we all know that if you tell someone that a subject is difficult the shutters come down and the 'I don't want to know' syndrome kicks in. Unfortunately it appears that, at A-level at least, it is more difficult to achieve in science in comparison with other subjects. In a study carried out by Fitz-Gibbon and Vincent

---

Things to consider

Reviewing the quality of tests

- What do you consider to be the purpose of the test? (practise in answering questions that are similar to those used in external examinations, checking that pupils have remembered all that they have been taught, checking to see if they can apply the knowledge they have learnt etc.)
- To what extent does the test cater for pupils of different abilities?
- How many of the questions test recall of knowledge?
- How many of the questions require pupils to understand the information and apply it to new situations?
- How many of the questions require pupils to analyse information and make decisions about its value?
- What does the test tell you about pupils' understanding of the topic and your teaching?

(1994), they found that chemistry and physics A-levels were at least one grade harder than other subjects. In a more recent study, Fitz-Gibbon (1999) looked at the long-term consequences for students who opt to study mathematics and science at A-level. She found that certain departments were considerably better at attracting students than others, and that this was generally due to their high academic standards and prior achievement. In addition, she was able to draw some tentative conclusions about the individuals' lifestyles five years after leaving school. Students who had included mathematics-science subjects in their A-level choices reported **quality of life** and **expected earnings** that were higher than those of students who did not follow these subjects at A-level. Information like this clearly strengthens arguments for pursuing difficult subjects. In a study carried out in 1996 (SCAA, 1996a), it was reported that a substantial majority of teachers were against reducing the level of difficulty of the science A-levels. Instead, they considered that the best way of encouraging more pupils to study advanced courses in science would be to improve the image and the status of the subjects.

Another problem faced by teachers, but this time originating from the general public and the media, is that examinations are getting easier. As teachers, we are well aware of the damage such comments can make to pupils' morale. Monitoring standards over time is not an easy process, as it needs to consider such things as changes in the specifications, changes in question type and assessment methods, mark allocation matched to question difficulty and, dare I say it, any influence the government may have on exam boards with regard to moving grade boundaries to adjust the number of candidates awarded each grade. Reports from the assessment authorities (SCAA, 1996b; QCA, 2001) highlight the changes that have taken place, and indicate marginal declines in some areas and an increased demand in others (see examples in Table 7.7).

Table 7.7 *A selection of comments from 'The five-yearly review of standards reports' (QCA at http://www.qca.org.uk). NB: 1, the dates for the reviews cover different periods as indicated; 2, no report was available for science*

Comments common to each science specification Examination demand had increased and standards of performance had been maintained. There were no significant differences between the awarding bodies in their expectation of candidates.

GCSE physics (1977–1997)
The main factors behind the increase in demand were the increase in demand in the practical component and the movement overall away from simple recall towards higher-level process skills. At grade C, there were some differences between tiers within an awarding body but no pattern suggesting the achievement of a C in one tier required higher performance than in another.

GCSE chemistry (1995–1998)
There was a conscious move to reduce demand for the most able pupils in coursework, but there was an increased demand for lower-attaining pupils.
There was some increase in the testing of chemical equations and calculations, making the examination more demanding.
It was harder to get a grade C on the Higher Tier because the Foundation Tier candidates were not required to show enough higher-order skills.

GCSE biology (1978–1988)
The increased focus on application rather than recall had increased the demand.
Some question papers did not always provide candidates with the opportunities to demonstrate their skills.
It was hard to be confident that there was any comparability across tiers.

Some headteachers like to compare the examination results of different departments in a school and use the information to generate a competitive climate. They may argue that a comparison of the core subjects of English, maths and science is fair, as the cohort being examined is the same for each subject. However, even if this were true there are problems with making such a simple comparison – such as the level of difficulty of the subject and understanding required to get each grade. Borrows (1997) suggests that the use of 'performance quotient', Q, for judging A*–C grades for each subject leads to fairer comparison, where:

$$Q = \frac{\text{number of pupils achieving A*–C in the subject at school}}{\text{number of pupils achieving A*–C in the subject nationally}}$$

National data can be obtained from the schools' PANDA (Performance AND Assessment) report or the performance section of the DfES website. These Q values tend to eliminate the factors over which the teacher has no control.

Earlier on in this chapter we looked at target setting as part of the ongoing feedback given to pupils. A process involving the use of pupils' test marks is also used in schools. Some schools may prefer this approach, perhaps because it can be less time-consuming (particularly if data are stored on a computer) and it is relatively clear to all concerned (e.g. pupils should achieve a higher mark in the next test). Statistical approaches have always been adorned with the cloak of respectability, and knit comfortably into the technicist and quantitative approach of Ofsted. There are drawbacks, however. Using this method on its own does not provide pupils with small step targets throughout the topic, and can perhaps cause them to limit their effort to a short period before the test. The method also presents the narrow view of education that test results are the only things that matter. It would be nice to think that other aspects of education were as highly valued by the media; however, we live in an era where numbers of GCSEs are considered to be extremely important, and sometimes we may have to resort to force-feeding to get the pupils to succeed.

It is becoming increasingly common for schools to use examination data to predict future results. Schools use KS2 test results and Cognitive Ability Tests (CATs) to predict future performance. In addition to forming a basis for target setting, the data have also been used to judge school, and subject departments', performance in terms of value added. In some schools there has been some unease about the use of KS2 teacher assessment and test results as a means of baseline data (Bunyan, 1988; Baxter, 2000). Bunyan investigated the belief held by some teachers that the KS2 national tests are easy and give rise to inflated levels for pupils. He arranged for a sample of pupils across a number of secondary schools to sit both KS2 and KS3 tests towards the end of Y9. The papers were compiled from previous examination papers, and they were marked by the teachers using the published mark scheme. The results showed that 53 per cent of the pupils achieved the same level in both tests, 35 per cent achieved one level higher in the KS3 test, and the remainder achieved a higher level in the KS2 test. Bunyan suggests that this provides strong evidence to refute the suggestion that it is easier to obtain a higher level in the KS2 test in comparison to the KS3 test. He then poses the question: if KS2 test results are a valid reflection of pupils' ability at that stage, why do so many make little progress during KS3? This may be answered in part by the fact that each level description covers a wide range of ability and it applies to the programme of study for the key stage, and therefore, as mentioned in Chapter 4, level 4 at KS2 is not the same thing as level 4 at KS3. Knowing that NC levels represent a very broad-brush approach to assessment, it might be expected that they would be unreliable predictors of future performance. Moody (2001) has in fact shown that there is no highly significant relationship between KS2 test data, teacher assessment and CAT average scores and the KS3 test results for science. The comparable figures for mathematics are better and, not surprisingly the scores on the CAT quantitative test correlate strongly with KS3 test results. Instead of using science KS2 results to predict science KS3 results, some schools adopt the DfES approach of converting the levels to points and calculating an average point score over the three core subjects at KS2. The performance data provided by DfES plot this average against the predicted points for KS3 science. Similar data are available for the KS3 to GCSE transition.

Whatever method a school uses for this type of target setting, it is worthwhile reflecting on the validity of the data from time to time and thinking about how the data are being used. Underperformance from individuals needs to be identified early on, and therefore the data need to be easily accessible and in a form that gives useful information. Is it sufficient to set a target for a pupil that his or her marks should improve in the next test by X per cent? Pupils tend to put long-term targets to the back of their minds and, although they may put on an extra spurt as the next test looms, day to day progress may remain largely unchanged. A combination of this statistical target setting with the type of regular feedback mentioned earlier is likely to be more productive. However, if target setting is really going to work it needs to be acceptable at all levels from the pupils to the headteacher and governors. As Flecknoe (2001) points out, pupils come to school with a whole range of private and personal targets that they are striving to reach, and these academic targets may or may not form part of that package. In order to accept a target, the pupil has to see it as valuable and worthy of effort. Experienced teachers regularly come across cases where it requires considerable persuasion to convince the pupil that the hard work will pay off in the end. The task can be made more difficult when there are negative influences on the pupil from others such as parents and fellow pupils and the local economic environment. While the prime responsibility for achieving the target rests with the pupil, the role of the school in establishing the right sort of climate and providing support, the role of the local community in providing suitable role models and employment, and the support from the government in terms of raising morale and providing appropriate funding, all have a part to play.

Things to consider

Review the system of target setting used in the science department by answering the following questions:

- To what extent does the department take into account the national targets for pupils' achievement at KS3 and GCSE?
- Are individual pupil's targets realistic and challenging?
- Are the aggregated targets in line with the English and maths departments and/or other benchmarks?
- To what extent do you use the data and pupils' achievement of targets to monitor the performance of teachers in the department and the strengths of the curriculum being taught?

References

Assessment Reform Group (1998) *Assessment for Learning: Beyond the Black Box*, Cambridge: University of Cambridge.

Baxter, M. (2000) 'Monitoring progress and target setting in the secondary school: finding appropriate methods of data collection and analysis' (available at: http://www.leeds.ac.uk/educol/documents/00001635.htm).

Bell, B. (2000) 'Formative assessment and science education', in Millar, R., Leach, J. and Osborne, J. (eds) *Improving Science Education: the Contribution of Research*, Buckingham: Open University Press.

Bell, B. and Cowie, B. (2001) 'The characteristics of formative assessment in science education', *Science Education*, **85**, 536–553.

Black, P. (1998) 'Formative assessment: raising standards inside the classroom', *School Science Review*, **80**(291), 39–46.

Black, P. and Harrison, C. (2001) 'Feedback in questioning and marking: the science teachers' role in formative assessment', *School Science Review*, **82**(301), 55–61.

Black, P. and Wiliam, D. (1998a) *Inside the Black Box: Raising Standards Through Classroom Assessment*, London: Kings.

Black, P. and Wiliam, D. (1998b) 'Assessment and classroom learning', *Assessment in Education*, **5**(1), 7–75.

Black, P., Harrison, C., Lee, C., Marshall, B. and Wiliam, D. (2002) *Working Inside the Black Box*, London: Kings.

Borrows, P. (1997) 'Analysing examination statistics', *School Science Review*, **79**(286), 47–49.

Brophy, J. (1981) 'Teacher praise: a functional analysis', *Review of Educational Research*, **51**(1), 5–32.

Bunyan, P. (1998) 'Comparing pupil performance in key stages 2 and 3 science SATs', *School Science Review*, **79**(289), 85–87.

Butler, R. (1988) 'Enhancing and undermining intrinsic motivation; the effects of task-involving and ego-involving evaluation on interest and performance', *British Journal of Educational Psychology*, **58**, 1–14.

Carr, D. (1998) 'The art of asking questions in the teaching of science', *School Science Review*, **79**(289), 47–50.

Clarke, S. (1998) *Targeting Assessment in the Primary Classroom*, London: Hodder & Stoughton.

Dann, R. (2002) *Promoting Assessment as Learning: Improving the Learning Process*, London: RoutledgeFalmer.

DfES (2002) *Key Stage 3 National Strategy Framework for Teaching Science: Years 7, 8, and 9*, London: DfES.

Estyn, (2001) *Good Practice in Science*, Cardiff: HMSO.

Fitz-Gibbon, C.T. (1999) 'Long term consequences of curriculum choices with particular reference to mathematics and science', *School Effectiveness and School Improvement*, **10**(2), 217–232.

Fitz-Gibbon, C.T. and Vincent, L.S. (1994) *Candidates' Performance in Science and Mathematics at A-level*, London: SCAA.

Flecknoe, M. (2001) 'Target setting: Will it help raise achievement?', *Educational Management and Administration*, **29**(2), 217–228.

Henry, J. (2001) 'Teachers' marking habits failing to make the grade', *Times Educational Supplement*, 19 January, 3.

James, M. and Gipps, C. (1998) 'Broadening the basis of assessment to prevent the narrowing of learning', *The Curriculum Journal*, **9**(3), 285–297.

Kerry, T. (1998) *Questioning and Explaining in Classrooms*, London: Hodder & Stoughton.

Koufetta, C. and Scaife, J. (2000) 'Teachers' questions – types and significance in science education', *School Science Review*, **81**(296), 79–84.

McCallum, B. (2001) *Formative Assessment: Implications for Classroom Practice* (available at: http://www.qca.org.uk).

Moody, I. (2001) 'A case study of the predictive validity and reliability of key stage 2 test results, and teacher assessments, as baseline data for target-setting and value added at key stage 3', *The Curriculum Journal*, **12**(1), 81–101.

Newman, D., Griffin, P. and Cole, M. (1989) *The Construction Zone: Working for Cognitive Change in School*, Cambridge: Cambridge University Press.

Ofsted (1998) *How Teachers Assess the Core Subjects at Key Stage 3*, London: OHMCI.

Parkinson, J. (2002) *Reflective Teaching of Science 11–18*, London: Continuum.

QCA (2001) 'The five-yearly review of standards reports' (available at: http://www.qca.org.uk/nq/mar/summary.asp).

SCAA (1996a) *Standards in Public Examinations 1975 to 1995: A Report on English, Mathematics and Chemistry Examinations Over Time*, London: SCAA.

SCAA (1996b) *The Take-up of Advanced Mathematics and Science Courses*, London: SCAA.

Selley, N. (2000) 'Wrong answers welcome', *School Science Review*, **82**(299), 41–44.

Swain, J.R.L. (1996) 'The impact and effect of key stage 3 science tests', *School Science Review*, **78**(283), 79–90.

Torrance, H. and Pryor, J. (2001) 'Developing formative assessment in the classroom: using action research to explore and modify theory', *British Educational Research Journal*, **27**(5), 615–631.

Van Zee, E.H., Iwasyk, M., Kurose, A., Simpson, D. and Wild, J. (2001) 'Student and teacher questioning during conversations about science', *Journal of Research in Science Teaching*, **38**(2), 159–190.

Watts, M., Gould, G. and Alsop, S. (1997) 'Questions of understanding: categorising pupils' questions in science', *School Science Review*, **79**(286), 57–63.

Woodward, C. (1992) 'Raising and answering questions in primary science: some considerations', *Evaluation and Research in Education*, **6**(2/3), 15–21.

CHAPTER 8

Learning about the Nature of Science

Had the big bang been less violent, the cumulative gravity of all the cosmic material would have caused the entire Universe to fall back on itself after a brief expansion. Alternatively, had the big bang been even bigger, the cosmic material would have been spread out more thinly by the stretching of space and galaxies would never have formed.

(Davies and Gribbin, 1992: 162)

In the programme of study for KS3, in the section on ideas and evidence in science it states (DfEE, 1999: 28):

Pupils should be taught:

a. about the interplay between empirical questions, evidence and scientific explanations using historical and contemporary examples (for example, Lavoisier's work on burning, the possible cause of global warming)
b. that it is important to test explanations by using them to make predictions and seeing if the evidence matches the predictions
c. about the ways in which scientists work today and how they worked in the past, including the role of experimentation, evidence and creative thought in the development of scientific ideas.

Similar statements are made in the Welsh National Curriculum for science, under the heading 'Nature of Science'. But these are not new areas of the NC; a whole attainment target, AT17, was devoted to this area in the original NC of 1989, and this aspect of science has been included in one form or another in each version since then. However, for one reason or another, teachers have largely sidelined the nature of science. Up until fairly recently science textbooks have only made passing reference to the history of science (Monk and Osborne, 1997), and the availability of other resources has been fairly limited. Also, teachers are influenced by the types of questions that appear on external examination papers, and the questions on this topic have been few in number and relatively trivial in the demands made on pupils.

What is the Nature of Science?

There is no simple answer to this question, and that in itself could be a contributory factor to the confusion in schools. Ginev (1990: 64) points out:

> ... we have no well-confirmed general picture of how science works, no theory of science worthy of general assent.

Although there is no universally accepted definition of the Nature of Science, there is a lot of agreed common ground on the characteristics of scientific enterprise. The NoS refers to understanding about the social practices and organisation of science and how scientists collect, interpret and use data to guide further research (Ryder *et al.*, 1999). Through a review of eight international science standards documents, McComas (1998: 6) has identified the following fourteen characteristics of scientific enterprise:

1 Scientific knowledge, while durable, has a tentative character
2 Scientific knowledge relies heavily, but not entirely, on observation, experimental evidence, rational arguments, and scepticism
3 There is no one way to do science (therefore there is no universal step-by-step scientific method)
4 Science is an attempt to explain natural phenomena
5 Laws and theories serve different roles in science: therefore students should note that theories do not become laws, even with additional evidence
6 People from all cultures contribute to science
7 New knowledge must be reported clearly and openly
8 Scientists require accurate record keeping, peer review and replicability
9 Observations are theory laden
10 Scientists are creative
11 The history of science reveals both an evolutionary and revolutionary character
12 Science is part of social and cultural traditions
13 Science and technology impact on each other
14 Scientific ideas are affected by their social and historical milieu.

There are many things that trigger off developments in science, such as the need for improved armaments in war (e.g. the Haber process for the manufacture of ammonia) and the need for new materials to carry out specific tasks (e.g. optical fibre to transmit digital information). Figure 8.1 indicates the main areas of influence on present-day scientific development.

Faced with the fact that perspectives on the nature of science are both diverse and complex, the teacher needs to make decisions concerning the extent of understanding required and the teaching strategies to be used.

As the word 'explanations' appears in two of the three paragraphs of the NC programme of study mentioned above, a useful starting point is to seek clarification of this term. Explaining natural phenomena is one of the central aims of the

[handwritten margin note: Include in conclusion?]

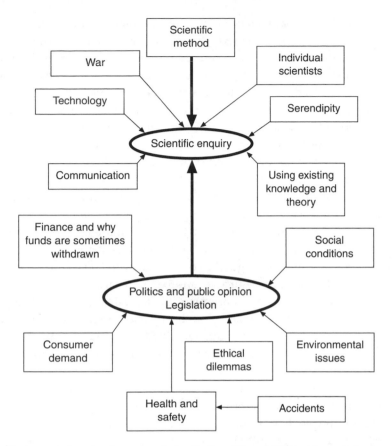

Figure 8.1 *The factors influencing the nature of scientific ideas (Warren, 2001) with permission from Royal Society of Chemistry*

scientific community, and involves providing solutions as to why things happen or giving an understanding as to why something exists in the way that it does. Pupils need to understand the relationship between evidence from experiments and possible explanations. Explanations don't simply emerge from the data or observations; they require the pupil (scientist) to use imagination or conjecture to make statements that are consistent with the available evidence. Pupils need to be aware that it is often the case that scientists interpret the same evidence differently, formulate different hypotheses to explain the evidence, and then fiercely defend their position. There are two types of explanations that pupils are likely to come across (Driver *et al.*, 1996):

1 Empirical generalisations (e.g. theories or laws formed by going beyond the available experimental data, such as Boyle's law)
2 Theoretical models (e.g. particle theory, wave model).

A traditional way of teaching tends to portray an image of scientists drawing conclusions from one or two simple experiments. For example, when pupils test a number of metals and non-metals to see if they conduct electricity, the teacher quickly leads the pupils to the conclusion that metals conduct and non-metals are insulators. By doing this we are leading pupils to believe that secure knowledge always comes from experience (empiricism). However, sometimes our experiences can mislead us, resulting in our drawing entirely inappropriate conclusions – e.g. heavy objects always sink in water. We are also leading pupils to think that it is appropriate to draw general conclusions from a series of specific observations (induction). Scientists don't work through a method of induction. You can look at the evidence from as many experiments as you like, but you can never identify the cause unequivocally. For example, how do we know that pure water always boils at 373 K under a pressure of 100 kPa when there are samples of water that have not been tested? Karl Popper (1902–1994) is recognised as having been the first to criticise the prevailing view that science is fundamentally inductive in nature. According to Popper, we can never prove anything correct, as there is always the possibility that we may find a case that is not in agreement with the results obtained so far. He suggested that the best way forward is to prove things wrong. Science, he argued, is concerned with conjectures and refutations – what he called a 'hypothetico-deductive' approach. In earlier versions of the NC this has been alluded to in statements concerning 'the tentative nature of theory'. Popper argued that progress in science takes place by realising that a current hypothesis is deficient, or false, and that a new hypothesis will be required to fit the new empirical evidence. The aim of experimental tests, according to Popper, is therefore the falsification of hypotheses.

This represents one view of science and, while it is reasonable to conclude that Popper was correct in terms of his criticism of induction, there are some deficiencies in his falsification principle. For example, when scientists are involved in so-called 'blue sky' research (researching an entirely new area), they have maybe no theories to disprove and their goal may be simply to collect data. Driver *et al.* (1996) point out that this mirrors the situation that pupils find themselves in when they are carrying out a practical task. Pupils are frequently unaware of the theory, and for them it is an exploration into the unknown. Also, if we are being honest with ourselves, we usually want our theory to be correct. It is simply not in human nature to want to be proved wrong, and therefore, in practice, is it likely that experiments will be undertaken to falsify a hypothesis?

Another major contributor to our thinking about the philosophy of science is Thomas Kuhn (1922–1996). He proposed a model of how science progresses. For most of the time scientists work in particular areas of study, clarifying or expanding on theory, identifying applications, solving problems etc. In each area of study there are accepted theories, defined methodologies and instrumentation, together with well-respected peer-reviewed journals and conferences to 'police' the system. He described this system of science as a 'disciplinary matrix' or a 'paradigm' (a set of accepted beliefs), and he called the stable state of a paradigm 'normal science'. However, when anomalies that do not fit into the accepted view are identified, scientists are put in a position where new ways of seeing thing or new ways of working are required. Kuhn called this 'revolutionary science'. If the new ideas are found to be more fruitful, then a new disciplinary matrix will take off and the old one will die. If the new disciplinary matrix is not fruitful, it will fade away. Critics of Kuhn argue that while his model might fit major scientific revolutions, much progress in science is more incremental and evolutionary.

This brief and sketchy account of some aspects of the nature of science gives an idea of the complexities involved in a study of the philosophy of science, and possibly leaves you thinking about how you are going to teach the NoS without causing whole-scale confusion.

Things to consider

The following two useful activities help teachers to reflect upon their own views about the nature of science, and can be done on an individual or group basis.

Activity 1

Wellington (2000: 266) provides 24 statements about science, and asks teachers to decide if they agree or disagree with the point of view using a scale of +5 (strongly agree) to −5 (strongly disagree). The total results for all the statements are plotted on a scale corresponding to: relativism to positivism; inductivism to deductivism; contextualism to decontextualism; process to content; instrumentalism to realism.

Activity 2

Nott and Wellington (1995: 43) provide a series of critical incidents and ask teachers for comments. The following is one of the ten incidents described:

- Below are two episodes from lessons.
  1 A teacher is doing the starch test on leaves. For inexplicable reasons the tests are indecisive.
  2 A teacher is demonstrating the non-magnetic properties of iron(II) sulphide. However, the freshly made sample sticks to the magnet.

  In both responses the pupils say the following:
  But science experiments never work.
  Anyway, we'll believe you, if you tell us the result.

List the kinds of things you could say at this point.

Why teach the Nature of Science?

Pupils need to be aware of the different ways in which scientists work in order to appreciate what a study of science involves. Previously this may have been implied in how the subject was taught, but more often it was completely ignored and hence pupils' views have been distorted, contributing to the development of many misconceptions. Driver *et al.* (1996) have proposed five arguments for the inclusion of the NoS in the curriculum. The first two are related to the value such a study would have in life beyond schools (the citizenship argument); the third and fourth are concerned with culture and morality, and the final argument is concerned with learning science:

1 It is essential to understand the NoS in order to make sense of science and manage the technological objects and processes they encounter.
2 In order to participate in the decision-making process, individuals must understand socio-scientific issues (see page 239).
3 The cultural divide initially described by Snow (1993) still lingers on today. The word culture summons up images of the arts, and rarely do we find people talking about scientific culture. Pupils need to have an appreciation of this culture as part of a balanced education.
4 Scientists frequently face moral dilemmas as part of their work. They need to be honest when reporting their findings, and to make ethical judgements about the investigation to be undertaken. These sorts of values are important in pupils' education, and science provides an authentic context with both past and present research.
5 This is concerned with making the context clear to the pupils and being explicit about what knowledge is static (scientific laws) and what is subject to change (scientific theories). Pupils are more likely to understand a theory if they have an appreciation of how the theory was devised. For example, in a study carried out by Songer and Linn (1991) of pupils' views about science and their understanding of thermodynamics, they found that those who had understood the dynamic nature of science acquired a more integrated understanding of the topic than those with static views. Teachers also need to bear in mind that some pupils may actually enjoy an approach to science that discusses 'real' people and 'real' situations. You only have to look at how popular history is as a school subject to appreciate the extent to which pupils relate to this approach.

Monk and Osborne (1997: 409) further propose that a study of scientific ideas in their original context will help pupils develop a conceptual understanding:

- because historical thinking often parallels their own (see, for example, Van Driel *et al.*, 1998)
- because the now accepted scientific idea was often strongly opposed for similar reasons to those proffered by pupils
- because it highlights the contrast between the thinking then and now, bringing into a sharper focus the nature and achievement of our current conceptions.

Problems facing teachers

There are two major problems facing science teachers. Most of them have not received any formal instruction in the NoS – traditionally it has not been part of the school curriculum, and there has been no place for it in degree courses. As a result, relatively simple terms (such as those shown in Table 8.1) are not properly understood. Second, some science teachers find it difficult to relate to the type of culture involved in teaching the NoS, which is more akin to the culture of teaching history rather than science. Donnelly (1999) points out that historians try to place pupils' interpretations and intellectual judgements at the centre of their work, whereas scientists place stronger emphasis on established knowledge and perceive uncertainty as threatening. Taken together, it is easy to see why many teachers tend to avoid any aspect of a topic that involves the NoS.

When setting out to teach something in a slightly different way, there is always the worry about the overall effect on pupils' progress. There is little evidence to indicate that a teaching approach involving an emphasis on the NoS improves or is detrimental to pupils' test scores. For example, Alan Irwin, a teacher from Northumberland, has reported on his teaching of the concept of the atom and the periodic arrangement of the elements to two parallel groups of 14-year-old pupils (Irwin, 2000). One group was taught by tracing the development of the atomic theory from the Greeks, through the work of Dalton, Newlands and Mendeleev on the Periodic Table, to the present day. The other group was taught without reference to any historical development, and presented with statements about chemical theory and the use of the Periodic Table. At the end of the four lessons on the topic pupils were given a test, and the results showed no difference in the understanding of the contemporary science between the two groups. Based on this example, teachers might ask, why bother to go to the trouble of teaching about historical events if it is not going to improve test scores? Irwin admits that he was disappointed with the result, but he saw the benefits in terms of the pupils' involvement in discussion and debate and believed that the gains made in

Table 8.1 *Common terms that are sometimes misunderstood by pupils (Driver et al., 1996; McComas, 1998)*

	Definition and clarification
Hypothesis	Three definitions 1 A supposition put forward to explain observed phenomena (generalising hypothesis) 2 A provisional theory (explanatory hypothesis) 3 A prediction about the outcomes of an experiment (prediction) **Relationship between hypothesis, theory and law** A generalising hypothesis might become a law An explanatory hypothesis might become a theory Under no circumstances do theories become laws
Theory	Theories are generalised explanations of laws. Theories are evaluated in the light of evidence. Evaluating a theory requires making predictions from the theory and testing the consistency of these with available data
Law	Laws are generalisations, principles or patterns in Nature. It is incorrect to believe that hypotheses become theories and theories become laws as the amount of evidence increases

understanding of how scientists work by the historical group were worth the effort. Not everything can be measured by written tests.

Teachers frequently make decisions about what to teach and how to teach it based on external examinations. Most of us will confess to leaving out parts of the specification (syllabus), particularly if we are not comfortable with the topic and there is pressure of time to complete the work before the examination. Teachers are influenced by the allocation of marks for a particular aspect of work, and when they read that a maximum of 5 per cent will be allocated to NoS questions in GCSE examinations they tend to give this aspect of the work a low priority. Arguments for excluding the topic are further enhanced when many of the questions asked are of a trivial nature requiring little scientific knowledge. Work is in hand to produce questions for KS2 and KS3 pupils that can be used for 'testing pupils' understanding of the processes and practices of science in contemporary or historic contexts' (Osborne and Ratcliffe, 2002: 122). The question below is a sample multiple-choice item presented in the paper that performed well in the initial trials:

1. **Scientists produce knowledge that is absolutely certain.**
   Which one of the following examples would NOT support this statement?
   A The explanation for photosynthesis.
   B Our description of the water cycle.
   C The view that matter is made of atoms.
   D The view that global warming is caused by carbon dioxide emitted by cars.

It is likely that in time, as the NoS becomes a more established part of teaching, the range and quality of questions and assessment activities will improve.

The heavy reliance on textbooks by some teachers can be a problem, as some books convey incorrect or conflicting messages about the NoS. Quite naturally a lot of science is simplified, but sometimes oversimplifications convey an image of science as being either black or white rather than having various shades of grey. Also it is common for textbooks to promulgate an inductivist approach to science in the way that they convey a view about the status of scientific knowledge and how that knowledge came to be. However, as with improvements in assessment procedures, new textbooks and resources are becoming available. The *Science Web* publications (e.g. Solomon *et al.*, 2000; Horsfall, 2001) provide teachers with an enquiry-based approach, mainly using activities that are already familiar to science teachers but with an emphasis on raising pupils' awareness of how scientists work. The *Thinking Through Science* publications provide activities based on the CASE project, and include sections that show how scientific understanding has changed with time (e.g. Cheney *et al.*, 2002).

Most teachers are aware that pupils have misconceptions about a number of science concepts (see page 92), and that it is often difficult to modify their initial views. However, it helps if the teachers have an understanding about how the pupils think about the phenomena and the logic they have employed. Similarly, pupils have varying ideas about the NoS prior to receiving any formal instruction, and these mental images are likely to remain unchanged unless they are challenged by teachers. Common misunderstandings held by pupils, as identified by Dunveen *et al.* (1993) and Driver *et al.* (1996), are:

- Pupils relate the word 'experiment' to an unthinking activity that gives surprising results, i.e. they do not appreciate that experiments are influenced by theory and are carefully planned. Confusion can be compounded by the incorrect use of the term by teachers who may refer to routine practical work as 'experiments'.
- Pupils think of theory as an idea or a guess, rather than as an explanation of phenomena.
- Many pupils think of science as a collection of facts. They consider that the purpose of experiments is to identify more facts, and would describe facts as 'true theories'.
- Some pupils see explanations as simply a re-description of an event or phenomenon.
- Pupils consider that unanticipated outcomes to experiments falsify the whole theory.
- The role of imagination and evidence in theory-building is rarely understood.
- Pupils rarely appreciate that science is a social enterprise. They generally see scientists as working in isolation, perhaps compiling 'facts' from a range of sources to reach 'the truth'. They do not appreciate that these 'facts' might be challenged or checked within the scientific community before becoming established.
- Pupils tend to see the purpose of science as providing solutions to technical problems, rather than providing more powerful explanations.
- Pupils are not clear about the use of models. They do not view scientific enquiry as the process of testing models and theories.
- Pupils consider that progress in science is entirely attributable to technological improvements.

Things to consider

Do your pupils recognise a scientific question? Leach *et al.* (1997) have identified a framework for considering pupils' reasoning about aspects of the nature of science by asking them to identify questions that are amenable to empirical enquiry and others that are not. They are told that scientific questions are questions that scientists might want to find out more about. Such an exercise can be given to pupils on an individual basis or in small groups. Examples from the paper are given below.

Question	Reason for inclusion
Which kind of fabric is waterproof?	Can be tested empirically, little theoretical background
Which is the best programme on TV?	Related to aesthetics
Is it wrong to keep dolphins in captivity?	Related to ethics
Is the Earth's atmosphere heating up?	Can be tested empirically: high level of theoretical background
Is it cheaper to buy a large or a small packet of a washing powder?	Related to economics

Teaching strategies

Matthews (1998) argues for a modest approach to teaching the NoS, saying that it is unrealistic for pupils to become competent historians, sociologists or philosophers of science. He goes on to say that philosophy is often present in science classrooms anyway, bubbling away just below the surface and emerging as pupils' questions or comments in class discussion.

One way of approaching the teaching of the NoS would be to teach about particular issues as and when they appear in the scheme of work. This usually involves taking a brief look at the development of a theory or the work of famous scientists in developing our understanding. As science teachers we are not used to teaching about historical developments, and there is the possibility that the lessons will turn out to be dry and uninteresting. They need to be brought alive by looking at the personalities involved and the situation that was prevalent at the time. Perhaps this is the time to seek advice from the history teacher. A dreary approach is likely to result in pupils being bored with this aspect of their science lessons and, as shown by research carried out by Stark and Gray (1999), learning about famous scientists can be one of the least popular learning activities. An episodic historical approach is likely to be sufficient for examination purposes, however, the NoS is not just a simple add on; and it should play a part in the way all science is taught. If pupils only learn about the NoS in isolated lessons, there is a danger that this could lead to overall confusion about how scientists work. Pupils may receive mixed messages about scientific activity as teachers take different stances in different lessons. A permeated approach will help pupils to appreciate the nature of the knowledge they have been learning – e.g. what is certain, what is theoretical, how we have come to our present understanding. It is easy to forget the underlying messages we give to pupils by the way we present science, and these are generally the things that stick with pupils for the rest of their lives. They may not be able to remember much of the content they have been taught, but may have an image of science as a lot of 'facts' to remember. Is this what we really want? In Chapter 9 I will talk about the confusion that can be caused when pupils are presented with different sorts of practical activities if no clear rationale for the task is given by the teacher. The same sort of thing can happen in many other teaching situations unless the pervading principles are made explicit. Learning *about* science will support pupils in their learning *of* science.

Teachers who prepare pupils for the International Baccalaureate are familiar with teaching the NoS, as it forms an important component of the diploma under the heading of Theory of Knowledge. Talbot (2000) suggests that this, and the Ideas and Evidence section of the NC, can be taught through case studies, and in his article he provides a number of examples. Finding background information in a form that is suitable for pupils can sometimes prove difficult, but the following are likely to prove useful:

- occasional articles in *Education in Chemistry*, e.g. 'In the beginning – was Ebonite' (Brown *et al.*, 2002), on the history of plastics;
- *The Faber Book of Science* (Carey, 1995);
- *I Wish I'd Made You Angry Earlier* (Perutz, 1998) – stories about science and scientists.

- some modern examples of physics controversies can be found in an article by Niaz and Rodríguez (2002).

Newspapers can be valuable resources for pupils to analyse in terms of how science is depicted in the media, as well as providing stories about famous scientists and cutting-edge science. One successful approach is to have a newsboard containing up to date clippings of science-related articles. Many teachers will use articles from newspapers on an *ad hoc* basis, mentioning things that they have recently seen that are relevant to lessons. At present, few teachers use newspapers in a systematic way to enhance their teaching (Jarman and McClune, 2002). This may be due to the difficulty in finding articles that closely match the curriculum and are also written in a suitable form. According to the research carried out by Jarman and McClune, biology teachers were the most frequent users of newspapers, followed by chemists, with physics teachers coming last by a significant margin. The research also showed that teachers tended to use newspapers more with older pupils, who they thought were more capable of understanding the articles. It would seem that while there is no external body producing detailed examples of how newspapers can be used to help pupils understand the nature of science, it is likely that their use in lessons will continue to be sporadic.

In planning work, teachers should look for opportunities where they can:

- make situations explicit (e.g. look at how evidence from a variety of sources leads scientists to draw conclusions, be clear about the use of models).
- explain why certain things are established knowledge and why our understanding of other situations is subject to change. As mentioned above, scientists reject the notion of attaining absolute truth and accept uncertainty as part of nature, however most scientific knowledge is durable. The modification of ideas, rather than their outright rejection, is the norm in science and reliable constructs tend to survive and grow to become more widely accepted.
- indicate why scientific theories have changed over time.
- provide pupils with opportunities to draw inferences from observations.
- help pupils to understand data and gain an appreciation of error in experimentation.
- present pupils with alternative explanations from a given set of data.
- use stories of real people and situations that pupils can relate to. Stories about scientists and their discoveries can make good reading, particularly for younger pupils. Care must be taken to ensure that the text is appropriate for all age groups, as over-simplified texts with cartoons may be treated with disdain by key stage 4 pupils. The stories are not necessarily concerned with teaching any science content; it is more likely that they will be aimed at teaching about the types of factors that affect scientific progress, such as the struggles, dilemmas and other real-life issues that face research scientists. An important factor in the production of the story is the building up of empathy with the characters in order to learn how theories are constructed and experiments designed (Solomon, 2002).
- explain the purpose of a practical activity to pupils (see Chapter 9). Pupils should appreciate that the experiments carried out by scientists are influenced by the theories they already hold, and that the results of the new experiment can lead to the development of new theories (Dunveen *et al.*, 1993).

- present pupils with problem-solving activities requiring them to work together in groups, collecting and disseminating information.

A few examples of opportunities to introduce NoS ideas are given in Table 8.2.

Table 8.2 *Some opportunities to raise issues concerned with the nature of science*

Topic	Notes
Light	Analogical modelling Huygens used water waves to help him understand light waves
Planetary motion	Analogical modelling Kepler developed his ideas by thinking about a clock's workings
Oxygen	Developments from unexpected results Priestley's discovery of oxygen (see page 18 in Solomon *et al.*, 2000)
Elements	The alchemist discovers phosphorus Phosphorus was discovered by accident. A KS3 unit produced by Charis (http://www.stapleford-centre.org/) provides teaching material on this and a variety of other topics involving moral and spiritual issues (Kempton, 2001)
Explanations	A discussion activity on the relationship between observation and explanation is provided in Warren, 2001
Periodic table	Mendeleev's prediction of the yet to be discovered elements together with deductions about their properties: scandium, gallium and germanium (an example of Popper's approach to science)

Things to consider

The following is a list of aims related to teaching the NoS to pupils. Do you consider them to be of relevance to teaching your pupils? How would you realise the aims?

Pupils should:

- understand that things and events in the universe occur in consistent patterns, and that that these are understandable through careful and systematic study
- appreciate that scientific ideas are subject to change
- appreciate that scientific knowledge is durable
- understand that science cannot provide complete answers to all questions
- understand that science demands evidence
- appreciate that science requires a blend of logic and imagination
- appreciate that science is a complex social activity.

What other aims do you consider to be important?

Review a group of lessons (five to ten) and consider what messages were portrayed about the NoS in these lessons. Ask other colleagues to do the same. Consider how you would ensure that an acceptable and consistent approach was used throughout the curriculum.

Modelling

Modelling is an important aspect of both science research and science teaching. Gilbert (1993) identifies the following four roles for modelling:

1 **Models are one of the main products of science.** Scientists produce models to simplify complex phenomena.
2 **Modelling is an element in scientific methodology.** Scientists use models to help them make progress in their understanding. They produce models and test their reliability in new situations.
3 **Pupils use models to help them learn science.** As pupils attempt to understand a concept or solve a problem in science, they construct their own mental models of the situation. Pupils should be able to appreciate the predictive power of a model and its ability to provide valuable insights into the fundamental nature of the phenomenon.
4 **Models are a major teaching tool in science education.** Teachers frequently use analogical models when trying to explain scientific phenomena. They do this in order to make abstract concepts more accessible to pupils. The particle model of matter is perhaps the most frequently used model throughout the whole of the secondary curriculum, and is used to explain things ranging from the behaviour of solids, liquids and gases to rates of reaction.

There are four different types of models commonly used in science teaching, as shown in Table 8.3. As we will see below, pupils do not always appreciate what type of model they are using, and as a result the desired clarification of the concept may not be realised.

Modelling is a complex process, and it must be assumed that it is only gradually acquired by pupils (Justi and Gilbert, 2002). Textbooks tend to oversimplify things or miss out important points. For example, atoms are often represented as coloured circles, sometimes of different sizes, but the books frequently neglect to point out that these are not scaled representations of atoms. If no explicit reference to the use of a model is given in these textbooks, and if teachers fail to bring this to pupils' attention, it is likely that they will leave the lesson with only partial understanding. It is not uncommon for pupils to believe that atoms actually look like the coloured spheres that

Table 8.3 *Different types of models used in science teaching*

Type of model	Description and example
Scale models	A version of the original that is easy to see, e.g. anatomical models
Analogue models	A simplification of the original used to explain certain phenomena, e.g. different types of atomic and molecular models
Mathematical models	Express a situation in terms of formulae, e.g. gas laws
Theoretical models	These put forward an explanation of a situation based on previous scientific knowledge, experiences and observations, e.g. the big bang theory

are often used to represent them. It is likely that if modelling is done superficially, it will ultimately tend to cause confusion and hinder understanding. Pupils (and adults) tend to think about abstract processes in concrete, everyday terms (Harrison and Treagust, 2000), as this helps them to understand the processes. They like the idea of the particle nature of matter because it makes sense, and they can play around with the idea of balls vibrating and colliding into one another. They 'collect' these simple mental models quite early on in their secondary career, and use them to explain things at various stages. These early images of how things work tend to become embedded in pupils' minds, and they find it difficult to upgrade their models in order to deal with the more sophisticated concepts they meet at a later stage.

In one lesson a teacher may be using a scale model of the ear, and in another lesson using a slinky spring as an analogical model to represent the movement of sound. However, the teacher may omit to point out to the pupils the differences between these two types of models. On the whole, pupils tend to appreciate that models are often used as explanatory tools (Treagust *et al.*, 2002). However, a teacher using a model to explain presumes that the pupils will interpret it in the same way as he or she does. This may not be the case, as the teacher comes to the situation with a great deal of experience of using models, and it is possible that he or she might make certain assumptions about the pupils' ability to understand the nature of the model that may or may not be valid. From a study of pupils and researchers as modellers, Grosslight *et al.* (1991) proposed three levels of understanding about models (Table 8.4). This research, and research carried out by Treagust *et al.* (2002), indicates that a significant number of pupils believe scientific models to be exact duplicates of reality – i.e. they are operating at level 1.

Possibly because of pupils' lack of understanding about the nature of modelling and their limited experience in using models, they are not always able to hold on to the full picture of the model. The mental models of particular phenomena can be unstable, and pupils may use their ideas to interpret one situation correctly but then manipulate their model incorrectly to respond to another situation (Harrison and Treagust, 2000). However, in a study of the use of modelling during the teaching of biological cells to Y7 pupils, Tregidgo and Ratcliffe (2000) identified a number of gains in pupils' learning. Two parallel groups of pupils modelled concepts of cell structure and function as they produced 2D or 3D representations of plant and animal cells. Conceptual changes and developments of the pupils were tracked and compared immediately after the

Table 8.4 *Progression in beliefs about the structure and purpose of analogical models (Grosslight et al., 1991)*

Level 1	Level 2	Level 3
The naïve learner The model is a small, incomplete copy of the actual object	As level 1, but the pupil believes that the modeller has chosen that items should be missing and sees the model's main purpose as communication rather than the exploration of ideas	**The expert** There are multiple uses of models. They are thinking tools and can be purposefully manipulated by the modeller to understanding of the concept

teaching, and 10 weeks later. In their responses to questionnaires, in contrast to 2D modellers, the 3D group:

- achieved accepted responses more frequently
- expressed new learning in their answers more often
- were more likely to apply their knowledge to novel situations and, these applications were more likely to be correct than those of the members of 2D group.

The gains were still apparent 10 weeks later, but the differences were less extreme.

Harrison and Treagust (2000) make the following five suggestions to improve pupils' understanding:

1 Teachers need to check pupils' visualisation of the analogy that they plan to use or work from, using a textbook or computer. There are particular dangers in some computer simulation models, as the image looks so 'real' the student can be led to the conclusion that it really does represent a scaled version.
2 Students cannot be expected reliably to interpret models they have not designed or previously experienced, and it is important for the teacher to explain what the model represents.
3 Teachers need to explain that models are thinking tools and that in some cases it is a good idea to represent the situation by a number of different models. Pupils need to understand why scientists use models and how analogies operate in order that they can appreciate that they are valuable things to learn.
4 The idea of multiple modelling should be introduced at an early stage and developed over time in order to help students become skilled modellers.
5 Teachers should provide opportunities for students to write explanations of model meanings, carry out model-based problem-solving, and 'play' with models. Using models can be a very powerful learning tool, but if used inappropriately it can lead to the development of misconceptions that may be very hard to replace.

Things to consider

- How do individual pupils internalise ideas about models and make them fit alongside their own mental models built from previous experiences? In order to get an insight into this, you will need to ask pupils to use models to explain new situations.
- To what extent does modelling feature in the science department's scheme of work?
- Are pupils given the opportunity to use models to predict and explain?

Conclusion

As science teachers we tend to be rather traditional in our approach, valuing what we have been taught and wanting to pass this on to the next generation. It could be said, however, that science teaching has got itself in a rut and is trying to cover a whole range of quite difficult concepts, some of which many pupils never understand. Might it not be better to spend more time on how scientists work, rather than requiring pupils to remember strings of unrelated facts?

References

Brown, T.M., Dronsfield, A.T. and Morris, P.J.T. (2002) 'In the beginning – was Ebonite', *Education in Chemistry*, **39**(1), 18–20.

Carey, J. (ed.) (1995) *The Faber Book of Science*, London: Faber & Faber.

Cheney, A., Flavell, H., Harrison, C., Hurst, G. and Yates, C. (2002) *Thinking Through Science*, London: John Murray.

Davies, P. and Gribbin, J. (1992) *The Matter Myth: Beyond Chaos and Complexity*, London: Penguin.

DfEE (1999) *Science: The National Curriculum for England*, London: DfEE.

Donnelly, J. (1999) 'Interpreting differences: the educational aims of teachers of science and history, and their implications', *Journal of Curriculum Studies*, **31**(1), 17–41.

Driver, R., Leach, J., Millar, R. and Scott, P. (1996) *Young People's Images of Science*, Buckingham: Open University Press.

Dunveen, J., Scott, L. and Solomon, J. (1993) 'Pupils' understanding of science: description of experiments or "A passion to explain"?', *School Science Review*, **75**(271), 19–27.

Gilbert, J.K. (ed.) (1993) *Models and Modelling in Science Education*, Hatfield: The Association for Science Education.

Ginev, D. (1990) 'Towards a new image of science: science teaching and non-analytical philosophy of science', *Studies in Philosophy and Education*, **10**, 63–71.

Grosslight, L., Unger, C., Jay, E. and Smith, C. (1991) 'Understanding models and their use in science: conceptions of middle and high school students and experts', *Journal of Research in Science Teaching*, **28**(9), 799–822.

Harrison, A.G. and Treagust, D.F. (2000) 'Learning about atoms, molecules and chemical bonds: a case study of multiple-model use in grade 11 chemistry', *Science Education*, **84**, 352–381.

Horsfall, P. (ed.) (2001) *Science Web: Enquiry Pack, Year 7 Units*, Cheltenham: Nelson Thornes.

Irwin, A.R. (2000) 'Historical case studies: teaching the nature of science in context', *Science Education*, **84**(1), 5–26.

Jarman, R. and McClune, B. (2002) 'A survey of the use of newspapers in science instruction by secondary teachers in Northern Ireland', *International Journal of Science Education*, **24**(10), 997–1020.

Justi, R.S. and Gilbert, J.K. (2002) 'Modelling, teachers' views on the nature of modelling, and implications for the education of modellers', *International Journal of Science Education*, **24**(4), 369–387.

Kempton, T. (2001) 'The Charis project: spiritual and moral development in science', *School Science Review*, **82**(301), 71–78.

Leach, J., Driver, R., Millar, R. and Scott, P. (1997) 'A study of progression in learning about "the nature of science": issues of conceptualisation and methodology', *International Journal of Science Education*, **19**(2), 147–166.

McComas, W.F. (ed.) (1998) *The Nature of Science in Science Education: Rationales and Strategies*, Kluwer: Dordrecht.

Matthews, M.R. (1998) 'In defence of modest goals when teaching about the nature of science', *Journal of Research in Science Teaching*, **35**(2), 161–174.

Monk, M. and Osborne, J. (1997) 'Placing the history and philosophy of science on the curriculum: a model for the development of pedagogy', *Science Education*, **81**, 405–424.

Niaz, M. and Rodríguez, M.A. (2002) 'Improving learning by discussing controversies in 20th century physics', *Physics Education*, **37**(1), 59–63.

Nott, M. and Wellington, J. (1995) 'Critical incidents in the science classroom and the nature of science', *School Science Review*, **76**(276), 41–46.

Osborne, J. and Ratcliffe, M. (2002) 'Developing effective methods of assessing *Ideas and evidence*', *School Science Review*, **83**(305), 113–123.

Perutz, M. (1998) *I Wish I'd Made You Angry Earlier: Essays on Science and Scientists*, Oxford: Oxford University Press.

Ryder, J., Leach, J. and Driver, R. (1999) 'Undergraduate science students' images of science', *Journal of Research in Science Teaching*, **36**(2), 201–219.

Snow, C.P. (1993) *The Two Cultures*, Cambridge: Cambridge University Press.

Solomon, J. (2002) 'Science stories and science texts: what can they do for students?', *Studies in Science Education*, **37**, 85–106.

Solomon, J., Murphy, J., Ratcliffe, M., Heslop, N. and Robinson, R. (2000) *Science Web Reader: Chemistry*, London: Nelson.

Songer, N. and Linn, M. (1991) 'How do students' views of science influence knowledge integration?', *Journal of Research in Science Teaching*, **28**(9), 761–784.

Stark, R. and Gray, D. (1999) 'Gender preferences in learning science', *International Journal of Science Education*, **21**(6), 633–643.

Talbot, C. (2000) 'Ideas and evidence in science', *School Science Review*, **82**(298), 13–22.

Treagust, D.F., Chittleborough, G. and Mamiala, T.L. (2002) 'Students' understanding of the role of scientific models in learning science', *International Journal of Science Education*, **24**(4), 357–368.

Tregidgo, D. and Ratcliffe, M. (2000) 'The use of modelling for improving pupils' learning about cells', *School Science Review*, **81**(296), 53–59.

Van Driel, J.H., De Vos, W. and Verloop, N. (1998) 'Relating students' reasoning to the history of science: the case of chemical equilibrium', *Research in Science Education*, **28**(2), 187–198.

Warren, D. (2001) *The Nature of Science*, London: RSC.

Wellington, J. (2000) *Teaching and Learning Secondary Science: Contemporary Issues and Practical Approaches*, London: Routledge.

CHAPTER 9

Learning through practical work

From a book about Sir Humphrey Davy:

> While in Rome, Davy was engaged for several successive days in the house of
> Morrichini, for the purpose of repeating with that philosopher his curious experi-
> ments on magnetisation. Mr Faraday was charged with the performance of the
> experiments, but never could obtain any results.
>
> (Paris, 1831: 42)

Practical work has been the key component of science teaching in the UK for over 150
years (Gee and Clackson, 1992; Jenkins, 1998). Projects and curriculum initiatives
have come and gone over the years, some with amazing alacrity, leaving the education
profession with a wealth of experience. Having tried the 'Nuffield approach' and the
'process approach' along with more traditional methods, and recognised the strengths
and weaknesses of each practical style, you might think that we should be in a position
to state the best way of carrying out practical work in schools. Yet, as you will see from
the rest of this chapter, we are still not quite there yet. Each teacher has his or her own
views about practical work, formed by the influence of a number of factors such as:

- his or her own experiences of science at school
- learning about practical work and classroom experiences during the period of initial
  teacher education and training
- the scheme of work and the textbooks used
- other teachers in the science department
- government initiatives, e.g. the National Curriculum, GCSE and A-level specifications.

The introduction of the statutory Science National Curriculum (NC) in 1989, with its
emphasis on an investigative approach, has forced all teachers to reflect on the nature
of their subject. The NC requires teachers to adopt a frame of thinking that is quite different to that required for a traditional teaching style. In the past, practical work has
mainly been concerned with illustrating the concepts taught. The investigative work of
the earlier versions of the NC required pupils to apply a scientific methodology to a
situation and, by following a procedure determined by the pupil, obtain a set of

results. In research carried out in 1997 on teachers' attitudes towards the aims of practical work, Swain *et al.* (2000) compared their results with earlier work carried out by
Beatty and Woolnough (1982). As can be seen from Table 9.1, the ratings for both dates
indicate that science teachers' aims for practical work have not changed a great deal in
recent years – indeed, there has been little change since the original survey carried out
by Kerr (1964). The introduction of investigative work has probably played a role in
increasing the level of importance of the aims given in the lower section of Table 9.1,
but these are not listed in the group of most significant aims. A similar exercise carried
out in Australia over six schools showed wide variation in teachers' views from one
school to another, indicating the different philosophies that prevail in individual
schools (Wilkinson and Ward, 1997). In this research, pupils' opinions were also
sought and were compared with their own teachers' views. There were mismatches for
many of the statements, but in particular the view that all teachers agreed, that laboratory work was useful to everyday life, was not shared by any of their pupils. There
was an indication that teachers' perceptions about practical work were not being conveyed to pupils. Whether or not this is true for the UK is yet to be determined, but my
experience of classrooms leads me to believe that there is some confusion between
pupils and teachers about the purpose of practical work. In the rest of this chapter we
will examine the different purposes of practical work, and consider how it can be used
effectively to help pupils to learn.

Table 9.1 *The aims of practical work as perceived by teachers: a comparison of a pre-National Curriculum with a post-National Curriculum survey (Swain* et al., *2000)*

Aims that have remained fairly constant over the period 1979 to 1997, rated in terms of importance	
High	To encourage accurate observation and description
	To promote a logical reasoning method of thought
	To arouse and maintain interest
	To make phenomena more real
Medium	To be able to comprehend and carry out instructions
	To develop specific manipulative skills
	To develop certain disciplined attitudes
	To develop an ability to communicate
Low	To indicate industrial aspects of science
	To prepare students for practical exams

Aims that were rated more highly in the 1997 survey than in 1979 (medium-weighted, i.e. within the middle group above)
To practise seeing problems and seeking ways to solve them
For finding facts and arriving at new principles
To develop an ability to co-operate
To develop a critical attitude

Why do we do practical work?

Some teachers do very little practical work possibly because:

- they consider it takes up too much curriculum time and that this time could be better spent in going over what pupils need to know for examinations
- when technician support is scarce, it requires a great deal of effort to get the apparatus ready and to put it away
- they are concerned about potential hazards.

Many studies have shown that pupils who have been taught using methods that involve practical activities exhibit significantly better attitudes towards science and achieve better marks in tests than those who have not used practical work (e.g. Yager, 1991; Stohr-Hunt; 1996; Thompson and Soyibo, 2002). However, there are reports in the literature of practical work causing pupils to become confused about science and, as a result, making no progress in their learning. Watson *et al.* (1995) carried out a comparative study of pupils' understanding of combustion, in Spain, where little practical work is used, and in England. The quality of understanding exhibited by the English pupils was only marginally better than that of their Spanish counterparts. Toplis (1998), in carrying out a small-scale research project with his pupils, found that practical work had done very little to enhance pupils' ideas about acid and alkalis. White (1996) is particularly critical of the way practical work is carried out in schools. His review of the literature indicates that laboratory work in its present form does little to improve pupils' understanding of science. He also questions the value of practical work in the development of learning in groups, and even as an activity that motivates pupils. So, is practical work worthwhile?

I share the view of Borrows (1999) that practical work is interesting and fun, providing pupils with the opportunity to work with materials that they may otherwise never come across. It helps to broaden their life experiences and, for a few, will inspire them to go on to study science at a higher level. Practical work is a fundamental part of scientists' work, and as such it should be part and parcel of the school curriculum. However, in a school world, where time and resources are limited, teachers need to consider carefully each teaching activity and make a judgement about its potential to achieve the planned learning outcomes. In order to help make a balanced decision, teachers need to have a clear picture of what each activity entails and how it can be presented to pupils. There are three distinct types of practical work commonly used in schools:

1 Illustrative work based on the concepts or the 'theory' that is taught in other parts of the lessons
2 Investigative work
3 Teaching pupils basic practical skills (these are now normally taught when they are needed to carry out an exercise, rather than as a separate unit on skills training).

Exactly what pupils take away from these practicals will depend, to a very large extent, upon what the teacher does in terms of:

- presenting the activity (making it clear what the pupils are supposed to do and what they should be looking for)
- supporting and questioning the pupils during the activity
- drawing together the key points at the end and reinforcing the learning outcomes from the practical experience.

The arguments for doing practical work have been grouped by Wellington (1998) under three broad headings: cognitive, affective and skills. The reasons for doing practical work and the counter-arguments given by Wellington are summarised in Table 9.2. The counter-arguments in the right-hand column are useful in terms of identifying problems that exist, and looking for ways of reducing them or eliminating them altogether.

Table 9.2 *Reasons and counter-reasons concerned with using practical work to promote pupils' learning in science (adapted from Wellington, 1998: 7)*

	Arguments for practical work	Arguments against practical work
Cognitive	• Improves pupils' understanding of science • Seeing is believing; helps to confirm 'theory' work	• Sometimes the 'noise' of the practical causes confusion • Sometimes the practical goes wrong, leaving pupils with mixed messages
Affective	• It is interesting and exciting • It helps promote positive attitudes towards science	• Some pupils don't like practical work • Some pupils like practicals because they see them as a social occasion, requiring little intellectual input
Skills	Practical work develops: • skills, e.g. manipulating apparatus, observing, measuring • processes, e.g. predicting, inferring, evaluating • the ability to work as a member of a team • an understanding of scientific enquiry	• There is little evidence that these skills and processes are transferable to other situations, i.e. they tend to be context-specific • Effective group work frequently does not happen, as pupils sometimes talk about non-science issues and/or one or two individuals carry out the work while the others watch • Pupils can become confused about approaches to scientific enquiry if the nature of the practical activity is not clearly explained

Things to consider

Carry out a review of the practical work your pupils have done during a 1–2-week period.

- What have been the aims of each practical? Are you happy that these were met?
- What exactly did you want pupils to remember from each activity? What did you want them to write down? How did you ensure that the key points were remembered?

The image portrayed

Pupils' perceptions of science and scientists are assimilated from a wide variety of sources outside the classroom, over which the teacher has no control. However, pupils are strongly influenced by the messages they receive through their science lessons. These messages are conveyed by what teachers do, how they behave, what they say, and how they present the science. For many pupils the people who teach them science are the only 'real' scientists that any of them will actually meet, and it is therefore up to the teachers to counter the often negative image of science that is portrayed in the media. In research carried out by Matthews and Davies (1999) it was found that pupils tended to view scientists as White males doing chemistry experiments, some of whom were mad. Putting this alongside the perceived difficulty of the subject, it is not surprising that many pupils are put off studying it.

Hodson (1998) points out that school science can often 'promote and perpetuate some grossly distorted views of science and scientists'. He identifies what he calls ten common myths that are sometimes present in science courses. These are:

1 Observation provides direct and reliable access to secure knowledge
2 Science starts with observation
3 Science proceeds via induction
4 Experiments are decisive
5 Science comprises of discrete, generic processes
6 Scientific inquiry is a simple, algorithmic procedure
7 Science is a value-free activity
8 Science is an exclusively Western, post-Renaissance activity
9 The so-called 'scientific attitudes' are essential to the effective practice of science
10 Scientists possess these attitudes.

Hodson suggests that these views may be transmitted for a number of reasons, such as:

• the nature of the curriculum (forces the teacher to project an oversimplified picture of science)
• the emphasis on examination results (tends to rule out anything that involves uncertainty)
• simply, the teacher is mainly unaware of the ways in which scientists operate.

To an extent the approach to science as presented in the National Curriculum has helped to eliminate some of these myths. For example, pupils are taught about the influence of creative thought in developing scientific ideas, they are taught to be critical of their experimental results, and there is no longer an emphasis of processes carried out in isolation from the content. However, many of these myths are still being taught either because of the National Curriculum or because of the way it has been interpreted by textbook writers and teachers.

It is during practical work that teachers have the greatest opportunity to do something about the image of science. Relatively simple things, such as getting the pupils prepared so that they know what they are doing, can help to convey the message that scientists work in a carefully organised fashion. There are also opportunities to encourage pupils to be honest about their results and to appreciate that scientists sometimes get the 'wrong' answer. Teachers occasionally go to great lengths to rig the experiment so that the 'right' results are obtained (Nott and Wellington, 1997), and they do this in order to ensure:

• that pupils end up with the correct facts (Nott and Smith, 1995)
• the smooth running of classroom life (Nott and Wellington, 1995).

Obtaining the 'wrong' answer, on the other hand, provides the teacher with the opportunity to discuss the experimental method and to look for reasons why the desired result wasn't obtained. So much depends on the practical competence and classroom experience of the teacher and the technician, but clearly getting too many 'wrong' answers is going to give the impression to the pupils that science never works.

Things to consider

Hodson and Bencze (1998) reported on an action research project carried out by a group of Canadian science teachers who were concerned about the nature of practical work carried out in their schools. Along with a researcher/facilitator they instigated a repeating cycle of action research comprising the following phases:

1 reflecting on and challenging each other's beliefs, ideas and practices
2 seeking alternative views, criticising them, and using them to develop new approaches
3 field-testing and evaluating these approaches in class.

Consider setting up a group within your school with the remit of reviewing the nature of the practical work done. If possible ask someone from outside the school to support your work (the researcher/facilitator), perhaps using funds from organisations such as the General Teaching Councils. This could be done by starting with one year group, probably Y7, to keep it to a manageable task.

The impact of the National Curriculum

There was a degree of shock when investigative work was introduced, first in the proposals of 1988 and then in the first statutory document in 1989, as this approach was new to the majority of science teachers. While teachers were still reeling from the effect, the government brought in a new version of the NC in 1991 with a tightly prescribed *Scientific Investigation* Sc1 section indicating how it should be both taught and assessed (Laws, 1996). The 1995 version saw Sc1 renamed *Experimental and Investigative Science*, accompanied by a reduction in emphasis on variables and their control and an increase in emphasis on the importance of evidence and its evaluation. However, all the way through the history of the NC the dominant approach has been one of manipulating variables. This model of promoting one way of doing science, one scientific method, has been heavily criticised (Wellington, 1998) for the false picture it gives of the way in which scientists operate.

In a study of teachers' experiences since the introduction of the NC, Jenkins (2000) found that the amount of time teachers spent on practical work had reduced since pre-NC days (see Table 4.2, page 62). In almost all cases, this reduction in time was attributed to the amount of science the NC required them to teach. In a similar study carried out by Donnelly (2000), teachers reported that, other than the introduction of Sc1, their overall practice had altered little. There was a strong emphasis on demonstration experiments, but there was nothing to indicate that this was an area of growth. The majority of teachers who commented on Sc1 were hostile towards it, and talked in terms of setting up contrived situations and devising hoops for pupils to jump through. Very few teachers appeared to base their approach on the notion of evidence, and there was little indication that the skills required for investigations were taught. This is supported by the work of Nott and Wellington (1999), who reported that teachers planned activities that provided access to all the levels and could be organised and completed in a relatively short time.

Information from Ofsted surveys paints a very similar picture:

> **Experimental and investigative science** often receives little explicit attention during Y7 and Y8. Teachers feel under pressure to cover content and see investigative work as time-consuming and less relevant to measurable performance.
>
> (Ofsted, 2000: 15)

> Scientific enquiry is developing slowly. In most schools, pupils undertake just two or three whole investigations a year often to a closely prescribed pattern. There is a growing separation between practical activity for coursework assessment and its use as part of normal teaching.
>
> (Ofsted, 2002: 2)

Clearly, the assessment of Sc1 strongly influences teachers' decisions when planning practical activities for pupils. Pupil-initiated investigations appear to be rare – unlike the situation in Scotland, where the 'question' comes from the pupil and is within the context of ongoing classwork (McNally, 2000). In England and Wales teachers use 'set investigations', which have been developed over the years to meet the demands of the examination (Nott and Wellington, 1999). Pupils quickly learn how to play the system and know what they have to do to obtain marks and what shortcuts they can take. Keiler and Woolnough (2002) report that the pupils in their survey were not motivated to produce a high-quality product when a less good one would still earn the desired marks.

I have painted a fairly gloomy picture of practical work so far, which, when put alongside the comments made by teachers reported in Jenkins' research (2000) about the reduction in fun and enjoyment brought about by the introduction of the NC, almost leads to despair.

Avoiding confusion

Pupils can become confused very easily, mainly because they are not paying attention, but sometimes because the teacher hasn't explained things clearly enough. It is becoming common practice in schools to make pupils aware of what they are going to learn at the start of the lesson (e.g. see Science Key Stage 3 Strategy). It is a good idea to use a similar approach at the start of a practical activity, making the purpose of the activity clear to the pupils. They may not understand why in one task they have to measure things very accurately and in another rough quantities are sufficient. They may query why in some practicals they are following fair testing procedures whereas in others these are completely ignored. They may find it difficult to identify which aspects of the practical are important: the final outcome, the steps on the way, the practical procedure, or all of these.

In some activities the purpose of the practical task will be to illustrate the principles and theories of science to pupils, and these will normally require some sort of detailed instruction about the steps to follow. In other activities the pupils will be learning about how scientists work, and will be using some of their knowledge of practical science and learning about the steps that scientists take in order to draw conclusions about a particular phenomenon. Confusion arises when these quite distinct forms of practical activity are mixed up.

In some practicals, pupils find it difficult to determine what is important and what is peripheral. This is particularly true of multi-stage activities and those involving complex apparatus. Johnstone and Wham (1982) have used the term 'noise' to label aspects of practical work that can result in the pupils being distracted. Noise can be something simple, such as telling the pupils information that they don't really need. This becomes another piece of information that has to be logged in the pupil's mind, and he or she has to make judgements as to the degree of significance of the information. In other instances it may be that the design of the task needs simplifying to reduce noise, or it may be that the teacher supports the pupils, giving them clear guidance as to what to look for and what to write down (for further suggestions, see Chapter 7 in Parkinson, 2002).

Critics of the recipe approach to practical work (a list of step-by-step instructions) maintain that this conveys the wrong sort of message to pupils about science, putting it on a par with cookery. They might also say that pupils learn little from this method of teaching, as they mindlessly follow the steps with little thought as to why they are doing so. It could justifiably be argued that pupils are in the process of learning about science, and they need to gain experience in this sort of way before they become fully-fledged practitioners. The lack of engagement and pupil learning can be taken care of by any of a number of well-established teaching methods (see examples in Table 9.3).

Observation is an important aspect of science, and yet we do little to point out to pupils the complexities of observation, and possibly do little to guide them in what they should write down about what they have observed (e.g. is it sufficient to say 'it went blue' when the observation tells them 'the solution turned from green to blue'?). Some pupils get mixed up between observations and inferences, and are too keen to write down what they consider to be an explanation of what has happened without appreciating that there is a big gap between the two processes. Each person will observe things from his or her own perspective (e.g. the glass of water that is half empty or half full), based on their previous experience and their understanding of the situation they are observing. Leach and Scott (1995) point out that pupils cannot develop an understanding of science simply through their observations; it is the inter-weaving of the observations with the 'theory' that leads to greater understanding. As teachers, we are sometimes guilty of thinking that pupils will see things in the same way that we do. McRobbie *et al.* (1997) showed that this was clearly not the case in research carried out on the effects of practical experiences for a group of physics pupils over a six-week period. It became clear that the pupils' existing conceptual frameworks relating to the topic affected what they observed. In a study carried out by Haslam and Gunstone (1998), looking at teachers' and pupils' perspectives on observation, it was suggested that teachers should encourage pupils to ask 'thinking questions' during practical tasks. These could be questions directed to themselves or other group members, or questions for the teacher. At the start of the practical the teacher would model the situation by providing the pupils with a few examples.

Many important aspects of science can pass us by because of poor observation, or perhaps because we choose to ignore things. For example, when zinc is added to copper (II) sulphate solution we are happy when pupils see the brownish colour of the resultant copper and, if we are patient, the clear solution of the zinc sulphate.

Table 9.3 *Some ideas for promoting pupils' thinking about the design of a practical task rather than letting them follow a series of instructions*

Getting away from the recipe approach

1 Sequencing exercises (cards containing instructions for the experiment in random order). Pupils arrange the cards in the correct sequence and explain their reasoning.
2 Questioning pupils about:
   - the apparatus they should use
   - the quantities of materials to be used
   - safety issues
   - why they are doing things in a specific way.
3 Getting the pupils to plan a whole illustrative practical activity (i.e. starting with the question: If you wanted to show someone this, what would you use and why would you use it?).

The bubbles (of hydrogen) tend to be ignored because we don't want to go into an explanation that copper (II) sulphate solution is acidic and that a side reaction is taking place between it and the zinc. Morley reports an unplanned incident (Morley, 2002) in one of his lessons, where one of his Y10 pupils was particularly observant during a demonstration on exploding hydrogen in a test tube. The pupil observed a series of condensation rings in the tube, and so the teacher and pupils decided to see if the phenomenon was repeatable and what explanations could be made. OK, so perhaps the pupils weren't learning a great deal of science that would be of use to them in an exam, but they were learning something about the way scientists work and, just as importantly, it was fun.

Practicals without the mess

Videos of experiments have been around for a number of years, and these have been useful in showing pupils things that cannot be carried out in a school laboratory. They can excite pupils about science (e.g. the video of the reaction between caesium and water) and they can be used as a focus for discussion. More recently, computer software has become available that allows pupils to carry out practical work electronically (see page 214).

In order to teach pupils about the interpretation of data, it is worthwhile considering presenting pupils with the results from experiments and asking them to discuss, in groups, what the information tells us. The exercise can be extended to ask pupils about what additional information would be required in order to make the knowledge more secure. This approach can be used to look at data concerning industrial or environmental topics, to raise issues about such things as interpretation, bias and media coverage. An interesting example of this type of activity is given in the Salters Advanced Level Chemistry Course (2000) unit WM8, where students are presented with information about two drugs and asked to decide which one the company should develop. The exercise provides the students with a sufficient level of detail to discuss the marketing of drugs and the level of risk that we have to take when we take any medication.

Teaching scientific enquiry and investigations

There is a considerable amount of information available about pupils' performance in investigations. This has come from the work of the Assessment and Performance Unit (APU) set up by the government in the early 1980s (for details see Gott and Duggan, 1995), ongoing classroom-based research, and the experiences of teachers and examiners. This information can be used by teachers to help pupils understand more about key aspects of this particular approach to science. Through a deeper understanding it should help pupils gain high marks in the assessment of Sc1, but if gaining high marks is the teacher's sole aim, then clearly the best method is to stick to using tried and tested investigations and train the pupils to jump through the hoops.

Bearing in mind that pupils will have carried out a significant amount of work on investigations in the primary school, the secondary teacher needs to build on this expertise and consider how to incorporate continuity of experience into schemes of work through key stages 3 and 4. Continuity will need to be considered in terms of:

- contexts in which the investigations are set
- procedures that pupils will need to use
- concepts that pupils will need to understand and apply to the investigation.

The context can have a bearing on pupils' performance (Gott and Duggan, 1995). Pupils tend to do better if an investigation is set in a scientific context rather than an everyday situation. If an everyday scenario is used this may cue pupils into thinking that an everyday, 'non-scientific', approach is required. On the other hand, if the context is scientific, pupils choose to use a scientific methodology based on their previous experience. Obviously, their performance will depend on the extent to which their knowledge of the topic is secure. For example, if their understanding about a topic such as 'light' is weak, then they will feel unhappy about tackling investigations based on this context.

The NC and, to a greater extent, the assessment of Sc1 for GCSE has led many teachers to believe that the only type of investigation worth carrying out is the fair testing type. This conveys the message to pupils that this is the way that all scientists operate i.e. it is **the** scientific method. In order to show pupils a variety of methods used by scientists, teachers need to accept a broader interpretation of the word 'investigation'. Through the work of the ASE-King's Science Investigations in Schools (AKSIS) project, Watson *et al.* (1999) have proposed six different types of investigations. These are summarised in Table 9.4, and examples of lesson activities that can be used to help pupils learn about how the different approaches are given in a book by Goldsworthy *et al.* (2000). This wider view of investigations helps to create opportunities for discussions about the nature of science and, in particular, the relationship between knowledge and data.

Teachers tend not to elaborate on what particular data need to be collected in an investigation, as it is generally considered to be obvious. However, it is worth pointing out that the decision is made on the basis of prior knowledge (i.e. the knowledge and science theories that we hold influence what data will be collected). Also, the data that are obtained from the investigation will influence further understanding. Pupils tend to hold very fuzzy views about the collection of data and its use in drawing conclusions. In a study carried out by Lubben and Millar (1996), pupils were asked about the reliability of experimental data. In particular, they looked at pupils' understanding of:

- the reasons for repeat measurements
- anomalous results, and what to do with them
- the extent of scatter of results in a series of repeat measurements as an indication of reliability.

With each of the areas there was a pattern of progression in understanding with age and experience. For example, in considering the need for repeat readings, pupils'

Table 9.4 *Different types of investigations (Watson et al., 1999)*

Type	Typical characteristics
Classifying and identifying	Looking at patterns, trends etc. (e.g. from experiments or databases) Putting things into groups (e.g. from carrying out tests/experiments) Making predictions about 'new' members of the group based on the information from existing members Confirming predictions through experiment
Fair testing	Applies to situations where pupils can observe the relationship between variables One variable is changed (the independent variable) while the other factors are controlled (controlled variables) An outcome is measured (the dependent variable) as a result of making systematic changes of the independent variable Titles often begin with the phrase 'Investigation to find the effect of...'
Pattern seeking	Considers large samples of data in situations where variables cannot easily be controlled Pupils recognise the importance of having a large sample to ensure that any conclusions that are drawn are significant An effect is noticed (the dependent variable) and an investigation is structured around finding a possible cause for the effect Topics may include biological surveys where there will be natural variation within samples
Investigating models	Testing to see if science models explain certain phenomena (e.g. Scientist A thinks that this can be explained because..., where scientist B thinks ... Based on what you have just seen which one do you think is right and why?) Pupils put forward their own ideas about why something happens and then check to see if it holds up in a related situation
Exploring	Pupils make a study of a change over time (e.g. growth) through systematic observation They make decisions about the number and frequency of the observations Pupils use the observations to raise questions
Making things or developing systems	Pupils make decisions about the appropriateness of a particular artefact (piece of science equipment) for a particular job Pupils consider how the bench work they do applies to the real world In some D&T lessons, pupils apply knowledge and procedures that they have learnt in science

views varied considerably. At one end there was a complete denial of the need for repeat readings. In the middle there were pupils who would search for recurring results, and there were those who considered the likely range of results. The research points to the need for teachers to explore pupils' views about data collection and the importance of carrying out a systematic programme of teaching to help pupils understand the nature of what they are doing.

With the experiences that pupils have had at primary school, they are generally quite good at brainstorming a list of variables and are adept at making decisions as to what to change and what to measure – that is, until the task involves two continuous independent variables. Then there is a considerable drop in performance, in terms of both identifying the independent variables and appreciating the need to control others (Duggan *et al.*, 1996). Teachers will recognise the importance of this, as investigations involving continuous independent variables are the type required for gaining the

---

Things to consider

Osborne (1998) refers to research carried out by Robertson on investigations, that indicates that pupils may have difficulties in:

- identifying key evidence
- wording hypotheses
- representing and manipulating two continuous variables.

Identify what you do to help pupils with each of these areas of difficulty.

---

highest marks in GCSE coursework assessments. Duggan *et al.* (1996) suggested that there is a need to ensure that pupils understand what continuous data means, and they suggest the following strategies for use at KS3:

- use simple practical activities that involve the use of continuous data, e.g. the extension of an elastic band in a catapult and the distance the catapulted object travels
- use exercises or activities that look at patterns in data, and ask pupils to sketch a graph to describe the event
- use activities that involve some sort of competition that encourages pupils to see the need for reliable data.

In carrying out their investigations, pupils need to consider what evidence they need to collect, as well as its reliability and validity. Decisions will have to be made about things such as:

- sample size (e.g. in investigations involving natural phenomenon)
- degree of precision required
- the number and range of readings to be made.

These require pupils to have a sound understanding and an appreciation of the scale of the phenomenon they are investigating. There is some research to show that pupils' ability to deal with evidence appears to decline in the early years of the secondary school (Duggan and Gott, 1996). There is little other research to corroborate these findings at present, but it may be worthwhile spending some time discussing what evidence should be collected and how this might be linked into drawing conclusions from the data.

The research described in this section makes a strong case for the teaching of the skills and processes involved with investigations. In addition, you may consider that it is worth aiming for a classroom environment in which the natural curiosity of children is nurtured (McNally, 2000) and where pupils are encouraged to make suggestions about things they would like to investigate. White (1996) argues for laboratory work that will promote effective learning, and he advocates the use of more open-ended investigations and problem-solving activities. It is difficult to break the current assessment stranglehold and, understandably, teachers are going to use activities that provide pupils with the opportunity to get maximum marks in each of the skill areas. However, it is worthwhile considering setting aside some time for pupils to carry out at least one investigation where they have been involved in raising the question themselves, perhaps as a project over an extended period of time. This quotation from Woolnough (1997: 70) sums up what is important in science teaching:

> To make our science teaching more effective, we need to concentrate on ways of developing the affective, of giving students a sense of satisfaction and personal achievement in their science. For, ultimately, it is not what our science students know or can do that is important, but what they want to do.

Things to consider

It could be argued that understanding and evaluating evidence should be a major part of any science curriculum, as in life after school the young adults will have to receive information through the media and make decisions about which is the best way to proceed. There are many opportunities during practical activities and during the teaching of controversial topics to discuss the reliability and validity of the data. These, and other terms to do with experimental work, are defined in Table 9.5. When teaching about investigations, you could ask pupils about:

- the design of the experiment (Will it give reliable information? Have all the control variables been accounted for?)
- the reliability of the results obtained (Have they used an appropriate level of precision? Have they taken sufficient readings to take into account random errors?)
- the conclusions they can draw from the evidence (What is the best way of presenting the data in order to help the conclusions to be drawn?).

In environmental situations and health-related issues, where large-scale data and statistics are involved, pupils could review published information and look at issues such as:

- the sampling technique
- the sampling size
- the method of presenting the results.

Table 9.5 *Terms related to the collection and use of data*

Precision
Precision refers to the level of detail of the measurements.
You can take readings with increased precision by using more precise instruments and/or techniques.
Advice to pupils (Fisher, 2002: 375):
- Choose a sensitive device that 'moves a lot'
- Use a big range of values to get significant variation
- Variable must change more than the size of the uncertainty
- Lots of significant figures due to small uncertainties
- Use a magnifying glass on analogue scales
- Measure a lot of things (e.g. 100 drawing pins to find the mass of an average drawing pin)
- Repeat readings and calculate an average.

Accuracy
Accuracy refers to the correctness of the measurements.
Accuracy depends on the ability of the user to use the measuring instrument.
Advice to pupils (Fisher, 2002: 375):
- Repeat values and review your method if there are large variations
- Check the zero and calibration of meters to avoid systematic errors
- Avoid parallax errors
- Check readings, calculations and graphs against agreed theory and known values. Review method if there are disagreements
- Triumph by using diverse methods. If there are disagreements, review your method.

Validity
Is concerned with the question: is the data I am collecting directly related to the phenomenon I want to measure?

Reliability
Is concerned with the question: are my measurements a good representation of the phenomenon I want to measure?

Repeatability
When the same person repeats the experiment, using the same equipment, and the results are close together.

Reproducibility
When the experiment is carried out by a different person(s), using different equipment, and the results are close together.

Reason for taking many measurements
Many careful measurements **may** get you close to the result you are measuring, but you can never be sure you have found it. Taking an average of several measurements allows for this.

Evaluating the results
Compare the results with those obtained by an authoritative source, e.g. data book.
The spread of measurements gives an indication of the reliability of the results.

Anomalous results
It is acceptable to ignore anomalous results before taking an average. The experimenter must make the decision.

Random and systematic errors
Both types of errors can be due to either the experiment or the person performing the experiment. Random errors can be detected by examination of the results. They can be eliminated by multiple readings. Systematic errors will shift the results in one direction.

Graphs

Many pupils find it difficult to draw and interpret graphs in science (Austin *et al.*, 1991; Swatton and Taylor, 1994). For example, pupils have problems with:

- placing a scale on the axes (e.g. using an inappropriate size so that the graph is either too small or too large, making it impossible to carry any extrapolations; the scale is not uniform);
- the origin (e.g. deciding on the need for a 0,0 point; deciding if the graph should go through this point)

- relating the graph to the situation it represents
- understanding errors in the data
- drawing the line of best fit.

Lenton *et al.* (2000) were a bit more optimistic in their research based on a group of Y10 pupils. They found that the pupils, of a wide range of ability, had no difficulty in transferring data from a table of results into a graph where the axes were already marked. However, in another part of their study they found that many pupils had difficulty in interpreting different types of graphs when they did this on an individual basis. In many cases, group discussion helped pupils to revise their answers and come to a correct understanding.

Graph work is also an important component of the National Curriculum for both mathematics and geography. In addition, pupils in England have had the benefit of following the National Numeracy Strategy in primary schools since 1999. All this should be starting to make a difference in pupils' abilities to work with graphs. A study carried out by Swan and Phillips (1998) investigated the graph interpretation skills of lower-achieving school leavers, and made some tentative comparisons with the results from earlier research. The sample group were pupils who had obtained D or E grades in GCSE mathematics and were planning to resit. An underlying purpose of the research was to identify the pupils' weaknesses and use this information to devise an appropriate course to help them to make progress. The results showed that more than half of the pupils could interpret data from line graphs and scatter graphs depicting familiar situations. Questions that involved the understanding of gradients, or concepts of ratio, were performed less well. For example, when pupils were asked to sketch a speed/distance graph from written information, only about 4 per cent produced a perfect response. Comparisons with previous data indicated a clear difference between results obtained 10 years ago and the present cohort insomuch that the present group were much better at interpretation skills but worse at other graph skills. This indicates that some progress is being made, but at the expense of continuing developments in other areas. The pupils tested in the 1980s were better at giving co-ordinates of points on a line and drawing a line through given co-ordinates, while present-day pupils are way ahead when it comes to extracting information from a scatter graph.

Part of the AKSIS research analysed pupils' use of graphs in investigations, and it was found that over 75 per cent of graphs were incorrectly constructed and most pupils regarded graphs as an end in themselves. Only a very few pupils referred to their graphs when considering evidence. As a result the research team produced a book containing exercises to help pupils, mainly within the age range 8 to 14, develop graphing skills (Goldsworthy *et al.*, 1999).

Things to consider

- There are clear links between Sc1 and Ma1 (Using and applying mathematics) and Ma4 (Handling data). How can the science and maths departments work together in a joint programme to improve graph work?
- A possible area of difference between maths and science is that in making scientific measurements there are always errors. How do you explain this to pupils, and how do pupils depict errors in their graphs?

References

Austin, R., Holding, B., Bell, J. and Daniels, S. (1991) *Assessment Matters No. 7: Patterns and Relationships in School Science*, London: SEAC.

Beatty, J.W. and Woolnough, B.E. (1982) 'Practical work in 11–13 science: the context, type and aims of current practice', *British Educational Research Journal*, **8**, 23–30.

Borrows, P. (1999) 'The changing face of practical work', *Education in Chemistry*, **36**(6), 158–164.

Donnelly, J.F. (2000) 'Secondary science teaching under the National Curriculum', *School Science Review*, **81**(296), 27–35.

Duggan, S. and Gott, R. (1996) 'Scientific evidence: the new emphasis in the practical science curriculum in England and Wales', *The Curriculum Journal*, **7**(1), 17–32.

Duggan, S., Johnson, P. and Gott, R. (1996) 'A critical point in investigative work: defining variables', *Journal of Research in Science Teaching*, **33**(5), 461–474.

Fisher, N. (2002) 'Teaching accuracy and reliability for student projects', *Physics Education*, **37**(5), 371–375.

Gee, B. and Clackson, S.G. (1992) 'The origin of practical work in the English school science curriculum', *School Science Review*, **73**(265), 79–83.

Goldsworthy, A., Watson, R. and Wood-Robinson, V. (1999) *Investigations: Getting to Grips with Graphs*, Hatfield: ASE.

Goldsworthy, A., Watson, R. and Wood-Robinson, V. (2000) *Investigations: Developing Understanding*, Hatfield: ASE.

Gott, R. and Duggan, S. (1995) *Investigative Work in the Science Curriculum*, Buckingham: Open University Press.

Haslam, F. and Gunstone, R. (1998) 'The influence of teachers on student observation in science classes'. Paper given at the Annual Meeting of the National Association for Research in Science Teaching, San Diego, April 1998.

Hodson, D. (1998) 'Science fiction: the continuing misrepresentation of science in the school curriculum', *Curriculum Studies*, **6**(2), 191–216.

Hodson, D. and Bencze, L. (1998) 'Becoming critical about practical work: changing views and changing practice through action research', *International Journal of Science Education*, **20**(6), 683–694.

Jenkins, E.W. (1998) 'The schooling of laboratory science', in Wellington, J. (ed.) *Practical Work in School Science: Which Way Now?*, London: Routledge.

Jenkins, E.W. (2000) 'The impact of the National Curriculum on secondary school science teaching in England and Wales', *International Journal of Science Education*, **22**(3), 325–336.

Johnstone, A.H. and Wham, A.J.B. (1982) 'The demands of practical work', *Education in Chemistry*, **19**(3), 71–73.

Keiler, L.S. and Woolnough, B.E. (2002) 'Practical work in school science: the dominance of assessment', *School Science Review*, **83**(304), 83–88.

Kerr, J.F. (1964) *Practical Work in School Science*, Leicester: Leicester University Press.

Laws, P.M. (1996) 'Investigative work in the Science National Curriculum', *School Science Review*, **77**(281), 17–25.

Leach, J. and Scott, P. (1995) 'The demands of learning science concepts: issues of theory and practice', *School Science Review*, **76**(277), 47–51.

Lenton, G., Stevens, B. and Illes, R. (2000) 'Numeracy in science: pupils' understanding of graphs', *School Science Review*, **82**(299), 15–23.

Lubben, F. and Millar, R. (1996) 'Children's ideas about the reliability of experimental data', *International Journal of Science Education*, **18**(8), 955–968.

McNally, J.G. (2000) 'Teaching investigative science: preliminary theorizing from the shared reflections of teachers', *International Journal of Science Education*, **22**(2), 159–176.

McRobbie, C.J., Roth, W.-M. and Lucas, K.B. (1997) 'Multiple learning environments in a physics classroom', *International Journal of Educational Research*, **27**, 333–342.

Matthews, B. and Davies, D. (1999) 'Changing children's images of scientists: can teachers make a difference?', *School Science Review*, **80**(293), 79–85.

Morley, R. (2002) 'Hydrogen pop condensation bands and the "Danielle Effect"', *School Science Review*, **83**(305), 132–133.

Nott, M. and Smith, J. (1995) '"Talking your way out of it", "rigging", and "conjuring": what science teachers do when practicals go wrong', *International Journal of Science Education*, **17**(3), 399–410.

Nott, M. and Wellington, J. (1995) 'Critical incidents in the science classroom and the nature of science', *School Science Review*, **76**(276), 41–46.

Nott, M. and Wellington, J. (1997) 'Producing the evidence: science teachers' initiations into practical work', *Research in Science Education*, **27**(3), 395–409.

Nott, M. and Wellington, J. (1999) 'The state we're in: issues in key stage 3 and 4 science', *School Science Review*, **81**(294), 13–18.

Ofsted (2000) *Progress in Key Stage 3 Science*, London: Office for Standards in Education.

Ofsted (2002) *Secondary Subject Reports 2000/01: Science*, London: HMSO.

Osborne, J. (1998) 'Science education without a laboratory?', in Wellington, J. (ed.) *Practical Work in School Science: Which Way Now?*, London: Routledge.

Paris, J.A. (1831) *The Life of Sir Humphry Davy: Volume II*, London: Colburn & Bentley.

Parkinson, J. (2002) *Reflective Teaching of Science 11–18*, London: Continuum.

Salters Advanced Level Chemistry Course (2000) *Activities and Assessment Pack*, Oxford: Heinemann.

Stohr-Hunt, P.M. (1996) 'Analysis of frequency of hands-on experience and science achievement', *Journal of Research in Science Teaching*, **33**, 101–109.

Swain, J., Monk, M. and Johnson, S. (2000) 'Developments in science teachers' attitudes to aims for practical work: continuity and change', *Teacher Development*, **4**(2), 281–292.

Swan, M. and Phillips, R. (1998) 'Graph interpretation skills among lower-achieving school leavers', *Research in Education*, **60**, 10–20.

Swatton, P. and Taylor, R.M. (1994) 'Pupil performance in graphical tasks and its relationship to the ability to handle variables', *British Educational Research Journal*, **20**, 227–243.

Thompson, J. and Soyibo, K. (2002) 'Effects of lecture, teacher demonstrations, discussion and practical work on 10th graders' attitudes to chemistry and understanding of electrolysis', *Research in Science and Technology Education*, **20**(1), 25–35.

Toplis, R. (1998) 'Ideas about acids and alkalis', *School Science Review*, **80**(291), 67–70.

Watson, R., Prieto, T. and Dillon, J. (1995) 'The effect of practical work on students' understanding of combustion', *Journal of Research in Science Teaching* **32**(5), 487–502.

Watson, R., Goldsworthy, A. and Wood-Robinson, V. (1999) 'What is not fair with investigations?', *School Science Review*, **80**(292), 101–106.

Wellington, J. (ed.) (1998) *Practical Work in School Science: Which Way Now?*, London: Routledge.

White, R.T. (1996) 'The link between laboratory and learning', *International Journal of Science Education*, **18**(7), 761–774.

Wilkinson, J. and Ward, M. (1997) 'A comparative study of students' and their teacher's perceptions of laboratory work in secondary schools', *Research in Science Education*, **27**(4), 599–610.

Woolnough, B.E. (1997) 'Motivating students or teaching pure science?', *School Science Review*, **78**(285), 67–72.

Yager, R.E. (1991) 'The centrality of practical work in science-technology–society movement', in B. Woolnough (ed.) *Practical Science*, Milton Keynes: Open University Press.

CHAPTER 10

Learning through ICT

Almost all educational changes of value require new (i) skills; (ii) behaviour; (iii) beliefs or understanding ... changes, to be productive, require skills, capacity, commitment, motivation, beliefs and insight, and discretionary judgement on the spot. If there is one cardinal rule of change in human condition, it is that you cannot make people change. You cannot force them to think differently or compel them to develop new skills.

(Fullan, 1993: 22–23)

In comparison with other curriculum subjects, science has tended to drag its heels in terms of the use of ICT in lessons (e.g. Harris, 1998; Ofsted, 2002). We can only speculate as to the possible reasons for this, but it is reasonable to assume that:

- some science teachers consider it to be an additional burden on their already busy teaching schedule
- some teachers (perhaps a relatively small number) do not feel confident in using ICT
- booking the computer room and moving the class can prove difficult
- some teachers are not convinced of the benefits of ICT in helping pupils to learn.

It is also worth considering how the introduction of ICT will impact on existing subject culture within a science department. Certain teaching styles have become embedded in the way science is taught in the UK, and the introduction of computers will have a distinct effect on the style of teaching used and the classroom interactions that take place. New entrants to the profession will have been educated in an environment where the use of ICT is a fundamental aspect of the day to day life of a practising scientist and are likely to see science without computers as strange. It may be the case that these new teachers will be the driving force for change. Not only do they have first-hand knowledge of relevant computer use in the development of science, but frequently they are also experts in a wide variety of computer applications.

The anti-computer lobby will always be able to quote instances where pupils' confusion can be directly related to their use of computers, and will argue strongly that the activity could have been carried out more effectively using more traditional methods. In some cases it will be true that objectives are more readily achieved by other means and, as in other instances where there is more than one way of teaching a topic, the teacher will have to make decisions about the best approach to use.

There are many benefits of using computers cited in the literature, some with a firm research base to substantiate the claims and others derived more from teachers' everyday observations of how their pupils work. The following gains are commonly attributed to the use of ICT:

- pupils can be motivated to learn science through computer use with appropriate planning and guidance from the teacher
- some pupils are keen to spend longer on the task and are prepared to continue the work outside normal lesson time voluntarily
- the opportunities for study directed by the teacher out of normal lesson time are increased
- the computer forms a focus for pupils' learning and has the potential for improving attention to task
- group discussion can be promoted
- a rich variety of learning materials is readily available
- pupils can develop skills that will help them to become more independent learners
- pupils can try things out on the computer without fear of being humiliated by their peers
- clear simulations can help teachers explain a topic
- pupils are more prepared to write about science using a word processor, desk-top publishing package or presentational software, and their writing tends to have greater clarity than when asked to do the same activity using pen and paper
- ICT can often compensate for the communication and learning difficulties of pupils with physical and/or sensory impairment
- ICT provides pupils with the opportunity to investigate situations that have hitherto been unavailable to them (e.g. global experiments through the Internet, data-logging over very short or very long time periods).

Recent research carried out on behalf of Becta (the British Educational Communications and Technology Agency) indicates that the use of ICT improves pupils' performance in science at both KS3 and KS4 (Harrison *et al.*, 2002).

Current educational thinking is based on a scenario of lifelong learning, where individuals will be required to 'pick up' knowledge at various stages of their working life in order to deal with situations in a rapidly changing world and a flexible job market. At present the science curriculum, in this country and in many other countries, is failing to promote this type of culture. In the USA work is in progress to help pupils develop skills and knowledge, through the learning of science, that will help them in later life. The project, called the Knowledge Integration Environment (KIE), is based on four principles:

1 Making science accessible, e.g. by encouraging pupils to investigate personally relevant problems and revisit their science ideas regularly
2 Making thinking visible, e.g. by scaffolding pupils to explain their ideas

3 Helping pupils to learn from one another, e.g. by designing social activities to promote productive and respectful interactions

4 Promoting lifelong science learning, e.g. by establishing a generalisable inquiry process suitable for diverse science projects (Linn, 2000).

This chapter will review the use of ICT in science lessons in the light of established theories of pupils' learning, and will identify a number of teaching approaches that can be used at all levels of secondary schooling and hopefully promote lifelong learning skills.

Motivation

The majority of pupils are motivated to learn through a use of ICT, as shown through the ImpacT (Impact of IT on children's attainment) (Watson, 1993) and PLAIT (Pupils' Learning and Access to Information Technology) (Gardner *et al.*, 1994) research projects. Pupils also have positive attitudes towards using computers, and they generally recognise that they can help them to learn (Kennewell *et al.*, 2000). There are possibly a number of factors that contribute to these motivational and attitudinal benefits, such as the following:

- Computers can present information in new and exciting ways using graphics, video and sound
- In youth culture, computers are still seen as being 'cool' and part of the technological world that it is important to know something about
- Using a word processor generally results in a neat and tidy looking product, which helps to raise pupils' self-esteem and pride in their work (Levine and Donitsa-Schmidt, 1996)
- It can remove the tedium of having to search for information from a variety of physical sources e.g. books, pamphlets, charts
- Through the Internet, pupils have access to practising scientists, science institutions (e.g. NASA, the Science Museum) and global experiments (e.g. accessing and/or adding to databases on environmental issues), and can communicate with other pupils in other parts of the world (e.g. through the ASE's Science Across the World project).

Using computers in science lessons can help to promote a modern image of science and give a sense of the importance of ICT at all levels of learning about the subject. Tasks can be performed at school level, such as carrying out an enquiry into a particular topic, that in may ways mirror the processes that take place at research level. Robinson (1994) suggests that the use of the Internet helps to raise pupils' awareness and understanding of science and technology in the 'real' world.

A severe drop in motivation occurs when computer systems fail or when the machines available in the school are significantly less powerful than those in pupils' homes. This puts an onus on the teacher to have a working knowledge of the system used in school and to appreciate its capabilities and limitations. The school must also accept the responsibility for ensuring that the technology available is reasonably up to date and in good working order. Pupils can also become demotivated if they are presented with routine, undemanding tasks, or if they are asked to do something that requires a great deal of unfruitful searching.

Teaching and learning

Becta's research into the impact of ICT on teaching, learning and standards produced two key findings for secondary schools, which were (Becta, 2002: 7):

- Secondary schools with better ICT resources achieved, on average, better results in the 1999 Key Stage 3 tests in English, mathematics and science. This difference was also true for Key Stage 4 and held true for the 2000 test results.
- Individual subject use at secondary school level is enhanced by the use of ICT across the curriculum. This suggests that a whole school policy of support across the curriculum is necessary and that the development of pupils' ICT skills is transferable from one subject to another.

Such improvements will only be achieved through careful planning and the formulation of precise objectives matched to appropriate technology (McFarlane and Sakellariou, 2002).

In this section I want to explore what ICT can offer science teachers in terms of providing learning experiences for pupils. Notwithstanding that the use of ICT in science is a part of the statutory National Curriculum, I argue that it should form a natural component of a teacher's repertoire of techniques.

In 'traditional' lessons, pupils learn from the teacher, other pupils and the resources available. In a lesson involving the use of ICT there is the possibility of pupils learning directly from the computer and by means of situations that arise because of computer use. Some have speculated that the computer might one day take over from the teacher as the main contributor to pupils' learning, but any consideration of the complex nature of how pupils learn leads to the conclusion that we are a very long way from mass teacher redundancies. Much of the tutorial type of software available at present provides pupils with structured information and then poses a series of questions to check understanding. These packages are very good at drill and practice routines, and are useful in helping pupils to pass examinations. The more sophisticated packages are able to monitor the interactions between the pupil and the computer, and can respond to individual's needs. These so-called Integrated Learning Systems (ILS) are designed on the basis of a one-to-one pupil-to-computer relationship, and can monitor a pupil's progress over time. An alternative approach is to consider how the teacher might set up conditions where the computer is one of a number of means of supporting pupils' learning. The computer is eminently able to create situations that encourage pupils to interact with the teacher, other pupils and the computer itself. The computer display affords the possibility of constructing such conversations in a coherent fashion. The ever-present screen provides pupils with a means for co-ordinating and structuring what they are talking about (Roth *et al.*, 1996). The term used to describe the potential for action and the capacity of an environment or object to enable pupils to achieve their goals is **affordances**. The affordances of a particular environment include the opportunities presented to the pupil by the technology in support of the task, the social support for learning provided by the teacher or other pupils, and the contextual support in which the activity occurs (Kennewell *et al.*, 2000). Looked at in this way, the computer can be one of the contributors to the scaffolding of learning (see page 96), alongside the teacher or a more competent peer. The teacher can set up situations that prompt pupils to think and discuss things with fellow pupils and their teacher, and from time to time it may be the computer that supplies the additional information that moves the learning along. Wild and Braid (1996) note that working with computers can increase pupils' participation in discussion, and provides them with an environment where they feel uninhibited in using exploratory language to arrive at decisions. In some instances the affordances of the technology reduce the total cognitive load on the pupil by taking care of the mechanical or routine tasks. For example, the computer may carry out a number of tedious calculations, or it may plot a graph, leaving time for the pupil to concentrate on the interpretation of the data. In these situations, as in all other teaching situations, the teacher needs to make decisions about how much information and help to give to pupils and how far to leave the pupils to their own devices. For effective learning to take place, there must be a gap between the pupils' abilities and the requirements of the problem to be solved. The width of the gap can be adjusted by the nature of the written information supplied, the explanations and questions posed, and many of the other techniques that enable pupils to focus on a particular task. The trick is to make the gap sufficiently wide so that to bridge it some effort is required. If the gap is too small, the result will be shallow understanding. If the gap is too large, the result may be failure to learn anything.

Taking the view that the computer is a teaching partner raises questions about the management of pupils' learning and organisation of the resources. Leaving aside for the moment how the teacher can work with a computer on a whole-class basis (discussed in the 'Obtaining knowledge' section below), we will look at strategies concerned with pupils working on computers in groups. The most likely situation we are going to experience for the foreseeable future is a small number of computers available in the science laboratory, and the possible occasional use of a computer room. In some schools the science department may have a dedicated computer suite, or they may share it with a small number of other departments. Therefore, for the majority of the time teachers have little option but to arrange some type of group work based around the computer. Most of the research on collaborative group work using computers has been carried out in primary schools (e.g. Hoyles *et al.*, 1994; Mercer, 1994; Jackson and Kutnick, 1996; Wegerif, 1996; Wild, 1996); however, there are a number of important outcomes that are of relevance to learning science in secondary schools. These are:

- The nature and quality of any computer-based activity is almost entirely defined by the software
- The procedures and outcomes of the activity are shaped by the talk and joint activity of teachers and pupils

- The pupils must be sufficiently mature to manage themselves, the task requirements and the resources, but the group must be unimpeded by antagonism
- Efforts must be made to ensure that any individual does not dominate the discussion or the interaction with the computer
- Reflecting on ideas 'away' from the computer is beneficial.

In a study carried out by Roth *et al.* (1996), looking at group work during the use of a modelling package in physics in a sample of Canadian schools, it was noted that the computer environment contributed in significant ways to the maintenance and co-ordination of pupils' physics conversations. However, the researchers were concerned that pupils spent more time learning about the software rather than on learning the physics. Important features of successful group work are the use of software that is not over-demanding for pupils, and the nature of the direction given by the teacher. Pupils need to be clear about how they are going to work with the computers, and the nature of the desired outcome. Table 10.1 indicates the main areas of pupil discussion that can take place. A considerable amount of low-level conversation is possible, but this can be reduced by the use of clear instructions and structuring of the task.

In research carried out in Hawaiian High Schools, Churach and Fisher (2001) monitored the effect of using the Internet on pupils' learning. As in the UK, pupils tended to work in groups around each computer. The researchers reported that this encouraged discussion about science, and generally promoted a more socio-constructivist classroom environment. Some pupils enjoyed the work so much they didn't appreciate that they were learning – something that they associated with more formal teaching.

Group discussion doesn't always have to be centred on a piece of science software or a website; generic packages such as word processors can act as the focus, as shown in the following examples.

Table 10.1 *Types of verbal interactions that can take place when pupils work in groups at a computer, based on Wild (1996)*

	Types of activity	Examples of questions that need to be answered
Preparation	Determining requirements and roles Determining methodology and deciding on the desired outcomes Sequencing the tasks to realise the desired outcomes	What additional resources do we need? Who is going to do what? What software should we use? How much should we write? What should the final product look like? Is it best to look at all the information first and then write the report, or should we write it up section by section from each item we come across?
Working on the computer	Making sure that the group keeps on target	Are we getting there? What other information do we need? How much time do we have?
	Discussion about science	Why did it (the computer) say that? How can we find out if it is correct? Shall we try this and see if it works?
	Recognising the value of the product	Have we done what we set out to do? Have we done a good job? What have we learnt in this lesson?

The computer can be used to explore the exploratory talk in group work, or to summarise the key points from discussion. For example, in a brainstorming session pupils may be asked to put forward ideas as to why something happens. These ideas can be recorded on the group's computer in a word processing package, and in doing so it helps to improve the clarity of thought processes and provides a written focus for discussion. The next stage is to see which ideas fit the available evidence. This can be done by the teacher supplying the information on a new word-processed file, and the pupils looking at each one of their ideas and checking for compatibility with the evidence. In any group discussion it is a good idea to get one member of the group to write down the key points. If a computer is used, it is easy for the group to edit the work and produce a polished product for presentation to other members of the class.

Another approach is for the teacher to provide each group with text that requires modification in some way. The following examples could be used:

- The pupils could be presented with an electronic DART-type exercise
- The pupils could be given some text that contains statements that are correct and some that are incorrect, and asked to decide on what is correct and why
- The pupils could be asked to add to existing text using information they have collected from other sources.

In all of these cases it is possible for pupils to have a print-out of notes that could be useful for revision purposes.

In planning any lesson involving the use of ICT, it is worth bearing in mind the following points:

- Keep pupils sharply focussed on the task in hand through both a clear description of what is required and by support throughout the lesson. A written worksheet or checklist for the pupils is likely to be helpful. Some pupils may find it is easy to move off task.
- Keep reminding yourself that your job is to teach science and not ICT. If it looks as though the technology is taking over and you are spending valuable lesson time trying to help pupils to carry out some sophisticated ICT skill, then stop and consider alternative strategies.
- Make sure that the task you set is within the pupils' ICT capabilities.

There is a recognisable growth in teachers' personal expertise in using the equipment, together with an increased understanding of how it can be used in teaching. Clearly there are many different ways of using ICT in science, and the remainder of this chapter will examine these under the five broad headings proposed by Newton and Rogers (2001: 40):

1 Obtaining knowledge
2 Practice and revision
3 Exploring ideas
4 Collating and recording
5 Presenting and reporting.

Things to consider

What views do members of the science department hold about:

- the value of ICT in helping pupils to learn
- the most appropriate way of organising computers for use in science lessons
- how the use of ICT affects their style of teaching
- the frequency of using ICT in science
- who should be responsible for keeping the department up to date with developments in ICT and the availability of new software?

Obtaining knowledge

Pupils obtaining knowledge from the teacher

There is a growing number of schools where one or two of the science laboratories are equipped with a computer, data projector and, in some instances, an electronic whiteboard. This has opened up the possibilities of using electronic media in the day to day teaching of science. Even in laboratories where data projectors are not available, teachers have been using large monitors or even gathering a class of pupils round the normal computer screen to use some sort of computer-based learning. This type of teaching raises new questions about teacher–pupil–computer interactivity and how to avoid reverting to a didactic teaching mode (Parkinson and Hollamby, 2003). Presentational software, such as PowerPoint, can influence teachers' decision-making about classroom methodology, and can push them in the direction of a lecture-type approach. In order to overcome this, and other problems associated with presentational software, teachers will need to consider the effect it will have on the pupils. Initially there will be the 'wow factor' as the new toy is introduced into the classroom, but it won't be too long before it becomes routine and pupils pay more attention to the content rather than the special effects. Also, the teacher may be initially fired with enthusiasm to work with the new technology, but as time goes on and day to day activities take over it is possible that the machinery will be left to gather dust. Rather than rush into the production of presentations, it is worthwhile thinking about:

- How to use the various features of the software to the best advantage
- How to structure the information so that it builds into an appropriate learning sequence
- How to teach using the software
- What sorts of messages about science are being conveyed through the use of the presentation
- How the teacher's use of ICT with the class can help the pupils to think about how they can use computers for their own learning.

It doesn't take all that long for a teacher to become familiar with the vast array of features available in software such as PowerPoint. In preparing the slide, the same principles apply as those concerned with the preparation of overhead transparencies, i.e.:

- use a clear font with reasonably large letters (no smaller than 18 point)
- do not overcrowd the slide with writing (use spacing and limited text to obtain a clear layout)
- remember that you don't need to put everything down on the slides (you will be talking to the pupils and you may want to use other media to get the best overall effect).

The special features of PowerPoint raise other considerations, and it may be beneficial to follow some of the guidance shown in Table 10.2.

Preparing a sequence of slides is a valuable learning experience for the teacher, as

Table 10.2 *Preparation of slides (Parkinson and Hollamby, 2003)*

Layout	Keep it simple. Avoid too much clutter and text overload. Be selective about what information is placed on the slides.
Background	What looks good on the computer may not look good on a screen. Use a good contrast between the background colour and the font colour, and keep the same background all the time. Be aware that the colour you choose may evoke an emotional response, e.g. red – creative thinking, short-term high energy; green – productivity, long-term energy; yellow/orange – conducive to physical work, exercise, positive moods; blue – slows pulse, lowers blood pressure, helps study and concentration; light colours – provide minimum disruption across all moods and mental activity (Smith, 2001). Black and white tends to cause a short attention span.
Font	Keep mainly to one clear font, e.g. Times New Roman or Comic Sans. Don't use more than two fonts on any one slide. Don't use all capital letters. Remember that italic script is more difficult to read.
Bullets	Avoid 'bullet-itis'. Include no more than four bullet points of text on a single slide. Consider using the 'dim body text' feature, so that only the highlighted bullet point is predominant during your discussion.
Graphics and pictures	Be very selective. A few excellent graphics work better that a number of mediocre ones. Include photographs where relevant.
Sound	Only add sound when it adds an important extra dimension to the text; pupils quickly get bored with trivial sound effects.
Number of slides	Avoid using too many slides. Keep the slide presentations to about 10–15 minutes long.
Transition from slide to slide	Use smooth and simple transitions from one slide to the next. If a slide is a continuation of the last slide, label it as such.
CD-ROM or website	Hyperlinking to a CD-ROM, website or prepared documents in Word and Excel helps to break up the slide show, and can provide additional useful material.
Ending	Whenever possible, finish with a slide that summarises the key points. In any case, it is a good idea to have a slide that shows that it is the end.

he or she has to think carefully through the logic behind the teaching sequence. The teacher also has to consider how this work links to previous work on related topics, and how this can be built into the presentation.

In most cases it is not a good idea to go through a sequence of slides one after another, otherwise you are going to get the same sort of reaction as you would from showing a set of holiday snaps. It is likely that many of the slides will generate class discussion and opportunities for questions. The system has the ability to reveal additional information when required, and can backtrack to previous slides to refresh pupils' memories.

It may be the case that the presentation comes across to the pupils as a series of slides containing bullet-pointed 'facts'. There is the danger here that pupils will receive an image of science as a list of facts to be remembered, and forget about science as being a method of enquiry. The teacher needs to consider what sort of point is being put across on each slide, and how the classroom discussion will lead to an interpretation of the information by the pupils.

There is a golden opportunity when using ICT with a class to show pupils how they can use the technology themselves to learn science. They will pick up many messages subliminally from the way in which the presentation is put together, but there will be times (for example when you divert to the web or a CD-ROM) when you can talk about things such as searching for and selecting information, using information to draw conclusions etc.

Teachers will also use the web and CD-ROMs independently of using presentational software, and in both cases it is a matter of deciding how much information to select and how reliable the source will be when it is needed in the classroom. You obviously don't want to spend valuable teaching time searching for information or waiting for it to download. It is worth considering printing out sections of the text or diagrams for pupils to work on at a suitable time, or emailing the information for pupils to follow up on their own.

The extra dimension brought to presentations by the use of interactive whiteboards creates additional opportunities for teaching. One of the main attractions of these boards is the way in which they can affect the classroom climate. Computer manipulations, writing and data can be carried out directly on the screen. Using a wireless (RF) or infrared mouse or keyboard enables the teacher to work on the board from any position within the classroom. The screen tends to focus pupils' attention, and the images can help to stimulate class discussions. Pupils tend to be enthusiastic and eager to contribute using the electronic pens or the remote control devices. Another one of its stated potential advantages (see Interactive Whiteboards on the Becta website at www.becta.org.uk) is that it can enable pupils who have missed the lesson to catch up by scrolling back to previous lesson files. The following examples illustrate some uses in science:

1 Working with simulation software. For example, with *Crocodile Clips* software (see www.crocodile-clips.com) pupils can build up the apparatus on the board and carry out an electronic practical, perhaps in preparation for carrying out an investigation using real equipment.

2 Using software that contains diagrams or pictures or simply the board's own software or word-processor software. Pupils can label apparatus, parts of the body etc., and produce a flow diagram or chart.[1] They can put symbols in the correct places, complete equations and carry out calculations. Using the dropdown menu in the frames option (under *Insert* in Word), teachers can place a number of optional words as part of a cloze procedure exercise. In other words, pupils can complete an electronic worksheet as a whole class activity.

3 Using the board with its own software or with word-processor software. This can act as a focal point for a brainstorming discussion as a starter activity, or in producing a class-agreed summary of things learnt as a plenary activity. It can also be used in this mode for collating information from a survey or class practical, or as an electronic notebook where various points made during the lesson are recorded and then, at a later date, printed off for the whole class.

4 Working with a word-processor, the teacher can help pupils to structure a piece of writing by showing them where each item of information should be situated within the whole text and illustrating the type of language that should be used.

5 It could be used to teach the techniques of researching a topic by using the Internet.

6 Whiteboards can be used to illustrate how to use certain packages, e.g. the teacher can show how to put formulae into a spreadsheet or discuss with the class the best way of representing the stored data.

7 When data-logging equipment is not available for whole-class practical work, it is possible to carry out a demonstration and interact with the equipment directly through the board.

Pupils obtaining knowledge by themselves

While we may appreciate that encouraging pupils to become more independent learners is a good idea, there are many teachers who are concerned that pupils will not learn what they are supposed to learn. However, computers can help to promote a classroom climate where pupils are willing to take on more responsibility for their own learning (Levine and Donitsa-Schmidt, 1996). The pupils may go off at a tangent, following their own particular interest; give up early and not learn a great deal; or go

---

Things to consider

Review a sample, or all, of the software available in the science department in terms of:

- suitability for the target age range in terms of presentation, language and content
- relevance to the National Curriculum
- the image it portrays of science
- how it helps pupils to learn science.

well beyond the point you want them to reach, making it difficult for you to follow on in a coherent fashion with the whole class. Pupils need to be taught how to learn from the various types of information technologies, and to have a clear indication about what they have to learn. Corbett (1997) suggests that the following may be of use to pupils working on the Internet:

- Worksheets with instructions for pupils to follow. Printed worksheets containing web addresses, together with teachers' notes, are commercially available, e.g. Sang (2000) and Becta (2000).
- Interactive guides where the instructions are web pages themselves.
- Restricting the use of sites to those bookmarked by the teacher.
- Teacher led work, with the teacher 'guiding' the pupils around the site and drawing their attention to key points.
- Question sheets based on the content of web pages.
- Making notes for use at home or class for use in a piece of extended writing, leaflet or poster (care needs to be taken to ensure that pupils don't simply copy the information from the screen and regurgitate it in their own written work).

Similar sorts of guidance may be required for pupils working from CD-ROMs if they do not contain any sort of stimulus that prompts the pupil into action. Just like reading a book or watching the television, pupils can see everything that is there but they will not internalise it unless they have to do something with the information. Multimedia packages can use a combination of still and animated graphics, sound and video to produce an all-round interesting and valuable piece of software that requires a significant amount of pupil interaction. They can be used to teach about topics where first-hand experience is likely to be difficult or impossible, such as industrial processes, space exploration and the investigation of certain biological processes. A study of the internal organs of animals no longer requires dissection, as there are software packages available that illustrate all that is required. In a study of university pharmacology students, Sewell *et al.* (1995) found that multimedia software concerned with the heart and muscle function of the frog was received enthusiastically by the students and that their final understanding of the topic was good.

The number of pupils with access to computers in the home is increasing all the time. At present 60–70 per cent of all pupils have home computers, but in more affluent areas this increases to 85 per cent or more (Kennewell *et al.*, 2000; Sutherland *et al.*, 2000; Becta, 2001). Playing games is the largest area of use for both boys and girls, and is slightly more popular with boys. Girls tend to spend more time emailing friends (Mumtaz, 2001). However, all children spend a significant amount of time on the sort of activities that we want them to use in school. Kennewell *et al.* (2000) found the breakdown of use to be: word-processing (82 per cent); retrieving data from a CD-ROM (64 per cent); revision programs (44 per cent); and Internet use (26 per cent). Teachers are faced with the problem of having to deal with two groups of pupils: those who have computers at home, are confident in carrying out procedures and generally see the benefit of computer use in everyday life, and those who have no computer at home and tend to be anxious about using computers in school. You may see it as part of your job as a teacher to encourage pupils to use ICT, and may set homework tasks based on the use of a computer. This doesn't seem to be an unreasonable request, as in most schools there are opportunities for pupils to use computers at lunchtime and after school. In addition to the usual tasks of asking pupils to find things out or prepare a piece of written work, it is possible to supply them with electronic copies of Power-Point presentations that have been used in lessons so that they can work through things themselves and perhaps use the information to complete a linked electronic worksheet.

Practice and revision

Revision books, software and Internet sites appear to be a growth industry. As mentioned elsewhere (page 214), there is a danger that this 'drill and practice' approach can lead to shallow learning and an image of science that is one of a list of facts to be remembered. Having said that, most of the software packages are excellently presented and fun to do, and it would be wrong to dismiss them out of hand. It is a good idea to look at a variety of packages and incorporate them into the teaching schedule from time to time. For the most part, these exercises are designed for individual pupils working on a computer by themselves. The Integrated Learning Systems (ILS) are, perhaps, the ultimate version of this type of program, as the linked management system is able to monitor a pupil's responses and provide individualised programs to meet the pupil's needs. However, even at this level of sophistication there are still doubts over the benefits for pupils (Wood, 1998).

Things to consider

How do members of the science department ensure that pupils don't waste time during sessions on (1) using the Internet to locate information, and (2) locating graphics when preparing a poster?

Exploring ideas

Exploring ideas with others through the use of the Internet

This type of approach matches the principles of the Knowledge Integration Environment mentioned at the start of this chapter. It has the potential to create situations that enable pupils to connect science concepts and develop a deeper understanding of scientific phenomena.

In the previous sections we have looked at group discussions within the classroom; now we will go on to look at how the Internet and email can open up the possibilities of holding discussions about science with:

- pupils in other schools, both in the UK and across the world
- scientists and science-based organisations.

Mistler-Jackson and Songer (2000) studied a group of 11–12-year-old pupils who were being taught about the weather. The pupils were in schools throughout North America, and the first stage of the project was for them to introduce themselves through email. The next step involved small groups selecting a focus for their study from one of the topics, such as clouds/humidity, precipitation, and pressure/temperature. The pupils then collected local weather data, identified patterns, and shared their results with others studying the same topic in different locations. They were also able to use real-time satellite maps, investigate severe weather and environmental issues, and communicate with professional meteorologists. In the final phase, the pupils applied their understanding through data comparisons and made predictions of current weather events. Towards the end of this phase the group shared personal stories and expertise through an on-line newspaper. The researchers found that pupils who were initially poorly motivated became keen to spend time working on the project. One of the key reasons for this appears to be the increase in self-esteem generated by being part of a project where their voices were valued and respected, thereby allowing them to view themselves as capable participants of the new learning. While weather is not part of the Science National Curriculum at present, the topic opens up the possibility of cross-curricular work with the geography department, linking it to work on artificial satellites (KS4). Other topics, such as those concerned with the environment or health, readily lend themselves to this type of approach. The ASE-based *Science Across the World* project helps to bring together schools in different countries that are keen to work on joint activities. Exchanging information can have the additional benefit of raising pupils' awareness of global issues, and thus make an important contribution to citizenship education.

Interpreting graphs

ICT has the potential to help pupils understand graphs through the various types of software that offer graphical display. Published exercises in graph interpretation (e.g. Goldsworthy *et al.*, 1999; Bell, 2002) frequently contain electronic versions of exercises along with their paper-based equivalent. Simulation software can simultaneously show the macroscopic situation and the microscopic situation, and plot the change taking place graphically. Graphs can be obtained from information in databases and spreadsheets, and also through the use of data-logging. As pointed out by Rogers (1995) and Barton (1997), computer-aided graphing removes the tedium of having to draw the graph manually and provides more time for studying the interpretation of the data. Barton's research also indicates the importance of asking pupils to make sketch graph predictions prior to plotting the data, and then to discuss why their prediction did or did not match the computer-generated graph. While a case for paper-based graphs can still be argued, their days may be numbered as computer graphs offer the opportunity for pupils to develop higher order skills of evaluating and predicting without having to go through the laborious plotting process.

Exploring through simulations and modelling

A computer simulation is a program that contains a model of a system – e.g. human respiratory system, the particulate nature of matter, the stages of an industrial process. The dynamic and often interactive nature of the computer-based simulation frequently makes it more useful in explaining phenomena than other types of simulation. However, the situation is far from perfect, and pupils may sometimes have difficulties in relating what they see on the computer screen to real-life situations. In a review of literature on the effect of simulation-based learning on examination results, de Jong and van Joolingen (1998) noted that there is no clear outcome in favour of simulations. In many cases the pupils are unable to make the required gain in knowledge because they are unable to bridge the gap between reality and the simulation. Each situation will therefore require prompting and guidance from the teacher to help the pupils develop the relationship (Roth *et al.*, 1996).

In a study of university students in the USA, Williamson and Abraham (1995) looked at the students' understanding of the particulate nature of matter in relation to chemical phenomena. They found that all the students who had seen the simulations as part of the lectures on the topic, and those who had personal experience of the program, had increased conceptual understanding of the topic, in comparison to a control group who had only used visuals such as transparencies and diagrams on the board. While this is fine for university students, secondary teachers need to be aware that many pupils believe that the properties at the macroscopic level represent the properties at the microscopic level (Anderson, 1990). Simulation images can look so 'real' that they lead some pupils to conclude that what they see on the screen represents a scaled version of reality. This can result in confirmation of pupils' misconceptions – for example, that individual particles of a substance are coloured (Harrison and Treagust, 2000).

A study of 15-year-old pupils carried out in Israel looked at the role of simulation in promoting understanding of electrical circuits (Ronen and Eliahu, 2000). They found that the use of the simulation contributed to pupils' confidence and enhanced their motivation to stay on task. The software also helped pupils to realise their misconceptions and correct them. In addition, the manipulation of the simulated models may have contributed to the pupils' ability to produce a correct diagram representing the real circuit.

A number of pieces of software, e.g. *Crocodile Clips* and *Science Investigations*, enable pupils to carry out computer-based 'experiments' which can help them in the planning of real practical work. They can also provide the pupils with a set of results to evaluate and analyse without having to deal with the complexities of the physical apparatus.

However, the major drawbacks to this sort of approach as alternative to practical work are that:

- pupils are working in a 'perfect' world where nothing can go wrong, and therefore they fail to appreciate significant aspects that are important in real practical work
- pupils miss out on practical skill development and the experiences that motivate some pupils to go on to study science at a higher level
- it conveys a message to pupils that science is about carrying out tried and tested routines rather than about investigating situations.

Computer-based modelling is concerned with pupils trying out different possibilities to answer the question 'what if?'. Some simulation software enables these sorts of exercises to be carried out, where pupils are able to alter variables and study the outcome – e.g. heat loss from a house, the dynamics of a predator–prey relationship, electronic versions of usual class-based investigations. Spreadsheets allow pupils to investigate mathematical relationships between variables by the introduction of different formulae – e.g. the ratio of volume to surface area in modelling heat loss from animals or respiration in plants. As a teacher, you will have to consider when the complexity of the mathematics begins to hide the planned learning outcomes of the science. As with other examples of modelling, it is worthwhile devoting some class time to discussing the validity of the model and the importance and limitations of using modelling in science. In his review of the effective use of computers, Thomas (2001) identifies computer modelling as an important component of science teaching, particularly when the deficiencies or strengths of the models embedded in the software are elaborated on.

Exploring through concept mapping and concept cartoons

Concept mapping (see page 244) helps pupils to think through their understanding of science topics and recognise the links between different concepts. Traditionally it is carried out by groups of pupils, or pupils working on their own, using paper and pencil. Software, e.g. *Inspiration* (see www.inspiration.com) is now available to enable pupils to carry out the same processes on a computer screen. The advantages of using a computer-based approach are that it is easy for the pupil to modify and update the concept map, and the product is neat and easy to read.

Concept cartoons (see page 242) are also available in electronic format (see http://www.conceptcartoons.com/index_flash.html). The speech bubbles can be left empty for the pupils to write in their ideas, or they can be filled with text supplied by the authors. In either case, the cartoon acts as a stimulus for group discussion.

Both of these packages can be used with an electronic whiteboard, enabling the teacher to hold whole-class discussions around the computer screen.

Collating and recording

Using databases

There are many different sorts of databases available to teachers, both on CD-ROM and on the Internet. Common ones in use include those containing information on the elements, planets, and nutritional values. The search mechanisms are almost invariably very easy, and pupils have no difficulty in finding the information they require. In order to provide some sort of intellectual challenge, it is necessary to consider what the pupils should do with the data in terms of looking for trends or relationships. The first stage might be to try to interpret what the data actually means, particularly in circumstances where the numerical values are far from the pupils' everyday experiences. The next step could be to get pupils to interpret or use the data in a scientific way. In a study of Australian pupils using a computerised database on *Birds of Antarctica*, Maor and Fraser (1994) found that the activity had enabled pupils to focus on their problem-solving techniques. Working with this authentic database had promoted the development of inquiry skills such as analysing relationships, discovering commonalities or differences between groups and events, and looking for patterns or trends.

In order to help pupils understand how scientists collect and record information, it is useful to get pupils to produce their own simple databases. This can be done by looking at group data on related aspects of a class investigation, or pupils can construct a modification of an existing database. This gives pupils an insight into data collection and the importance of consistency in presentation.

Using spreadsheets

In most instances pupils will be presented with spreadsheets already containing data (e.g. from pre-prepared worksheets or through data-logging), but there will be times when it is appropriate for pupils to enter data themselves. This is a useful exercise because it prompts pupils to think about units and scale and how to deal with non-numeric data.

Using data-logging

In a study of teachers' views about the use of data-logging, carried out by Newton (2000), it was found that in spite of some teachers' relative enthusiasm for using the technology, there were a number of problems associated with its implementation. The first is concerned with teachers' confidence in being able to operate the system and deal with it when it malfunctions. Familiarisation takes time, and if the system is not used frequently the method of operating will have to be re-learnt each time it is used. The other major issue is concerned with the technical complexity of the task, which, if high, can reduce the accessibility for pupils. Newton suggests that simple data-logging activities are more likely to win teachers' support, and that greater emphasis should be given to interpreting the data rather than the data-logging activity itself.

Presenting and reporting

As mentioned earlier in this chapter, word-processing can help pupils to think. Pupils should be encouraged to jot things down in note form as they work in groups or as individuals in order to help them to clarify their understanding. The jottings can be refined and compiled in a more acceptable form if they are required for presentation to the whole class or the teacher.

Pupils on the whole tend to be competent at word-processing and desktop publishing, but they often find it difficult to know what to write. In order to help them, teachers usually produce templates or writing frames containing clues as to what to write about in each section. Sometimes it is appropriate to include images such as digital photographs (e.g. of apparatus used or location visited), scanned images, graphics or clip art. Pupils can waste a considerable amount of time searching for these images and contemplating how they can best fit into their work. Teachers may consider supplying pupils with a limited range of artwork from which to choose, and asking pupils to carry out some preliminary planning about design and layout away from the computer so that they can concentrate on the presentation of the science concepts during the lesson. In order to minimise time wasting on trivia, the teacher may consider setting strict time constraints. One way of doing this is for the teacher to tell pupils that they are writing a report for the local newspaper and that a deadline has to be met.

Things to consider

The science National Curriculum (DfEE, 1999) for KS3 recommends the use of ICT for the following:

Sc1
- data-handling software with fieldwork data (2d page 28)
- data-handling software to create, analyse and evaluate charts and graphs (2j page 29)

Sc2
- simulation software to model changes in populations of bacteria in different conditions (2n page 31)
- use of sensors to record or simulation software to model factors that affect photosynthesis (3a page 31)
- simulations to explore toxic materials in food chains (5f page 31)

Sc3
- use of the Internet to find up to date information about environmental issues (2i page 33)
- use of video or CD-ROM to see reactions that are dangerous issues (3a page 33)

Sc4
- use of video or CD-ROM to study the solar system (4a, c, e page 35)
- use of the Internet to find up to date information about energy resources (5a, c page 35).

Does your department follow these recommendations?

Problems with computers

Unfortunately we have all had to deal with situations where the computers have not been working or the Internet has been down. These are the sorts of situations that put you off using computers for life. However, until the computers become totally reliable (which will probably never happen), teachers need to have some sort of back-up plan.

Another potential problem is that of the easy availability of 'unsuitable' sites. According to Lawson and Comber (2000), the main strategies used by schools to combat the issue are:

- restricting access to supervised sessions
- using filtering software
- using AUP (acceptable use policies) strategies
- virtual surveillance strategies.

Each strategy has drawbacks, and it may be that there are sites you want to use but can't because of the restrictions imposed. In cases like this, and when the Internet connection is unreliable, you need to consider if it is appropriate to download the site from your home computer onto a CD-ROM.

Most of us at one time or another have been worried about who has actually done a piece of work. Significant amounts of help might have come from a parent, a private tutor, or someone trying to make a fast buck somewhere out there on the web. Increasingly pupils are encouraged to use ICT for their coursework, and some pupils are taking advantage of this situation to plagiarise other people's work. Very little research has been carried out regarding the issues of dishonesty, plagiarism and cheating in connection with ICT. Pupils of all ages tend to regard cheating in coursework as less serious than cheating in formal examinations. Some pupils don't see it as dishonest at all to provide fellow pupils with work to copy; they see it more as a sign of friendship and helping one another to save time. Clearly teachers aren't getting the right sort of messages across, and pupils are putting themselves in danger of having the marks from all their papers cancelled. In research carried out into plagiarism of coursework, Williams (2001) identified four main strategies being used to combat the problem. One approach was the development of a culture of honesty amongst the pupils. Teachers emphasised the nature of cheating, and the importance of self-respect and taking pride in your own work. They also pointed out the negative aspects of being found out, and the public shame that the pupils would be exposed to. Another approach was based on the fact that many of the teachers knew their pupils very well and were able to recognise anything that was at a level beyond the pupil's normal contribution. A third technique was to ask the pupils to produce a first draft or plan by hand in class. The teacher would collect these, mark them and return them to the pupils, who then continued to develop the piece of work over time. The teacher would see and comment on it several times during the process, and for the final product the whole series of drafts would also be submitted. The fourth method involved the teacher talking to the pupil at various stages about the development of the piece of work to determine whether the work had been fully understood. Clearly this is a significant problem, and teachers at all levels need to look at a variety of approaches to combat cheating.

Information for teachers

As well as using ICT to prepare worksheets and maintain records, teachers can use the technology to support them in their professional development through Internet sites such as those listed in Table 10.3. Chat rooms and discussion groups now provide teachers with the opportunity to discuss any aspect of science teaching with colleagues in other schools. Such networks have been operating successfully in the USA for a number of years (Muscella and Dimauro, 1995), providing teachers with a platform for electronic conversations. More recently in the UK, an active discussion group based loosely around 'learning science concepts' provides a forum for discussion on topics ranging from the optimum arrangement of laboratory benches to Piagetian levels (see http://uk.groups.yahoo.com/group/learning-science-concepts).

Table 10.3 *Some useful websites for teachers (NB: website addresses may change from time to time)*

http://www.dfes.gov.uk/index.htm	DfES
http://www.becta.org.uk/index.cfm	Becta – advice and help about using ICT in schools
http://vtc.ngfl.gov.uk/resource/cits/science/ideas.html	Ideas for using ICT in science teaching
http://www.ofsted.gov.uk/	Ofsted and inspection reports
http://www.canteach.gov.uk/home.htm	Teacher Training Agency
http://www.ase.org.uk/	Association for Science Education
http://www.rsc.org	The Royal Society of Chemistry
http://www.chemsoc.org	
http://www.iop.org/	Institute of Physics
http://www.iob.org/	Institute of Biology

Things to consider

- To what extent is good practice in the use of ICT shared between staff within the department and the different departments within the school?
- Is the science department aware of the availability of computers in pupils' homes?
- How can the department make use of this availability?
- To what extent do you see it as a science teacher's job to improve pupils' ICT capability?

References

Anderson, B. (1990) 'Pupils' conceptions of matter and its transformation (age 12–16)', *Studies in Science Education*, **18**, 53–85.

Barton, R. (1997) 'Computer-aided graphing: a comparative study', *Journal of Information Technology for Teacher Education*, **6**(1), 59–72.

Becta (2000) *Science On Line: Practical Ideas about Using the World Wide Web*, Coventry: Becta.

Becta (2001) *Home–School Links and ICT* (available on the Becta website, www.becta.org.uk).

Becta (2002) *Connecting Schools: Networking People*, Coventry: Becta.

Bell, S. (2002) *Speak To Me Graph*, Hatfield: ASE.

Churach, D. and Fisher, D. (2001) 'Science students surf the web: effects on constructivist classroom environments', *Journal of Computers in Mathematics and Science Teaching*, **20**(2), 221–247.

Corbett, A. (1997) 'Unleashing the power of the Internet as a Classroom Learning Tool,' *Computer Education*, **85**, 14–17.

de Jong, T. and van Joolingen, W.R. (1998) 'Scientific discovery learning with computer simulations of conceptual domains', *Review of Educational Research*, **68**(2), 179–201.

DfEE (1999) *The National Curriculum for England: Science*, London: DfEE/QCA.

Fullan, M. (1993) *Change Forces: Probing the Depths of Educational Reform*, London: Falmer Press.

Gardner, M., Morrison, H., Jarman, R., Reilly, C. and McNally, H. (1994) *Personal Portable Computers and the Curriculum*, Scottish Council for Research in Education.

Goldsworthy, A., Watson, R. and Wood-Robinson, V. (1999) *Getting to Grips with Graphs*, Hatfield: ASE.

Harris, S. (1998) 'What TIMMS tells us about the use of computers in mathematics and science in secondary schools', *Computer Education*, **90**, 3–6.

Harrison, A.G. and Treagust, D.F. (2000) 'Learning about atoms, molecules, and chemical bonds: a case study of multiple-model use in Grade II chemistry', *Science Education*, **84**(3), 352–381.

Harrison, C., Comber, C., Fisher, T. *et al.* (2002) *Impact2: The Impact of Information and Communications Technologies on Pupil Learning and Attainment*, Coventry: Becta (available at http://www.becta.org.uk/research/impact2/index.cfm).

Hoyles, C., Healy, L. and Pozzi, S. (1994) 'Groupwork with computers: an overview of findings', *Journal of Computer Assisted Learning*, **10**, 202–215.

Jackson, A. and Kutnick, P. (1996) 'Groupwork and computers: task type and children's performance', *Journal of Computer Assisted Learning*, **12**, 162–171.

Kennewell, S., Parkinson, J. and Tanner, H. (2000) *Developing the ICT Capable School*, London: RoutledgeFalmer.

Lawson, T. and Comber, C. (2000) 'Censorship, the Internet and schools: a new moral panic?', *The Curriculum Journal*, **11**(2), 273–285.

Levine, T. and Donitsa-Schmidt, S. (1996) 'Classroom environment in computer-integrated science classes: effects of gender and computer ownership', *Research in Science & Technology Education*, **14**(2), 163–178.

Linn, M.C. (2000) 'Designing the Knowledge Integration Environment', *International Journal of Science Education*, **22**(8), 781–796.

McFarlane, A. and Sakellariou, S. (2002) 'The role of ICT in science education', *Cambridge Journal of Education*, **32**(2), 219–232.

Maor, D. and Fraser, B. (1994) 'An evaluation of an inquiry-based computer-assisted learning environment', *Australian Science Teachers Journal*, **40**(4), 65–70.

Mercer, N. (1994) 'The quality of talk in children's joint activity on the computer', *Journal of Computer Assisted Learning*, **10**, 24–32.

Mistler-Jackson, M. and Songer, N.B. (2000) 'Student motivation and Internet technology: Are students empowered to learn science?', *Journal of Research in Science Teaching*, **37**(5), 459–479.

Mumtaz, S. (2001) 'Children's enjoyment and perception of computer use in the home and the school', *Computers & Education*, **36**, 347–362.

Muscella, D. and Dimauro, V. (1995) 'Talking about science: the case of electronic conversation', *Journal of Information Technology for Teacher Education*, **4**(2), 165–181.

Newton, L.R. (2000) 'Data-logging in practical science: research and reality', *International Journal of Science Education*, **22**(12), 1247–1259.

Newton, L.R. and Rogers, L. (2001) *Teaching Science with ICT*, London: Continuum.

Ofsted (2002) *Secondary Subject Reports 2000/01: Science*, London: HMSO.

Parkinson, J. and Hollamby, P. (2003) 'PowerPoint: just another slide show or a useful learning aid?', *School Science Review*, **84**(309), 61–68.

Robinson, M. (1994) 'Using email and the Internet in science teaching', *Journal of Information Technology for Teacher Education*, **3**(2), 229–238.

Rogers, L.T. (1995) 'The computer as an aid to exploring graphs', *School Science Review*, **76**(276), 31–39.

Ronen, M. and Eliahu, M. (2000) 'Simulation – a bridge between theory and reality: the case of electric circuits', *Journal of Computer Assisted Learning*, **16**, 14–26.

Roth, W.-M., Woszczyna, C. and Smith, G. (1996) 'Affordances and constraints of computers in science education', *Journal of Research in Science Teaching*, **33**(9), 995–1017.

Sang, D. (ed.) (2000) *Science @ www: Getting Started*, ASE: Hatfield.

Sewell, R.D.E., Stevens, R.G. and Lewis, D.J.A. (1995) 'Multimedia computer technology as a tool for teaching and assessment of biological science', *Journal of Biological Education*, **29**(1), 27–32.

Smith (2001) *Accelerated Learning in Practice*, Stafford: Network Educational Press.

Sutherland, R., Facer, K., Furlong, R. and Furlong, J. (2000) 'A new environment for education? The computer in the home', *Computers & Education*, **34**, 195–212.

Thomas, G.P. (2001) 'Toward effective computer use in high school science education: Where to from here?', *Education and Information Technologies*, **6**(1), 29–41.

Watson, D.M. (ed.) (1993) *The ImpacT Report: An Evaluation of the Impact of Information Technology on Children's Achievements in Primary and Secondary Schools*, London: Kings College.

Wegerif, R. (1996) 'Collaborative learning and directive software', *Journal of Computer Assisted Learning*, **12**, 22–32.

Wild, M. (1996) 'Investigating verbal interactions when primary children use computers', *Journal of Computer Assisted Learning*, **12**, 66–77.

Wild, M. and Braid, P. (1996) 'Children's talk in co-operative groups', *Journal of Computer Assisted Learning*, **12**(4), 216–231.

Williams, S. (2001) 'How do I know if they're cheating? Teacher strategies in an information age', *The Curriculum Journal*, **12**(2), 225–239.

Williamson, V.M. and Abraham, M.R. (1995) 'The effects of computer animation on the particulate mental models of college chemistry students', *Journal of Research in Science Teaching*, **32**(5), 521–534.

Wood, D. (1998) *The UK ILS Evaluation; Final Report*, Coventry: Becta.

CHAPTER 11

Learning through written and oral work

Teachers with any class must be careful to check that 'obvious' words have a meaning which is shared by pupils and teachers. For classes with an ethnic mix, this procedure has to be more carefully applied. Explanations in pupils' own words should be encouraged, to avoid mere 'parroting' of rote-memorised, teacher language. In this way pupils and teachers can arrive at a shared meaning.

(Johnstone and Selepong, 2001: 26)

Looking back over the last 20 years or so of science teaching there have been a number of ideas that were fashionable for a short time and then, for one reason or another, disappeared. The issue of language and its relation to learning first came to prominence in the late 1960s with the work of Barnes *et al.* (1969), who looked at spoken and written language in a variety of classrooms. This was quickly followed by a DES publication, the Bullock Report (1975), which made a large number of recommendations, including the establishment of the post of school co-ordinator for language across the curriculum. While it seemed an excellent idea at the time, even those schools that created such a post soon found that it had to be abandoned because of the difficulties in obtaining a common approach to language development across the subject specialisms. In the early 1980s the Schools Council (an early incarnation of QCA) produced guidance for science teachers on the use of reading activities for pupils (Davies and Greene, 1984; Lunzer and Gardner, 1984). This led to the birth of the so-called DART (Directed Activities Related to Text) activities. These came in a variety of forms, from the simple cloze procedure to annotating and analysing a piece of text. Science textbooks at this time were considerably more wordy than those available now, and it was easy to find pages of text that could be used as the basis for a DART exercise involving the location of key items of information. Pupils could then reformulate the information to produce a piece of their own writing. The ASE-produced SATIS (Science and Technology in Society) materials which contained examples of DART exercises, along with other activities to promote learning through language. However, resources of this type were sparse and, apart from a few books written to promote pupils' reading of science (e.g. Berry and Kellington, 1986), teachers were left to produce their own resources. Many science textbooks have retained short cloze procedure exercises, and these are also a common feature of school-produced workbooks. There are various versions of these exercises, ranging from no clues at all to providing pupils with one or two letters to help them to 'guess' the word. There are even electronic versions that confirm that the correct word has been placed in the gap. In many cases pupils work on their own to complete these tasks, and they often end up guessing the missing word. The final product may be a piece of writing that is useful as a note for revision, but it could be argued that, as a learning activity, it makes little demand on the pupil.

A fresh impetus to language and learning was given in the early 1990s through the production of *Active Teaching and Learning Approaches in Science* (Harrison, 1992). Like the earlier Schools Council work, it was based on the principle that in order for pupils to learn they have to be actively involved in the learning process. Little (if any) learning is likely to occur if pupils are simply passive recipients of information from the teacher, television, book or any other knowledge base. The author suggested that active learning can have significant gains (Harrison, 1992: 6):

> Active learning techniques frequently can enable students to attain a higher level of understanding in science than with more traditional passive learning approaches. The key to this is a sense of ownership and personal involvement that active learning creates. Students see their work as important because **they** feel important and **their** ideas and findings are valued. Student satisfaction is enhanced and there is greater motivation.

The book is a rich source of ideas for group discussions, active reading and writing, pupil presentations, games and simulations etc. comprising guidance for teachers and sample activities for pupils.

The information we have about current classroom practice comes from classroom observations by researchers and the completion of questionnaires by teachers indicating the frequency of use of certain activities. Observational studies indicate that classroom discourse is largely teacher dominated, and consists of teachers either telling pupils what to do or providing them with explanations (Sands, 1981; Newton *et al.*, 1999; Galton, 2002). In a survey looking at teachers' ratings of the frequency of use of activities, group discussion work was placed fairly high but role play and drama were rarely used (Donnelly, 2000). This does not agree with the findings of Newton *et al.* (1999), who found that 'group discussion was notable by its absence'. The discrepancy could possibly be explained by different understandings of 'group discussion'. Some teachers might think of group work as any activity where pupils' work together on a task, with practical work being the most common example used in science lessons.

In summary, the ideas about the use of language in science lessons have been bubbling away in the background for many years but have never really taken off and made the impact that they should have done. Why should it happen now?

Grasping the moment

There are three strong arguments for giving greater emphasis to language work than has been the case in the past. We now have a greater understanding of pupils' misconceptions, and have begun to appreciate the need for pupils to talk about their understanding of scientific phenomena. The principles of socio-constructivism are incorporated into the QCA SoW in many of the topics in terms of elucidating prior knowledge and providing activities to get pupils talking about science. Talking is also a prominent feature of the starter activities suggested in the KS3 National Strategy for Science. It may be the case that some of the misconceptions held by pupils arise, and then become embedded, as a result of confusion over the language used during the initial explanation given by the teacher (Clerk and Rutherford, 2000). Teachers need to ensure that pupils fully understand the words they are using and consider how this aspect of language inter-relates with strategies they might adopt to bring about conceptual change.

If pupils are to gain a thorough understanding of a science concept, they must be given the opportunity to use the language associated with that concept in a variety of situations. We cannot assume that a pupil will take 'on board' what the teacher has said and go through the process of internalising the knowledge simply by completing a 'filling in the gaps' exercise or carrying out some other low-level task. A report on the KS3 tests indicates the increased emphasis on language skills:

> There were opportunities this year [2002] for more extended written responses. Generally, the ability to generate continuous prose in relation to scientific facts has improved but needs further attention.
>
> More care needs to be taken by all pupils to read the question carefully, think, formulate their ideas, and select their words before writing a response.
>
> (ACCAC, 2002)

The second argument relates to the introduction of national literacy strategies into primary and secondary schools. As pointed out by McKeon (2000), an enormous amount of work is being devoted to the development of literacy skills in primary schools, and much of this is potentially very useful for learning science. She goes on to provide the following examples from the strategy that have a direct bearing on secondary science work:

- pupils use dictionaries to check the meaning of words, particularly words that have one meaning in everyday conversations and another meaning in science
- primary teachers provide pupils with the opportunity for using words in a variety of contexts in order to help them mentally construct their meaning
- pupils learn how to locate information from a variety of sources, e.g. books, Internet etc.
- pupils carry out exercises that help them to learn how to summarise information by recognising important elements in the original text
- pupils learn how to identify the strengths and weaknesses of different points of view
- pupils learn about different writing styles and an appreciation of the sense of audience.

Some schools may occasionally choose science texts as the context for the Literacy Hour, for example using Nuffield Primary Science (1996). The purpose of these is to introduce pupils to a scientific style of writing and methods of analysing text. Pupils may learn some science through the text, but the main aim is to provide them with skills that can be used in their science lessons (Peacock, 2001). The introduction of Key Stage 3 National Literacy Strategy (DfES, 2001) reintroduced the principle of a whole-school approach to raising the standard of pupils' use of language. The strategy was introduced to combat the significant literacy problem that exists across the whole of the UK. The DfES has produced a substantial amount of material to support this pro-gramme, including:

- an INSET pack with audio CD and accompanying video
- six 'Literacy Progress Units', covering *Spelling*, *Writing organisation*, *Information retrieval*, *Reading between the lines* (using inference and deduction in interpreting liter-ary texts), *Phonics* and *Sentences*, designed to support teachers in providing addi-tional help for pupils who are falling below the expected standard.

The third argument for taking a fresh look at language work is that more and more people are recognising its importance in pupils' learning. The National Curriculum, the QCA SoW and many of the new science books concerned with the teaching of Scientific Enquiry mention the need for key literacy skills. While looking at good prac-tice in science teaching, Estyn (2001: 2) noted the contribution language work can make to learning.

Things to consider

The introduction of any new government initiative usually results in the publication of a large number of new resources. Not unnaturally, teachers rush to buy them, hoping that they will solve all their problems and save them a considerable amount of preparation time. While many of these resources are likely to be of excellent quality, there is a danger that whole-scale adoption might lead to a piecemeal approach to liter-acy across the school. 'Off the shelf' items alone are unlikely to achieve the goals of language for learning. Commitment and a fully integrated approach across the school are important ingredients for success.

- To what extent does the science department liaise with the co-ordinator of the KS3 literacy strategy within the school?
- To what extent does the science department meet the statements made in the school policy on literacy?
- How can the science department make best use of pupils' growing expertise in literacy?

Pupils achieve good standards when they think rigorously about scientific concepts and communicate their ideas by speaking and writing. The quality of their thinking has a major influence on the standards they achieve in all aspects of their work in science.

There is a strong link between high standards in science and good application of pupils' key skills of listening, speaking, reading and writing. Plans for good science lessons identify opportunities to develop and apply these key skills.

Words

How do pupils come to understand the meaning of words used in science? If they are introduced to a new word in a modern foreign language lesson, they will hear it used many times by the teacher and then will have the opportunity to use it themselves, perhaps in paired work or as part of a whole-class activity. This rarely happens in science, even though some of the words used have complex meanings. Sometimes science teachers are guilty of using words incorrectly, with the classic example being phrases such as 'the weight of this object is 2g'. It is all too easy to slip into everyday language use, but teachers need to be aware that using words like 'power', 'energy' and 'molecule' in sentences that are scientifically incorrect can cause confusion.

However, it is not just scientific vocabulary that is a barrier to pupils' learning; there are also major problems with pupils' understanding of non-technical words. Cassels and Johnstone (1985) carried out a large-scale study of pupils' understanding of words that are commonly used in discussions about science but do not have a special place in scientific vocabulary. Table 11.1 lists the main words that caused problems for pupils. In some cases the level of understanding was so low that it would have been impossible for any pupil to have understood a science concept where these words were used. Other more recent studies show very similar results (Pickersgill and Lock, 1991; Prophet and Towse, 1999). The work carried out by Prophet and Towse compared pupils whose first language was English with pupils who were second-language English speakers. Understandably, there were considerable differences between the two populations. For example, approximately 82 per cent of first-language English-speaking Y7 pupils understood the word 'dehydrate', but only about 39 per cent of the second-language pupils understood the word. Many pupils also have difficulty in understanding the meaning of some everyday words, such as 'thus', 'essentially', 'conversely', 'in practice' and 'moreover'. Research carried out in the 1970s by Gardner (1975) indicated that of a group of 200 logical connective words, less than 70 per cent of secondary-age pupils were able to use them correctly. Byrne *et al.* (1994) carried out a further study based on a sample of 14-year-old pupils, and found that many of them had difficulties in using logical connectives and that these were exacerbated when pupils were required to use them in scientific contexts. Teachers frequently use logical connective words when explaining things to pupils, and there is clearly a danger that some pupils may not understand the logic being applied. This has massive implications for schools where there are a significant number of EAL children (see page 138). One obvious way of helping pupils is to question them to ensure that they

Table 11.1 *Difficult non-technical words used in science (Cassels and Johnstone, 1985; Prophet and Towse, 1999)*

Word	Some pupils' understanding of the word
abundant	scarce, shortage, poor supply
accumulate	take from, use up, accommodate, calculate
adjacent	opposite
complex	natural, simple, clever
component	pupils guessed at the meaning
composition	*how* it is made, forcing together
conception	generally unsure about the meaning
constant	generally poor understanding
constituent	equated with words to which it is normally attached, e.g. mixture
contract	get larger, become longer, become slacker
contrast	contract, similar
converse	imprecise understanding
emit	mixed up with omit and admit
excess	essential, very good, except, dilute
exert	urge, exempt, exit
immerse	float, wipe with oil, coat
initial	with greatest care, best effort, crucial, final
linear	liner, linen, ascending, descending
negligible	most important, great, negligent, a lot
omit	put in, collect in, repeat, finish off
random	appeared regularly, well ordered
relevant	imprecise understanding
sequence	sequel, planning
spontaneous	quick, vigorous, steady, loud
stimulate	end, slow down, deactivate, smother
tabulate	interpret, allocate, solve, construct
valid	no pattern of responses

have understood, but there is also a strong argument for providing pupils with the opportunity to use these types of words in their own writing.

Wellington and Osborne (2001) have proposed a taxonomy of words that are used in science teaching. This is useful in drawing teachers' attention to the range of difficulties that can be experienced by pupils. Such a classification could be used in considering when to introduce pupils to new words and in helping them to think about how to explain meaning.

There are many ideas for helping pupils to spell and understand the meaning of words as they are used in science (see Figures 11.1, 11.2). It is obviously important to keep stressing the meaning of words and their correct use in science, but there also needs to be freshness in the way that it is done. Being over repetitive with a technique or using a method that is inappropriate for the age range is not going to work. Word walls are an effective way of reminding pupils of new words and their spelling (see Table 11.2) but, as suggested by Ford and Versey (2001), it is best to restrict the display to the topic being taught at the time, and for the teacher to use the display regularly during lessons.

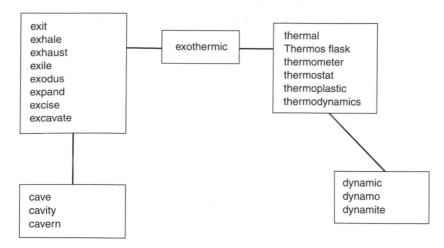

Figure 11.1 *A word web*

Figure 11.2 *A calligram for pressure*

Talking in groups

There are many possible explanations for the lack of group work carried out in science. Some teachers may not see group work as a natural way of teaching the subject. They may say that it is fine for subjects such as English and history, where pupils' opinions are sought, but less appropriate for science, where we tend to deal with a lot of facts. Other teachers may not use group work because they feel insecure in a lesson where they are not controlling what is happening from the front of the classroom. They may say that you can never be sure of what is going to emerge from a group discussion. There will also be teachers who say that they are unhappy about using group work because of the amount of time it takes. They may say that you can get the same results by providing the pupils with the information through teacher explanation, or by pupils reading about the topic in a textbook.

Table 11.2 *Some ideas for helping pupils become more familiar with science words and their spelling*

Strategy	Suggestions
Science dictionaries	In addition to having an English dictionary in each laboratory have a science dictionary Prepare a science dictionary yourself, preferably with pupils' help, containing the key words they will come across in each topic and display this in each laboratory Build up an electronic dictionary on the school intranet
Worksheets	Highlight key words on worksheets
Spelling log	Pupils keep a record of words that they find difficult to spell, either at the back of their exercise book or in some other significant place Pupils build up their own spelling log as a computer file
Bookmark	Issue each pupil a strip of card that can be used as a bookmark in his or her exercise book, and ask pupils to write the key words for the topic on the card
Word wall	Banks of science words can be purchased, or the teacher can add to an ongoing list
Word web	Starting from one science word, pupils create a list of other words stemming from the beginning and ending of the original word. The new words must all have the same root as used in the original word ('ex' relating to 'going out' and 'thermic' relating to 'heat' in the example given in Figure 11.1)
Calligram posters	Calligrams are visual representations of a word that reflect its meaning. Letters in the word can take up the shape of the object or can somehow or other depict the concept as shown in Figure 11.2 (see Heselden and Staples, 2002; Staples and Heselden, 2002a, 2002b for further examples)
Word and definition cards	Pupils match a card containing a word with another card containing a definition
Games	Crosswords, word bingo (teacher reads out a definition and pupils have bingo cards containing the words)*, wordsearches with definitions, 'Blockbusters'

*See examples at: http://www.sycd.co.uk/can_we_should_we/explore/fun_size.htm

As mentioned on page 230, the most frequently used approach to teaching in science is the transmission mode, where the teacher dominates most of the classroom discourse and presents information and 'facts' to pupils. This teaching strategy can lead to pupils gaining a false impression about the nature of the subject, as they come to see 'science as a fixed body of facts primarily accessed though authoritative sources (e.g. the teacher)' (Newton *et al.*, 1999: 568). Past experiences show that such teaching, when it is done well, can give rise to good examination results. However, research into pupils' misconceptions indicates that many of them have only a superficial level of understanding of the concepts taught, and, while they may be able to answer examination questions on the topic that are similar to those completed in class, they are unable to apply their understanding to new situations. Pupils need opportunities to reason things through and to use the words and expressions that give meaning to science concepts to explain different types of phenomena. While group work in science is sometimes about opinion, the activity serves a much wider function. It presents pupils with the opportunity to talk about their understanding and to work with others to co-construct knowledge. Osborne (1997) points out that in 'real science', ideas are introduced and then discussed and explained through dialogue with peers, giving rise to an opportunity to elaborate and question. Words in science are linked to particular ideas and can only be used in certain ways, and it is only when pupils are given the opportunity to use these words that they begin to understand the concepts. Group work allows pupils to use these science words and to explore their meaning with others through personal reflection in a non-threatening environment. Sutton (1996) refers to science learning as learning to talk in new ways, and sees science lessons as opportunities for being taught about this new language. Sceptics will say that there is a danger that group work might result in pupils learning incorrect science. While that is possible, it is also worth bearing in mind that pupils can misinterpret what a teacher says. There is some evidence to show that learning can be directly attributable to group work. Kempa and Ayob (1995) studied the conversations of pupils who were planning their investigations in groups of three or four without being directly supervised by the teacher. They were able to identify aspects of problem-solving and understanding of science concepts that were learnt (or re-learnt) from other group members. Conwell *et al.* (1993) also reported that pupils' verbal interactions during group work were positive. The authors supported the idea of using mixed sex groups, as they found that the girls tended to encourage members of the group to contribute.

Group work needs to be managed so that pupils are given the opportunity to talk through the science to ensure that any misunderstanding is eliminated. Pupils need to be given clear tasks to do, and in large groups, individual group members will need specific roles. Some group activities will need to be designed to give pupils the opportunity for exploratory talk by providing them with stimulus material that forces them to engage critically, but constructively, with each other's ideas. Mercer (2000) points out that this type of conversation does not occur naturally in group discussions, and that pupils will need to be made aware of its value and learn how to use it effectively. The KS3 National Literacy Strategy recognises the importance of critical interaction and identifies the following as a priority for Y8:

> Use talk to question, hypothesize, speculate, evaluate, solve problems and develop thinking about complex issues and ideas.
>
> Year 8 Cross-curricular priorities (DfES, 2001: ohp 1.7)

Osborne *et al.* (2001) have also made the case for using group work that requires pupils to justify or question statements about science. As pointed out above, this models the very process that takes place in 'real science', and therefore the inclusion of this type of activity will help pupils to appreciate aspects of the nature of scientific reasoning. In addition, such activities lead to greater understanding of science concepts, as pupils are required to think through situations and identify evidence that supports their argument. Working with a number of science teachers in the South East of England, the authors devised a number of tasks to promote argument, such as the competing theories activity shown in Figure 11.3. While the group discussion was taking place, the teacher's role was that of an initiator of argument. He or she would use a selection of

---

Competing theories

Theory 1: Light rays travel from our eyes to the objects and enable us to see them

Theory 2: Light rays are produced by a source of light and reflect off objects so that we can see them

Which of the following pieces of evidence supports theory 1, theory 2, both or neither?
Discuss

a) Light travels in straight lines
b) We can all see at night when there is no sun
c) Sunglasses are worn to protect our eyes
d) If there is no light we cannot see a thing
e) We 'stare at' people, 'look daggers' and 'catch people's eye'
f) You have to look at something to see it

Figure 11.3 *An example of a task card designed to promote argumentation in group discussion (Osborne, 2001: 65)*

arguing prompts to help pupils identify evidence and structure their reasoning by asking questions such as:

- Why do you think that?
- What is your reason for that?
- Can you think of another argument for your view?
- Can you think of arguments against your view?
- How do you know?
- What is your evidence?

(Osborne, 2001: 67)

As with any group activity it is useful for the group to produce some sort of product, whether an oral presentation of their findings, a poster or a written report. There is strong evidence to show that talk combined with writing enhances the retention of science learning over time (Rivard and Straw, 2000).

Kibble (2002) has designed similar tasks to those of Osborne *et al.* (2001), based on the literature about pupils' misconceptions. These are aimed at primary school pupils, and are therefore much simpler in their design. Pupils are given a number of cards containing a picture and a statement, and are asked to discuss and decide if the statement is true or false. This is the sort of task that can be carried out by pupils working in pairs, and could form the basis of a starter activity for any new topic.

The question then arises as to how long should pupils spend on group discussion. Osborne *et al.* (2001) found that at least 30 minutes were required for pupils to develop a coherent line of reasoning in the argumentation tasks. Other group activities vary from 2–3 minutes for a brainstorming session, to a whole lesson (or longer) for rainbow and jigsaw tasks. The skill is to set a strict but realistic time limit, and to monitor the level and nature of the discussion taking place.

Group size is generally determined by the nature of the task set. In some instances teachers will choose to use whole-class discussion as a useful method for generating ideas. In this mode, the teacher maintains control and is able to keep the discourse focussed. The argument against using this technique is that a significant number of pupils may not involve themselves in the activity, and may even be completely cut off from the learning process. Pair work is also particularly good at generating ideas, and has the added benefit of involving all members of the class (Swain *et al.*, 1999). Table 11.3 summarises a number of common group arrangements. Relatively short tasks are best accomplished by small groups of two to four pupils, and it is often useful for these groups to exchange ideas with another group before reporting back to the whole class. Longer tasks require larger groups (four to seven) pupils, with each person having to fulfil a specific role.

Many teachers will have had the unpleasant experience of setting up a group activity only to find that the pupils are unwilling to talk. This situation was vividly illustrated by a TES cartoonist, who depicted the teacher shouting out to her class 'Stop not talking at the back' (TES, 1999: 24). Such situations can be eliminated by following a few simple guidelines:

1 **Clarity of purpose.** Pupils need to know why they are doing the task, and the nature of the intended outcome. Written guidelines for the task are particularly useful for longer activities, as they help to focus the group and serve as a reminder during the discussion. Sometimes it will be a good idea to start pupils off with a key phrase such as 'What do you think would happen if...' 'What about...' 'What if...?' Examples of different types of stimulus materials for group discussion are given in Table 11.4. Some tasks may require the use of a framework for summarising the outcomes of the discussion, containing a list of points to be included or questions to be answered.

2 **Good management.** Teachers need to decide on the composition of the groups, rather than letting pupils choose. Teachers may have specific reasons for deciding on grouping pupils, according to gender, ability and friendship. The best advice is to construct the groups so that the pupils work well together. If pupils are left to their own devices, there is a danger that valuable time will be taken up with squabbling. In large groups, the teacher also needs to allocate specific roles to each person.

3 **Matching the task to the age and ability of the class.** Experienced teachers are unlikely to find this difficult for most situations, but they are likely to come unstuck where the discussion takes pupils into uncharted territory. This can be problematic for discussions based on socio-scientific issues, when conversations can spill over into areas where there are no right or wrong answers. While the starting point for such exercises should be a good understanding of the relevant science, Ratcliffe (1998) suggests that pupils should be allowed to express their feelings and personal beliefs based on as much evidence as they can muster.

Table 11.3 *Ideas for group discussion*

Group strategies	Organisation	Comments
Pair talk	Pupils talk to a neighbour	• Easily organised, requiring no movement of desks or chairs • Useful for brainstorming and quick-fire reflection • Best chance of getting everyone to talk – a non-threatening situation • Provides pupils with the opportunity to think things through before presenting information to the whole class
Pairs to fours	Pairs join with other pairs to compare ideas	• May require movement of chairs in traditional laboratories • Opens up the discussion without creating too much stress for individual pupils • Possibility of the discussion deteriorating into casual chat if the situation is allowed to continue for too long (pupils may see that all the work has been done in the paired situation)
Listening triads etc.	Each member of the group takes on a role: • the talker • the questioner • the recorder	• Requires limited movement of chairs, but groups have to be far enough away from other groups to avoid being interrupted • Each person can be asked to research a separate topic prior to the session and then take it in turns to carry out the three roles. The questioner can ask for facts, opinions, explanations • Helps to build pupils' confidence, as each person is given a responsibility
Discussion group	Each group is set a task based on the resources given to the group	• Four or five pupils per group, and therefore movement of pupils might be necessary • Tasks set for each member of the group helps to ensure that everyone makes a contribution • Useful for preparation for class discussion, debates or role-play activities* • Members of the group work together on arguments or the role to be played, and one pupil represents the group at the next stage (presents information / acts out a role) • Helps to develop team work
Rainbow groups	Initial discussion takes place in a group, and each member of the group is given a colour. A second round of group discussion takes place, with the new groups being composed of pupils with the same colour	• Pupil movement needs to be organised • Pupils have the responsibility of taking information from the original group to the new group • Each original group can be given a different remit, thereby making the second phase an opportunity to bring together different aspects of information
Jigsaw	The topic is divided up into suitable sections. Pupils are allocated to a 'home' group of four or five pupils. Each member of the home group is allocated a different section of work. Secondary groups of pupils work together on their section of work and become experts, and each expert reports back to his/her home group	• The activity gives responsibility to pupils for their own learning, and all pupils are involved • There may be a lot of pupil movement, which will require well thought through management and vigilance • Teachers need to select the resources carefully, and the support available with the resources. Pupils may simply copy verbatim from the resource and take that back to their home group

*Ideas for role-play activities can be found in Harrison (1992) and SATIS units

Table 11.4 *Examples of stimulus materials for group discussions*

Technique	Example
True/false statements	In your groups, discuss each of the statements. Decide if they are true or false. Be prepared to say why you have reached your decision.

Statement	True	False	Don't know
Acids are corrosive			
Acids dissolve most things			
Dilute hydrochloric acid is a weak acid			
The salt that you put on your chipps can be made from dilute hydrochloric acid			
All metals react with hydrochloric acid			
You have got hydrochloric acid inside you			

(For further examples, see Wellington and Osborne, 2001: Chapter 6)

Concept cartoons

> We need to reduce the number of cars because their fumes endanger the ozone layer.

> Catalytic converters remove all the harmful gases.

> It's the heat from all the car engines that is causing global warming.

> Cars still give off CO_2, and that gives us acid rain.

Cartoon characters could accompany the speech bubbles. Alternatively the information could be written in terms of 'Emma says: "We need ...", Jeelna says "Catalytic converters ..." etc. What do you think?' It is usual to include a correct answer as one of the speech bubbles (not given in the example above).

The statements above are based on pupils' misconceptions of the environment impact of cars (Boyes and Stanisstreet, 1997).

(For further examples of Concept Cartoons, see Naylor and Keogh, 2000)

Concept maps

Part of a concept map based around the concept of an element.
(For further examples, see Learners' Co-operative, 1996)

4 **The role of the teacher during the discussion.** This needs to be defined from the outset. In most cases the teacher will provide help when needed, remind pupils of the issues to be discussed and the questions to be answered, and, where appropriate, ask additional questions to promote further thinking. Although undesirable, it may be necessary to stop the discussion and provide the whole class with clarification. It is also worth bearing in mind that some pupils may see their discussions as personal, and may not want the teacher to interfere.

5 **After the group discussion.** Teachers need to bear in mind that the group discussion has been a learning process and the production of some sort of outcome has helped to focus that learning. A plenary discussion may be useful in bringing together views or decisions from different groups, but it will serve little purpose if it is repetitive. A good plenary discussion draws key points from a number of groups, and perhaps results in something that is worthy of including in pupils' notes. Teachers may also consider it worthwhile to get some feedback on the kinds of talk that went on and pupils' perceptions of the value of the exercise. It is worth reminding the class that being able to work in a group, to recognise other people's points of view and to make decisions are very important skills.

A study into Y7 pupils' reactions to group work, looking at collaborative learning techniques and the social and emotional development of boys and girls (Matthews, 2001: 1), provided an interesting insight into the value of this technique. The study showed that following a series of lessons involving group work:

- pupils learnt to get on with each other, but they did not find it easy
- boys and girls talked more equally to each other
- they developed socially and understood each other more
- they felt more confident about working with the same and the opposite sex
- they supported each other in their learning
- they thought that it was important to learn together
- they enjoyed their lessons
- they found that group work increased their understanding.

Two types of stimulus material, concept cartoons and concept mapping, are discussed further in the sections below. These techniques have proved to be particularly valuable in helping pupils to appreciate their level of personal understanding of a topic.

Concept cartoons

These were first created in 1992 by Brenda Naylor and Stuart Naylor in an attempt to develop an innovative teaching strategy that took account of socio-constructivist views on learning science. The principal aim of a cartoon is to elicit a learner's understanding of a science concept so that the teacher can plan for future teaching, particularly the range of restructuring activities (see page 93). This is done by presenting pupils with a cartoon of a familiar context where there are three to four people, usually children.

The purpose of this is to help pupils identify with the situation and, perhaps, make links to their own experiences. Each of the cartoon characters is associated with a statement in a speech bubble, and pupils are invited to say what they think. They may agree or disagree with what is being said, or may come up with some ideas of their own. An evaluation of the use of these cartoons in primary and secondary schools indicated that pupils enjoyed working with the materials and that they led to significant improvements in the quality of group discussions and individual pupils' written work (Keogh and Naylor, 1999). In addition to their usual use in teaching the evaluation revealed that teachers had identified a number of other valuable ways of using the resource, such as:

- material for homework
- making worksheets more interesting
- presenting children's own ideas to them (in speech bubbles) in a non-threatening form
- enabling pupils to summarise their own ideas by drawing cartoons
- illustrating that the nature of science includes alternative viewpoints.

(Keogh and Naylor, 1999: 441)

Stephenson and Warwick (2002) have investigated the use of concept cartoons with primary school pupils being taught about light. They found that practical investigations stemming from the cartoons helped the pupils to explore their ideas further. They also looked at how making small changes to the cartoons could extend pupils' discussions and help the teacher monitor some of the progression in understanding. In the first cartoon, the characters were considering the shadows cast when light hit two pieces of card, one black and one white. This was based on the common misconception that black objects produce darker shadows than light objects. In the next cartoon the black object was replaced by a mirror, and in the final cartoon two objects overlapped one another. All of the situations gave rise to really useful discussion, and overall the cartoons:

- encouraged the students and teacher to operate within the social dimensions of science
- recognised that learners hold a range of ideas about the world and these are important and generally based on reason
- identified the accepted scientific explanation
- identified the likely progression in conceptual understanding
- provided a means by which the teacher could both differentiate and assess learning
- demonstrated that a constructivist approach is possible within the tight constraints of a curriculum programme.

(Stephenson and Warwick, 2002: 139)

Concept maps

Concept mapping has a much longer history, dating back to the late 1970s, when it was used mainly in the USA and Australia as a means of teaching and assessing science undergraduates. Concept maps have since been used in a wide variety of educational contexts, from showing the connections between ideas in primary schools (e.g. Harlen *et al.*, 1990; Sizmur, 1994) to self-assessment of subject knowledge in teacher education (e.g. Bishop and Denley, 1997; Lenton and Turner, 1999). The versatility of concept mapping and the fact that the maps are easy to use with pupils of all abilities makes them a suitable learning activity for virtually every topic.

A map consists of two parts: the objects (or prime descriptors), which are usually placed in boxes, and the links (or propositions), which consist of arrows together with a word or short phrase showing the nature of the link (see sample of a section of a concept map in Table 11.4). The objects are key words (concepts or terms) related to the topic, and these may be given by the teacher or suggested by the pupils. The links are usually supplied by the pupils. There are a number of ways of completing a map, and the choice depends on the facilities available and the nature of the exercise. If it is a relatively short activity, involving only a small number of concepts, it can be done using pencil and paper. Using this approach, things can be quickly jotted down and rubbed out if there is a change of mind. When a larger number of objects is to be considered, it is useful to adopt a system that will lead to a clear and tidy product. If the map has lines crisscrossing one another it makes it difficult to see how the link words relate to the objects and understand the map in general. The problem can be overcome by providing pupils with cards with the words written on them, or blank cards for the pupils to write on themselves. These can be positioned and re-positioned on a piece of paper, and the links drawn in. Re-usable adhesive makes it possible to keep the cards secure while producing the map. Alternatively, concept mapping can be carried on a computer with the help of specialised software (see page 220).

Significant claims have been made in the research literature for the use of this technique, the vast majority of which indicate that they have a positive impact on learning. For example:

- Novak (1990) determined that the use of mapping significantly reduced anxiety and enhanced self-concept
- Novak (1991) said that mapping helps learners to reflect on existing understanding and, where necessary, construct new meanings in a subject
- Horton *et al.* (1993) showed that regular use of mapping produced a significant improvement in pupils' understanding of science
- Roth and Roychoudhury (1993) found that mapping fostered interaction between learners, enabled pupils to sustain scientific discussion and argumentation, and produced favourable attitudes towards science
- Rye and Rubba (1998) reported that mapping appeared to facilitate metacognition in pupils.

Although it is a simple technique to set up, its success depends to a large extent on the support given by the teacher. As pointed out by Roth and Roychoudhury (1993), without appropriate teacher intervention the technique can lead to scientifically incorrect notions becoming ingrained. In addition to encouraging pupils to self-check their maps, teachers need to monitor the situation and question pupils' decisions. Group work also helps to ensure that connections between concepts are fully aired (Sizmur, 1994; Wellington and Osborne, 2001), and there are opportunities for further checking when groups of two join to make groups of four. In cannot be assumed that pupils will be able to construct concept maps without any instruction on the processes involved. Research carried out by Brandt *et al.* (2001) showed no significant gains in learning by pupils who had used concept mapping to learn about electrochemistry. However, these pupils had been taught by watching the teacher construct the concept map in the first lesson, and were then required to draw a concept map themselves in the last lesson. It would have been more appropriate for the teacher to have modelled the process, rather than giving the pupils the 'answer', and then to allow them to build their personal maps.

Adamczyk *et al.* (1994) identified five different approaches to concept mapping:

1 The 'free range' map, where pupils have a completely free choice of words from a topic either supplied by the teacher or themselves
2 The 'object only' map, where objects are arranged on a page and the pupils have to complete the map with link arrows and link phrases
3 The 'link only' map, where the objects and arrows are provided for the pupils and only the link phrases have to be added
4 The 'propositional' or 'outline framework' map, where only the structure of the map and directional links are given and pupils have to place the objects and the links in the correct places
5 The 'picture' map, where pupils are given clues to help them construct the map either through drawings or shapes that match with object words written in an identical shape.

The use of concept mapping software and interactive whiteboards opens up the possibilities of starting off a mapping exercise as a class activity and then letting pupils finish it off.

Teachers may wish to give a mark for pupils' concept maps to indicate their level of understanding of the topic. Many of the systems given in the literature are complex, and put a great strain on the working memories of the scorers. Kinchin (2000a) suggests a more workable approach where the teacher concentrates on the correctness of the links between the concepts. Marks can be given for:

• the existence of a relationship between the concepts
• a correct label indicating the relationship
• correct use of the arrow.

Kinchin (2000b) suggests that a combination of concept cartoons and concept mapping may help in revealing pupils' beliefs and underlying assumptions about natural phenomena. In his article he takes the example of photosynthesis, a topic where misconceptions abound, and underneath the cartoon places fragments of a concept map which breaks down the words in the speech bubble into manageable chunks. The author maintains that this makes it easier for the pupils to handle during discussion.

Listening

In classrooms where the dominant teaching style is 'teacher talk', it is assumed that pupils learn by listening. But how many of the pupils are really listening? In many cases they will be half listening, in the same way that they are able to hold conversations while listening to music or the TV at home. Pupils tend not to be used to sustained listening and are likely to find it difficult, particularly when it is prolonged or when the subject matter is difficult. From time to time it is worth carrying out activities that help pupils to develop their listening skills. A technique that is commonly employed in science lessons is the use of a worksheet when pupils watch a video. The sheet helps them to identify specific information. When teachers talk to pupils they ask questions to check on understanding and to see if pupils are paying attention, but this only involves a sample of the class. In order to involve everybody, the teacher could mention that today pupils are going to do a listening exercise, something that they are familiar with from their English lessons, and following a short talk ask pupils to write down the key points made.

Reading

As mentioned at the start of this chapter, science textbooks published in the last ten years or so contain the minimum number of words on any one page and the maximum number of pictures and diagrams. Key words and phrases are highlighted, and in many cases there is a list of new words prominently displayed in a box. All this was done in a response to reports written in the 1980s (e.g. Knutton, 1983; Johnson and Johnson, 1987) on the readability of science texts, which indicated that books and many worksheets were written at too high a level for pupils to understand. These remarks were based on the use of 'readability formulae' on samples of writing from textbooks. Applying the formulae resulted in a value for the reading age that was required in order to be able to understand the text fully. It was recommended that science texts should have a reading age two years below the pupils' chronological age (Harrison and Gardner, 1977), but the reading age of the published books was almost exclusively above the age of target pupils. Although there have been many critics (e.g. Slater and Thompson, 1984; Connaster, 1999) of the validly of using such formulae on science texts, where the technical language used tends to inflate the reading age considerably, there has been little move to increase the amount of text until fairly recently. There is an indication that some new science textbooks contain longer sections of writing, particularly when they are explaining something or writing about an historical event (e.g. *Science Web* published by Nelson-Thornes, *Absolute Science* published by Collins).

Some publishers produce two levels of textbooks, one containing less writing and a larger font size for less able pupils, and one containing more writing and smaller print for the more able (e.g. *Eureka*, published by Heinemann). It is probably true to say that most pupils could cope with more reading than they currently come across in science lessons.

There are four very good reasons for including reading in science lessons:

1 Science texts and worksheets can provide pupils with opportunities to use national literacy strategies in ways that are not always possible in other subjects (e.g. sorting technical information; evaluating the evidence)
2 Pupils can learn science concepts through active reading and the text can act as a stimulus for group discussion
3 Through familiarity with texts, pupils can learn about presentation of information and methods of structuring scientific arguments
4 Pupils develop independent learning skills that will be of use to them throughout their lives, and learn to identify comments that are based on opinion and those that are based on evidence.

As with all other teaching strategies, it is important to explain to pupils what they are doing and why they are doing it. Some of the reading activities have 'game-like' qualities and, while that is one of the reasons why pupils like them, there is the possibility that pupils may perceive them as trivial and, as a result, miss vital learning points. Table 11.5 summarises the main type of DART activities and suggests a general strategy for teaching. Texts can either be photocopied (after ensuring that photocopying regulations have been complied with) or constructed by the teacher. Examples of different types of DART exercises can be found in a number of resources, e.g. Parkinson, 1994; Ross *et al.*, 2000; Wellington and Osborne, 2001.

Wray and Lewis (1997) have devised a model that incorporates DARTs into a much wider teaching framework, from the identification of prior knowledge through to the production of a product. This approach, which is featured in the KS3 National Literacy Strategy, is called the EXIT (Extending Interactions with Texts) model. Table 11.6 illustrates the process with examples of how it could be used in the teaching of the topic 'chemical weathering of rocks'.

Things to consider

Review the reading resources used in the department (textbooks, workbooks, worksheets etc.) in terms of the appropriateness for age and ability of the target pupils. To what extent do the resources used in the science department provide pupils with the opportunity to carry out analytical reading tasks? How could the use of texts be improved to help pupils become more independent in their learning?

Table 11.5 *Types of DART activities*

DART type	Method	Comments
Cloze	Pupils fill in the gaps in a piece of prose	Differentiation can be achieved through the number of clues given, e.g. initial letters of words or words placed at the end of the text. Useful in the production of a set of notes for pupils. Tasks are generally of low cognitive demand (pupils can guess or copy the missing word). Pupils need to attend to the sense of the sentences. Leaving gaps where a number of similar words could be inserted, only one of which is correct, can increase the difficulty
Sequencing	A piece of text on A4 card is divided and cut up into a number of sections (~6–12); pupils rearrange them into the correct sequence	Pupils need to pay careful attention to the reading and identify the logic of the text. Useful opportunity to emphasise the use of logical connective words. Asking pupils why they have chosen a particular sequence helps them to understand their own learning. The exercise will help them to sequence their own writing
Text marking	Includes a number of techniques, such as: highlighting or underlining, annotating and numbering	Preliminary discussion identifies what needs to be marked and how it should be marked. Older or more able pupils could be supplied with a longish piece of text that they can skim and scan for specific information
Text restructuring	Involves the identification of key pieces of the text, which are then used in another format – e.g. flow chart, labelling a diagram, producing a table, writing a summary	This can follow on from a text-marking exercise. It can be a useful learning exercise, as pupils are required to reformulate information supplied in the original text

Suggested teaching strategy
- Start with texts that are between 200 and 300 words. Check that it does not contain too many technical words and that the connective words (Table 11.8) are familiar to the pupils.
- Explain the purpose of the task to the pupils and identify the learning goals and outcomes. The technique can be modelled using an electronic whiteboard. Highlighting and annotating are easily done, and by placing each section of the text in a text box it can be dragged into position using the remote mouse.
- Guide and support the pupils through the task. Ask 'why' questions.
- Organise pupils to work on the text in groups of two to three.

Writing

Pupils sometimes come into lessons requesting practical work and saying that they don't want to do too much writing. Traditionally, the type of writing that has been done in science has been limited to the preparation of notes as a record of the topic being taught or the writing up of a practical activity. The type of writing described in this section is what is generally referred to as 'writing for learning'. There is growing evidence that writing can be particularly effective in helping pupils to learn about science, in addition to improving their ability to write. Prain and Hand (1999) carried out a study, over a period of four years, looking at pupils' perceptions of writing in science. Tasks were devised that required pupils to construct, revise, clarify and reflect on their understanding of scientifically acceptable concepts. The outcomes of their research indicated that:

- Pupils reacted overwhelmingly positively towards the tasks.
- Pupils perceived the tasks as having a positive effect on the quality of their learning. They said they forced them to reflect on their own thinking in more depth and believed that the process enabled them to retain the knowledge.
- Pupils' comments indicated that they had an increased sense of ownership and control over their learning. An important aspect of this was the opportunity they had to develop their thoughts before encountering authorised views.
- Pupils were not always clear about the purpose of the writing tasks. Many pupils gave little thought to how different learning activities could be beneficial.

Pupils' thinking processes during the writing of laboratory reports were investigated by Keys (2000), using think-aloud protocols and analysis of qualitative data. The study indicated that the majority of pupils in the survey generated new knowledge and explanations specifically from the act of writing, and there were some pupils who made no progress in their learning.

Hand and Prain (2002) have also examined how teachers present writing tasks, and how they manage pupils' learning while they are carrying out the activity. The research, which took the form of a case study of two teachers, indicated that a number of changes took place involving the teachers' views and concerns. Initially both teachers tended to see the main purpose of writing as testing pupils' knowledge after learning, but later on in the project they appreciated that it enabled them to identify misconceptions and get an insight into pupils' thinking. The teachers were concerned about sorting out the assessment of science from the assessment of writing. This issue was partly solved by the use of assessment grids that specified language target concepts that needed to be addressed in addition to science concepts. In addition, the teachers were concerned about the planning of activities, the scaffolding of pupils' learning and the development of manageable classroom routines. All of this presented a significant challenge to the teachers, and required ongoing reflection on practice and long-term support from colleagues.

The National Literacy Strategy identifies cross-curricular priorities for each year group for KS3. The following statements, taken from the priorities for Y9, indicate some of the aspects of literacy that are relevant for learning science:

Synthesize information from a range of sources, shaping material to meet the reader's needs.

Write with differing degrees of formality, relating vocabulary and grammar to context, e.g. using the active or passive voice.

Discuss and evaluate conflicting evidence to arrive at a considered viewpoint.

Year 9 Cross-curricular priorities (DfES, 2001: ohp 1.8)

Table 11.6 *Possible sequence of events when using the EXIT model for learning from a text*

Process stages	Pupil activities	Teaching concerns (based on the teaching of chemical weathering of rocks at KS3 as an example)		
Activating prior knowledge	• Brainstorming • Concept mapping	Prior knowledge may include some confusion between erosion and dirt deposition. Misconceptions may include: all erosion processes are physical; regarding all weathering processes as chemical; classifying processes as weathering because atmospheric elements (i.e. wind and rain) are involved etc. (Dove, 1997)		
Establishing purposes	• Clarifying learning objectives • Establishing what needs to be learnt and what will be done with the information	Consider using a KWL grid		
		What do I already **know** about this topic?	What do I **want** to know about this topic?	What have I **learned** about this topic?
		Water, wind and temperature changes can erode rocks	What chemicals are present in the air naturally? Do these cause rocks to erode? What man-made pollutants are there in the atmosphere? Which rocks react with these pollutants? etc.	
Locating information	• Using the Internet • Using reference books, etc.	Discussion about how to find out information from different sources – use of web searches and indices. Information from several sources may need to be collated to ensure that there is sufficient recap of previous work, and that the new information is covered in sufficient depth. Some schools have websites on the topic, e.g. http://www.moorlandschool.co.uk/earth/rockcycle.htm. Discuss refining searches to locate relevant information at the appropriate level for the pupil. Consider modelling the search procedures, indicating why some text is acceptable and some not. Consider providing pupils with texts, at least initially, to avoid wasting too much time		
Adopting an appropriate strategy	• Considering how to use the information to meet the objectives • Metacognitive discussion	Reading through the text to gain an appreciation of how the information is presented and the extent to which it meets the learning goals. This is a skimming (gaining an overall impression and the main points) and scanning (picking out specific information) exercise rather than detailed reading. Pupils should be looking for answers to who, what, when, why, where questions		

Interacting with the text	• DARTs activities	Pupils could carry out a text-marking exercise, identifying key points such as names of rocks that are subject to chemical weathering, the causes of chemical weathering, problems and possible solutions. Pupils need actively to engage with the text and ask themselves, what does it mean and do I understand it?
Monitoring understanding	• Pupils ask when there is anything they don't understand	Pupils need to be aware of their own understanding. They need to appreciate that they may need to read the text more than once, and may need to check the meaning of some words in a dictionary. Pupils need to appreciate that sometimes the meaning of earlier parts of the text only becomes clear once the text has been read through y complete]
Making a record	• Pupils produce a written summary	This may be in the form of notes or a more formal piece of writing. In both cases pupils will need guidance by the teacher modelling the process or through the use of writing frames
Evaluating information	• Pupils identify bias in texts • Pupils consider the impartiality of Internet sites	Pupils need to be critical and evaluative. They need to look for evidence and determine points that are based on sound scientific argument and those that are personal opinions. This is a good opportunity to show that people sometimes jump to conclusions about pollution that have no firm scientific foundation. Newspaper articles (real or made up) can be useful additional reading
Assisting memory	• Pupils consider how they are going to remember the information	Pupils need to make links with existing knowledge. They may need to revisit text and restructure their notes, or they may go back to their concept map and update it
Communicating information	• Further writing or oral presentation • Role play or drama	Further work could be done on chemical weathering in the local environment, perhaps in conjunction with the geography department. Further writing possibilities could include the production of a web page, an information booklet or poster (using software such as Publisher). This helps to clarify any uncertainties and establish the learning

Wray and Lewis (1997) have identified six main non-fiction text types. Within the Strategy these are identified as information, recount, explanation, instruction, persuasion and discussion. The Strategy adds a further two: analysis and evaluation. Some pieces of writing fit into more than one text type, and it is not helpful to think of them as discrete categories. Their use lies in providing a framework for planning for the inclusion of writing exercises in the curriculum to ensure that pupils experience different modes of expression. An outline of how these text types relate to learning science is given below.

1 **Information.**
   * Presents information in a logical way. Report writing can help pupils to organise their own learning and help them to develop the skill of synthesising information from a variety of sources, e.g. through project work on topics such as global warming, the misuse of drugs etc.
   * Uses the present tense and is impersonal.
   e.g. 'Sound waves are collected by the outer ear and passed to the eardrum, which then vibrates. The vibrations are passed to the oval window by three bones, which magnify the force of the vibrations.'
2 **Recount.**
   * Personal account of an event written in a logical sequence (written either from an individual's perspective or from the perspective of a fantasy figure). Hanrahan (1999) advocates the use of asking pupils to keep a journal where they can express their own opinions and feelings about science and reflect on their learning.
   * The text generally uses sequencing connectives.
   * Uses the past tense and is personal.
   e.g. 'When we went to Techniquest we tried to work out how the Bernoulli Blower worked. The ball stayed in the air when the blower was on. Andrew put a piece of paper in the airflow and we looked at how far it bent.'
3 **Explanation.**
   * Answers 'why' and 'how' questions in a series of scientifically accurate statements. According to Keys (1995), the construction of explanations is greatly enhanced by the use of collaborative talk amongst groups of pupils. There are opportunities for explanatory writing in virtually every topic taught.
   * The text uses cause and effect connectives.
   * Uses the present tense (sometimes the past) and is impersonal.
   e.g. 'When sodium reacts with water it turns into a blob of silvery metal and floats around on the surface of the water. This is because the heat given off from the reaction melts the metal and it floats because it is less dense than water.'
4 **Instruction.**
   * Clear series of steps describing how something should be done. Text uses sequencing connectives.
   * Uses the imperative tense and is impersonal.
   e.g. '1. Draw a faint pencil line 1 cm from the bottom of the paper, as shown in the diagram. 2. Using the glass spotter carefully put a spot of the dye on the paper, making sure that it is on the line and about 2 cm in from the edge.'

5 **Persuasion.**
   - Argues the case for a particular point of view. Text uses a range of connectives.
   - Uses the present tense and is usually impersonal.

   e.g. 'It is important to use public transport rather than take your own car because it is environmentally friendly. This is because you can get a lot of people onto a bus but you can only get four or five in a car. This means that a bus is more energy efficient.'

6 **Discussion.**
   - Presents arguments and information from different points of view. Text uses a range of connectives, but mainly cause and effect, qualifying and contrasting connectives. Using this genre pupils could also write about famous scientists and their work, perhaps giving an indication of the historical background and other factors relevant to the scientific development.
   - Generally uses the present tense and is usually impersonal.

   e.g. 'Some people believe that when iron rusts it loses weight because the metal turns into a crumbly powder. However, other people think that is has gained weight because the iron must have combined with something to form rust.'

7 **Analysis.**
   - Analyses a piece of writing or a product (e.g. the outcome of an investigation), identifying the key points and supporting these with quotations. Text uses contrasting connectives.
   - Uses the present or past tense as appropriate and is impersonal.

   e.g. 'Boyle had a difficult job in persuading people that gases were made up of particles. He had to argue against the alchemists, who thought that "chemistry was not a true science". Alchemists thought that all things were made up of earth, air, fire and water, whereas Boyle's experiments led him to believe that matter was made up of "simple, or perfectly unmingled bodies".' (Analysis of text from Morgan, 1995.)

8 **Evaluation.**
   - Recording the strengths or weaknesses of a performance or product. Text uses cause and effect connectives.
   - Uses past, present and future tenses as appropriate and is usually personal.

   e.g. 'I repeated the experiment three times for each temperature and took the average of the readings to draw my graph. I did this to improve the reliability of my results. However, I was not able to get the exact temperature each time, and sometimes the solution cooled down very quickly. This affected the accuracy of my results.'

Table 11.7 links these text types with a number of examples of exercises commonly used in science lessons. Sutton (1992: 89) points out that the key to success for a piece of writing appears to be:

- the clarity of **writer's sense of audience**
- the amount of **preparation** done before the writing begins, thinking it through, talking it over, considering what is needed in this particular situation, and
- **how the teacher responds** to the product.

Table 11.7 *Examples of writing exercises*

Text type	Idea	Comment
Information	Translating data into prose	e.g. Pupils are presented with information about a group of elements and are asked to write sentences about their physical state at room temperature, change in melting points etc.
	Pupils describe a series of observations	Pupils will need to be taught about making relevant observations
	Providing a report for a mythical organisation	This is a good opportunity for pupils to practise presenting information clearly and logically
Recount	Asking pupils to write down a summary of what they have learnt during the topic	Need to ensure that pupils don't simply copy previous work, by asking them to present it in a different format
	Reporting on specific exhibits following a visit to a science centre	Briefing before the visit is essential
	Writing from the position of being a fantasy figure, e.g. water droplet or a famous scientist, reporting, for example, the serendipitous discoveries made by scientists such as Ampere and Fleming	Pupils have the opportunity to use their imagination, but the science must be correct
	Pupils write a newspaper article	
Explanation	Asking pupils to write down a scientific explanation of an everyday event	e.g. Why clothes on a washing line dry quicker on a windy day, why a hard football goes softer at night
	Asking pupils to use their existing knowledge to explain new phenomena	This can provide an opportunity for pupils to bring together information from a number of topics
	Asking pupils to make careful observations and then explain these in terms of science concepts or theories	Gives an indication as to degree to which pupils' understanding is secure. Teachers need to check for completeness
Instruction	Rearranging text into the correct sequence	e.g. Instructions for a practical activity are jumbled up, leaving pupils to rearrange into the correct sequence
	Based on pupils' practical experience, they write a series of instructions for another person	Useful for investigations

Persuasion	Writing a letter Pupils put forward suggestions for a healthy diet Pupils present arguments for conserving biodiversity	e.g. Putting forward an argument for an environmental issue Can be used to link work done in the science lessons with food products Pupils will need guidance on selecting resources that are suitable for the age group
Discussion	Writing about a controversy in science Pupils can write about why certain scientific theories have not stood the test of time Writing about the advantages and disadvantages of different methods of electricity production	e.g. Phlogiston theory versus burning as combination with oxygen; pros and cons of siting an industrial plant in a particular area Helps pupils to understand that many factors need to be taken into account when coming to a decision as to which method to adopt
Analysis	Identifying key points within a text and using the information to produce a summary Pupils look for patterns and draw conclusions from sets of data	DART activity This could be from given data, or data obtained from an investigation
Evaluation	Pupils note the strengths and weaknesses in their approach to an investigation Pupils are presented with data and they have to comment on its reliability or generalisability Pupils are presented with a newspaper article or website and are asked to comment on the clarity of information and the accuracy of the science	Sometimes difficult for pupils; practice and modelling by the teacher are useful Helps pupils to understand these important terms Useful to collect articles over time. Some newspaper articles can be downloaded from the web

Pupils are sometimes confused about who they are writing for – the teacher, themselves or some unknown person, and as a result the writing is muddled and there is no coherent argument from start to finish. In order to avoid this problem, teachers need to explain the purpose of the writing and what it will be used for. One of the main conclusions drawn by Kelly and Chen (1999), arising from research into pupils' writing in physics, was the need for teachers to explain clearly the goals of the task to the pupils and provide them with guidance about the writing style. I have previously argued (Parkinson, 1994) for the use of a variety of writing genres in science, including poetry and rap. However, not everyone would agree that these are appropriate for learning science. Martin (1993) claims that narratives and poems have the wrong purposes and structures to suit science learning. When given this degree of freedom, pupils can introduce inaccurate understanding and personal irrelevancies. Keys (1999) also criticises the use of creative writing in science, saying that it reinforces the idea that scientific writing is inaccessible to most people and is inherently boring.

While some pupils will find it relatively straightforward to produce a piece of writing, the majority will require some sort of guidance. It may be helpful to provide pupils with examples of previously completed work on similar projects and point out how the text has been constructed. An alternative approach is to provide pupils with short paragraphs written by a number of fictional pupils. The class is asked to rank order the pieces of writing in terms of how well they achieved the aim of the exercise, and to consider how the writing could be developed from this original paragraph. Goldsworthy *et al.* (2000) suggest that this sort of activity is useful in helping pupils to write down what they plan to do in an investigation. In a sample exercise they provided statements, written by six pupils, who have written their individual interpretations of the investigative task set by the teacher: 'How does the temperature affect the time taken for sugar to dissolve in water?'. Following a group discussion, the teacher helps the class to build up a framework of the piece of writing based on questions and feedback from the pupils. An electronic whiteboard can be particularly useful here, as it allows the teacher (or pupils) to compose the work in front of the class using the contributions made by the pupils. Teachers can point out how text can be changed or moved to improve the overall meaning or to make the argument clearer, using the simple functions that the electronic whiteboard provides. Pupils should only be allowed to start the tasks once they have a clear idea about what they are required to do in each section of the piece of work. An alternative approach is for the teacher to provide the pupils with a writing frame containing a sequence of questions or starter sentences that provide a focus for pupils to construct their work. Both methods scaffold pupils' understanding of how to set out a piece of writing, but the former method has the added advantage of raising pupils' awareness of why the writing is structured in a particular way. An important aspect of producing a coherent piece of text is the correct use of connective words. As mentioned above, some pupils have difficulty in understanding the meaning of these words, and encouraging them to use such words in their writing may be of considerably benefit in helping them to understand logical thinking in science. A list of common logical connectives is given in Table 11.8.

The third point made by Sutton (1992) – how the teacher responds to the product – concerns the feedback given to pupils about their writing. In some situations the initial

Table 11.8 *Helping pupils to compose a piece of writing using connective words (adapted from 'Connectives as signposts', Handout 3.1* Literacy Across the Curriculum, *DfES, 2001)*

Adding		Cause and effect	
and	as well as	because	so
also	moreover	this shows that	thus
too	thus	consequently	but
hence	furthermore	this causes	therefore

Sequencing		Qualifying	
next	then	however	although
first, second, third	finally	unless	except
meanwhile	after	if	as long as
		apart from	yet
		nevertheless	but

Emphasising		Illustrating	
above all	in particular	for example	such as
especially	significantly	as revealed by	for instance
indeed	notably	in the case of	i.e.
		in practice	

Comparing		Contrasting	
in the same way	equally	whereas	instead of
similarly	likewise	alternatively	otherwise
as with	like	on the other hand	unlike
		conversely	while

feedback can be through peer review, where pupils exchange their work within a group and look for clarity and completeness of text. This can be phrased in terms of: 'what advice would you give to your friend about?', followed by a list of statements that are relevant to the writing exercise. Prain and Hand (1996) suggested that when the teacher comes to look at the work, he or she should respond sympathetically to pupils' use of exploratory language and grammatical accuracy. In many of the situations where writing is used, the exercise needs to be seen as part of the learning process rather than as an end product. The teacher needs to make the learning objectives clear to the pupils and let them know exactly what they will be looking for on this particular occasion.

Things to consider

Review the work carried out by one year group in terms of the number and nature of writing exercises they are required to do. In what ways do the exercises cater for pupils of different abilities? How do teachers scaffold pupils' learning during these tasks? How can the conceptual demand made on pupils be improved?

References

ACCAC (2002) *Implications for Teaching and Learning: Report on the 2002 Tests in Science at Key Stage 3*, Birmingham: Qualifications, Curriculum and Assessment Authority for Wales.

Adamczyk, P., Willson, M. and Williams, D. (1994) 'Concept mapping: a multi-level and multi-purpose tool', *School Science Review*, **76**(275), 116–124.

Barnes, D., Britton, J. and Rosen, H. (1969) *Language, the Learner and the School*, Harmondsworth: Penguin.

Berry, M. and Kellington, S. (1986) *Reading About Chemistry*, London: Heinemann.

Bishop, K. and Denley, P. (1997) 'The fundamental role of subject matter knowledge in the teaching of science', *School Science Review*, **79**(286), 65–71.

Boyes, E. and Stanisstreet, M. (1997) 'The environmental impact of cars: children's ideas and reasoning', *Environmental Education Research*, **3**(3), 269–282.

Brandt, L., Elen, J., Hellemans, J. *et al.* (2001) 'The impact of concept mapping and visualisation on the learning of secondary school chemistry students', *International Journal of Science Education*, **23**(12), 1303–1313.

Bullock, A. (1975) *A Language for Life*, London: HMSO.

Byrne, M., Johnstone, A.H. and Pope, A. (1994) 'Reasoning in science: a language problem revealed?', *School Science Review*, **75**(272), 103–107.

Cassels, J.R.T. and Johnstone, A.H. (1985) *Words that Matter in Science*, London: The Royal Society of Chemistry.

Clerk, D. and Rutherford, M. (2000) 'Language as a confounding variable in the diagnosis of misconceptions', *International Journal of Science Education*, **22**(7), 703–717.

Connaster, B.R. (1999) 'Last rites for readability formulas in technical communication', *Journal of Technical Writing & Communication*, **29**(3), 271–287.

Conwell, C.R., Algozzine, B. and Griffin, S. (1993) 'Gender and racial differences in unstructured learning groups in science', *International Journal of Science Education*, **15**(1), 107–115.

Davies, F. and Greene, T. (1984) *Reading for Learning in the Sciences*, Edinburgh: Oliver and Boyd.

DfES (2001) *Literacy Across the Curriculum: Key Stage 3 National Strategy*, London: DfEE publications.

Donnelly, J.F. (2000) 'Secondary science teaching under the National Curriculum', *School Science Review*, **81**(296), 27–35.

Dove, J. (1997) 'Student ideas about weathering and erosion', *International Journal of Science Education*, **19**(8), 971–980.

Estyn (2001) *Good Practice in Science*, Cardiff: HM Inspectorate for Education and Training in Wales.

Ford, S. and Versey, J. (2001) 'Secondary science and literacy: making the words work', *Education Today*, **51**(2), 16–21.

Galton, M. (2002) 'Continuity and progression in science teaching at key stages 2 and 3', *Cambridge Journal of Education*, **32**(2), 249–265.

Gardner, P.L. (1975) 'Logical connectives in science – a summary of the findings', *Research in Science Education*, **7**, 9–24.

Goldsworthy, A., Watson, R. and Wood-Robinson, V. (2000) *Investigations: Developing Understanding*, Hatfield: ASE.

Hand, B. and Prain, V. (2002) 'Teachers implementing Writing-To-Learn Strategies in junior secondary science: A case study', *Science Education*, **86**(6), 737–755.

Hanrahan, M. (1999) 'Rethinking science literacy: enhancing communication and participation in school science through affirmational dialogue journal writing', *Journal of Research in Science Teaching*, **36**(6), 699–717.

Harlen, W., Macro, C., Schilling, M. and Malvern, D. (1990) *Progress in Primary Science*, London: Routledge.

Harrison, B. (Project Director for the Centre for Science Education, Sheffield City Polytechnic) (1992) *Active Teaching and Learning Approaches in Science*, London: Collins.

Harrison, C. and Gardner, K. (1997) in Marland, M. (ed.) *Language Across the Curriculum*, London: Heinemann.

Heselden, R. and Staples, R. (2002) 'Science teaching and literacy, part 2: Reading', *School Science Review*, **83**(304), 51–62.

Horton, P.B., McConney, A.A., Gallo, M., Woods, A.L., Senn, G.J. and Hamelin, D. (1993) 'An investigation of the effectiveness of concept mapping as an instructional tool', *Science Education*, **77**(1), 95–111.

Johnson, C.K. and Johnson, R.K. (1987) 'Readability', *School Science Review*, **68**(244), 565–568.

Johnstone, A.H. and Selepong, D. (2001) 'A language problem revisited', *Chemistry Education: Research and Practice in Europe*, **2**(1), 19–29.

Kelly, G.J. and Chen, C. (1999) 'The sound of music: constructing science as sociocultural practices through oral and written discourse', *Journal of Research in Science Teaching*, **36**(8), 883–915.

Kempa, R.F. and Ayob, A. (1995) 'Learning from group work in science', *International Journal of Science Education*, **17**(6), 743–754.

Keogh, B. and Naylor, S. (1999) 'Concept cartoons, teaching and learning in science: an evaluation', *International Journal of Science Education*, **21**(4), 431–446.

Keys, C.W. (1995) 'An interpretative study of students' scientific reasoning skills in collaborative report writing intervention in ninth grade science', *Science Education*, **79**(4), 415–435.

Keys, C.W. (1999) 'Revitalizing instruction in scientific genres: connecting knowledge production with writing to learn in science', *Science Education*, **83**(2), 115–130.

Keys, C.W. (2000) 'Investigating the thinking processes of eighth grade writers during the composition of a scientific laboratory report', *Journal of Research in Science Teaching*, **37**(7), 676–690.

Kibble, B. (2002) 'Misconceptions about space? It's on the cards', *Primary Science Review*, **72**, 5–8.

Kinchin, I.M. (2000a) 'Using concept maps to reveal understanding: a two-tier analysis', *School Science Review*, **81**(296), 41–46.

Kinchin, I.M. (2000b) 'Concept-mapping activities to help students understand photosynthesis – and teachers understand students', *School Science Review*, **82**(299), 11–14.

Knutton, S. (1983) 'Chemistry textbooks – are they readable?', *Education in Chemistry*, **20**(3), 100–105.

Learners' Co-operative (1996) *Science Thinking Maps for Key Stage 3*, Plymouth: The Learners' Co-operative.

Lenton, G. and Turner, G. (1999) 'Student teachers' grasp of science concepts', *School Science Review*, **81**(295), 67–72.

Lunzer, E. and Gardner, K. (1984) *Learning from the Written Word*, Edinburgh: Oliver and Boyd.

McKeon, F. (2000) 'Literacy and secondary science – building on primary experience', *School Science Review*, **81**(297), 45–50.

Martin, J.R. (1993) 'Literacy in science: learning to handle text as well as technology', in Halliday, M.A.K. and Martin, J.R. (eds) *Writing Science: Literacy and Discursive Power*, London: Falmer Press.

Matthews, B. (2001) *Improving Science and Emotional Development (The ISED Project)*, London: Goldsmiths College, University of London.

Mercer, N. (2000) *Words and Minds: How We Use Language to Think Together*, London: Routledge.

Morgan, N. (1995) *History Makers of the Scientific Revolution*, Hove: Wayland.

Naylor, S. and Keogh, B. (2000) *Concept Cartoons in Science Education*, Sandbach: Millgate House.

Newton, P., Driver, R. and Osborne, J. (1999) 'The place of argumentation in the pedagogy of school science', *International Journal of Science Education*, **21**(5), 553–576.

Novak, J. (1990) 'Concept Mapping: A Useful Tool for Science Education', *Journal of Research in Science Teaching*, **27**(10), 937–949.

Novak, J. (1991) 'Clarify with Concept Maps', *Science Teacher*, **58**(7), 44–49.

Nuffield Primary Science (1996) *Science Coordinators' Handbook*, London: Collins.

Osborne, J. (1997) 'Practical alternatives', *School Science Review*, **78**(285), 61–66.

Osborne, J., Erduran, S., Simon, S. and Monk, M. (2001) 'Enhancing the quality of argument in school science', *School Science Review*, **82**(301), 63–70.

Parkinson, J. (1994) *The Effective Teaching of Secondary Science*, London: Longman.

Peacock, A. (2001) 'The potential impact of the "Literacy Hour" on the teaching of science from text material', *Journal of Curriculum Studies*, **33**(1), 25–42.

Pickersgill, S. and Lock, R. (1991) 'Student understanding of selected non-technical words in science', *Research in Science and Technology Education*, **9**(1), 71–79.

Prain, V. and Hand, B. (1996) 'Writing for learning in secondary science: rethinking practices', *Teaching & Teacher Education*, **12**(6), 609–626.

Prain, V. and Hand, B. (1999) 'Students' perceptions of writing for learning in secondary school science', *Science Education*, **83**(2), 151–162.

Prophet, B. and Towse, P. (1999) 'Pupils' understanding of some non-technical words in science', *School Science Review*, **81**(295), 79–86.

Ratcliffe, M. (1998) 'Discussing socio-scientific issue in science lessons – pupils' actions and the teachers' role', *School Science Review*, **79**(288), 55–59.

Rivard, L.P. and Straw, S.B. (2000) 'The effect of talk and writing on learning science: an exploratory study', *Science Education*, **84**(5), 566–593.

Ross, K., Lakin, L. and Callaghan, P. (2000) *Teaching Secondary Science: Constructing Meaning and Developing Understanding*, London: David Fulton.

Roth, W.-M. and Roychoudhury, A. (1993) 'The concept map as a tool for the collaborative construction of knowledge: a microanalysis of high school physics students', *Journal of Research in Science Teaching*, **30**(5), 503–534.

Rye, J.A. and Rubba, P.A. (1998) 'An exploration of the concept map as an interview tool to facilitate the externalization of students' understandings about global atmospheric change', *Journal of Research in Science Teaching*, **35**(5), 503–534.

Sands, M.K. (1981) 'Group work in science: myth and reality', *School Science Review*, **62**(221), 765–769.

Sizmur, S. (1994) 'Concept mapping, language and learning in the classroom', *School Science Review*, **76**(274), 120–125.

Slater, B.C. and Thompson, J.J. (1984) 'How useful are readability formulae', *Education in Chemistry*, **21**(3), 92–94.

Staples, R. and Heselden, R. (2002a) 'Science teaching and literacy, part 1: writing', *School Science Review*, **83**(303), 35–46.

Staples, R. and Heselden, R. (2002b) 'Science teaching and literacy, part 3: speaking and listening, spelling and vocabulary', *School Science Review*, **84**(306), 83–95.

Stephenson, P. and Warwick, P. (2002) 'Using Concept Cartoons To Support Progression in Students' Understanding of Light', *Physics Education*, **37**(2), 135–141.

Sutton, C.R. (1992) *Words, Science, and Learning*, Buckingham: Open University Press.

Sutton, C. (1996) 'The scientific model as a form of speech', in Welford, G., Osborne, J. and Scott, P. (eds) *Research in Science Education in Europe: Current Issues and Themes*, London: Falmer Press.

Swain, J., Monk, M. and Johnson, S. (1999) 'A quantitative study of the differences in ideas generated by three different opportunities for classroom talk', *International Journal of Science Education*, **21**(4), 389–399.

TES (1999) 'Talking is good for the brain', *Times Educational Supplement*, 15 January.

Wellington, J. and Osborne, J. (2001) *Language and Literacy in Science Education*, Buckingham: Open University Press.

Wray, D. and Lewis, M. (1997) *Extending Literacy: Children Reading and Writing Non-fiction*, London: Routledge.

CHAPTER 12

Where do we go from here?

And God said

$$\nabla \bullet E = \frac{\rho}{\epsilon_0} = 4\pi k \rho$$

$$\nabla \bullet B = 0$$

$$\nabla \times E = -\frac{\delta B}{\delta t}$$

$$\nabla \times B = \frac{J}{c^2 \epsilon_0} + \frac{1}{c^2} \frac{\delta E}{\delta t}$$

and there was light.

(apologies to James Clerk Maxwell)

Life before the National Curriculum

Some people will say that there is nothing new in education; the old ideas are dusted off and recycled in some bright new glossy format. We are all made to believe that what we are currently doing is not cutting the mustard and we must change our practices. So perhaps, in trying to predict the future, it is sometimes worth spending a short time looking at the past. Bearing in mind that the past is sometimes seen through rose-tinted spectacles, I shall try to keep the discussion as objective as possible; however, it is only my perspective on what has happened, and others may see things in a different light.

From the 1960s and to the late 1980s, pupils took courses in years 10 and 11 (called the 4th and 5th forms at the time) leading to either an O-level qualification (introduced in 1951) for the more able, or a CSE (Certificate of Secondary Education, introduced in 1965) for the less able. Science departments could choose between syllabuses produced by the examination boards, or they could devise their own mode 2 or mode 3 courses. These were courses that were designed to meet the needs of pupils in a particular school or area and to match the interests of the teachers. For mode 3 courses, teachers could write the syllabus and the course materials and devise the assessment scheme and, when final assessment was seen as appropriate, they could write the examination papers. The exam would also be marked by the teachers, but the exam scripts would be moderated by the examination board. In one school, for example, teachers produced a mode 3 O-level chemistry course with an emphasis on problem solving and pupil-based activities structured around project work (Greatorex and Turner, 1977). Another example involved a group of teachers from ten schools working together to produce a mode 3 limited-grade CSE course (Langdon and Harrison, 1980). The course was targeted at the least able, and therefore higher CSE grades were not attainable. The teaching material was based on a resource produced by ASE called the LAMP (Less Academically Motivated Pupils) project. Such was the freedom given to teachers in pre-GCSE days. In 1986 a new 'one size fits all' policy was introduced, and, in spite of criticism in terms of its ability to cater for the needs of pupils of vastly differing abilities, the GCSE has maintained its position as the principal examination for 16-year-olds. Running alongside these changes throughout the 1980s was the work of the Secondary Science Curriculum Review (SSCR). During this time groups of teachers got together to work on projects of common interest, under the auspices of the SSCR. They produced guidance material, resources and a vast array of publications so that their work could be shared by others. The aim of the review was:

> ... to stimulate the development of science studies so as to provide an appropriate education for all young people growing up in a scientific and technological society, whatever their abilities or career intentions.
>
> (SSCR, 1989: xi)

There was concern that some pupils ended their science studies as early as Y9 (the 3rd form), and that a significant number of pupils who continued studying science up to GCSE level only studied one or two science subjects. The gender imbalance in physics was of particular concern. The cry for science for all was taken up by the Government in 1985 with the publication of a policy statement looking at the provision of science education throughout compulsory schooling (DES and WO, 1985). The Conservative Government came into power in 1979 and was re-elected in 1983 and 1987, each time with a large majority. Conservative policy was to improve education through the use of a consumerist type of approach. This involved having a National Curriculum, where all pupils would study the same work, and a common system of assessment. This, as we are now well aware, enabled schools to be judged against one another. The ideals of the SSCR review became lost in the desire to manufacture a common template to measure all pupils, and no longer was it possible to have science courses that matched the needs of different groups of pupils. The refinements and adjustments to the Science National Curriculum and GCSE courses over the last 10 years have improved the situation, but have only tinkered with what has to be taught. What is needed now is a radical rethink, perhaps going back to first principles and asking 'Do all pupils need to be taught science?' and, if they do, 'What sort of science should they be taught?'.

Science for all

There are some very compelling arguments in favour of the case that all pupils should study science. In Chapter 8 it was mentioned that pupils need to know about the culture of science. In the same way that young people need to appreciate the contribution that art and music make to their lives, they also need to be aware of how an understanding of scientific thinking and knowledge about the products of science contribute to their perceptions of the world. Education in its broadest sense is not restricted to conceptual understanding; it is about values (e.g. honesty, tolerance, self-criticism), spiritual, moral and ethical issues, and the rights and responsibilities of individuals living in a community. Science has a role to play in each of these areas, and helps to provide pupils with a balanced perspective. All young people are entitled to an education that is concerned with 'all those things that as a society we have decided we value and which we wish to pass on to our successors' (Tate, 1999: 10).

If we accept that these are sound reasons for making a study of science compulsory, then we need to consider how effective the last 12 years of National Curriculum Science has been in providing a scientific education for all pupils. It would be expected that an increase in the number of pupils studying science pre-16 would lead to an increase in the number of pupils choosing to study science in their post-16 courses. Jenkins (2002) reports that there has been no significant increase in numbers wishing to study the physical sciences beyond GCSE. Moreover, mandatory science has not led to significant change in the long-established gender imbalance associated with physics. Figure 12.1 shows the general increase in the numbers taking GCSE Double Award Science courses, and Figure 12.2 shows corresponding data for A-level entries. There has been a general decline for both chemistry and physics since 1990, and a gradual increase in numbers for biology up to 1998, followed by a decline. The data for English have been included for comparison purposes and, as can be seen in Figure 12.2, there has been a sharp reduction in the numbers taking English in recent years. A possible

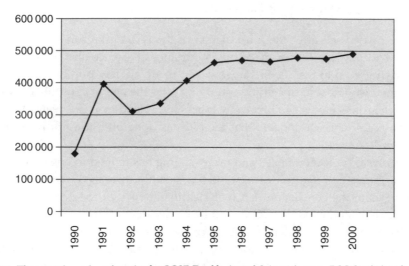

Figure 12.1 *The annual number of entries for GCSE Double Award Science (source: RSC Statistics of Chemistry Education)*

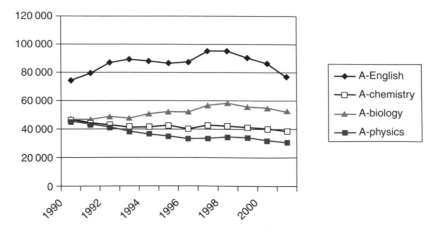

Figure 12.2 *The annual number of entries for A-levels in English, chemistry, biology and physics (source: RSC Statistics of Chemistry Education)*

explanation for this could be an increase in popularity of A-levels in subjects such as business studies, psychology and media studies, leading to each of the other subjects reducing its market share.

Another way of evaluating the success of the NC is to look at pupils' attitudes towards science. Does the curriculum make pupils interested and excited about science? Research carried out prior to the introduction of the NC consistently showed a negative image of science. Bennett (2001) highlights the key findings as:

- science is not perceived to be relevant to people's lives
- science is a cause of social and environmental problems
- science is a difficult subject
- science is about things rather than people
- science is for boys rather than girls
- scientists are generally rather odd people.

In a study carried out after the introduction of the NC, Parkinson *et al.* (1998) found that most KS3 pupils were aware of the importance of science and were keen to continue studying it up to the age of 16. However, relatively few pupils saw it as an area of study they would wish to continue studying after the age of compulsory schooling. Similar conclusions have been drawn by others (e.g. Hendley *et al.*, 1996; Ofsted, 2000) relating to NC science. It appears that the NC has done little to improve pupils' attitudes towards science.

The emphasis on league tables and target setting has helped to ensure that the percentage of pupils gaining grades A* to C has steadily increased over the years. This might lead us to the conclusion that the scientific literacy of the generation of young people who have followed the NC should be higher than of those who have not. Most of the surveys on scientific literacy study a cross-section of the population, and it is not possible to distinguish between people who have studied balanced science and those who have not. However, Murphy *et al.* (2001) studied the extent of understanding of science held by two groups of young people training to become primary school teachers. One group had followed science courses from 11–16, and the other had little or no experience of compulsory science. The level of scientific literacy was determined using questions originally set for KS2 pupils and aimed at levels 3–5 of the NC. Not unsurprisingly, the group that had followed a balanced science course performed better than those who did not, and the authors concluded that there is some evidence to show that compulsory science has been effective in raising the general level of scientific literacy. However, there were some areas of knowledge where there was a complete lack of understanding. These were the circulatory system, light, sound, electric circuits and the water cycle. It is a little disconcerting to find that the level of understanding of science concepts is so very low.

Scientific literacy

The term 'scientific literacy' has an interesting history, linked initially to the concerns of the science community in the USA about the public support for science at a time when the USSR was leading the space race. In the late 1970s and early 1980s it came into prominence again when the USA became concerned about the growing economic power of Japan and other Pacific rim countries when its own industrial leadership appeared to be on the wane. In the UK the debate has focussed more on the social and cultural relevance of science in a scientific and technological society, and the inclusion of social responsibility in the science education curriculum.

Scientific literacy is one of those terms that is difficult to define. Laugksch (2000) describes three different forms of scientific literacy that build upon one another in degree of sophistication. A country might aspire to having a population that could be described as being culturally scientifically literate (Laugksch's foundational level), defined in terms of people being able to read about science, make some sense of what they have read and express their views about scientific matters. Judging from the number of people who have bought *A Brief History of Time* by Stephen Hawkins (over 1.5 million in the UK by 2003), it might appear that a substantial proportion of the population is well on the way to higher levels of scientific literacy.

Teaching for scientific literacy will involve a considerable change in current practices (Jenkins, 1999):

- It will mean a move away from much of the physics, chemistry and biology that is currently taught to make way for issues where the science is less secure and sometimes controversial
- It is likely that school science curricula in different countries will be more varied than at present in order to accommodate local and regional scientific issues
- The contribution that science teaching makes to the education of the whole child and his or her development as a citizen will need to be reappraised.

Teaching will require an increased use of the techniques used in a science, technology and society (STS) approach, where pupils are required to read about science, discuss issues, role-play situations and make presentations. Solomon (2001) points out that the current provision is doing little to prepare future citizens, and suggests that time spent on activities that promote scientific literacy is likely to be both worthwhile and enjoyable for the pupils.

Citizenship

Citizenship was introduced into the National Curriculum in England in 2002, with a requirement that teachers should assess pupils' attainment for the first time at the end of KS3 in July 2004. The rationale for citizenship is based on three inter-related dimensions:

1 The global dimension to political literacy
2 The global dimension to social and moral responsibility
3 The global dimension to community involvement.

In certain topics, knowledge about science can play an important role in each of these dimensions. It may, however, be one factor in a situation that involves a myriad of inter-relating factors and where pupils have to make judgements based on the strengths of the various arguments. In his criticism of the inclusion of environmental issues into NC science, Chapman (1991) pointed out that the problems are not simply scientific or technological in nature but are more related to economics and politics on a global perspective. Perhaps a citizenship course might be more successful than a science course in dealing with these challenging issues. Schools will approach the teaching of citizenship in a variety of ways, such as:

* through specific citizenship timetabled lessons
* as part of the PSHE course
* by collapsing the timetable and running special citizenship days
* through different curriculum subjects.

Science can make a contribution to at least two of the units in the QCA SoW for citizenship; People and the environment at KS3 (unit 21), and Global issues, local action at KS4 (unit 12) (QCA, 2001). Reporting on science teachers' views of the cross-curricular approach to citizenship, Campbell (2002a) draws attention to teachers' anxiety about the effect of an overbearing assessment scheme on the quality of the teaching. At present teachers have to record progress and report to parents each year, and assess achievement at the end of KS3. At KS4 there is no statutory requirement for assessment and recording, but a comment on citizenship must be included in pupils' annual written reports.

Teaching about controversial issues can be extremely demanding on science teachers, who, in the main, are not used to deconstructing items presented by the media and to teaching ethical issues. Levinson (2001) points out that these teaching skills are more in line with the techniques used by humanities teachers, but points out that these teachers may be more interested in the persuasiveness of the argument rather than the technical accuracy of the science. He suggests that a way forward might be the production of guidance material containing examples of what teaching controversial issues (such as those related to the biomedical sciences) might look like, together with increased co-operation between humanities and science teachers. Campbell (2002b), along with others, has recognised the need for resources and provided some suggestions and activities whereby pupils can explore issues using a variety of activities. As mentioned on page 177, Jarman and McClune (2002) have pointed out the useful role that newspapers, TV and the Internet can play in linking school science with everyday life. Newspaper articles can act as stimulus material, e.g. on a laboratory bulletin board or as a starter activity, or can be used in a DART activity or as a resource for group discussion. Ratcliffe (1998) recommends that group discussion involving socio-scientific issues should follow a fairly tight format involving the clarification of the purpose of the activity, a clear indication of the tasks to be accomplished, and a class review of how the decisions were made. This last stage helps pupils to appreciate the value of the exercise, and promotes the development decision-making skills.

What should a future science curriculum contain?

Given the evidence of students' lack of understanding in so many basic areas, the guiding principle as regards curriculum content must surely be: do less but do it better.

(Millar, 1996: 12)

Were mistakes made in the 1980s? The principle of 'science for all' was very appealing at the time, and for various reasons it was decided to control the science curriculum so that everyone, more or less, studied the same work. Chapman (1991) was highly critical of the 'science for all' movement, and suggested that many of the perceived benefits expressed by the curriculum writers were unlikely to materialise. To a large extent, much of what he said has been found to be correct. 'Science for all' hasn't resulted in increased numbers entering science-related employment, it hasn't resulted in an uptake in A-level sciences, and it hasn't encouraged large numbers of young women to go into careers in physics or engineering.

In a recent paper exploring the views of employees and key members of the public about what should form the basis of a common curriculum, Duggan and Gott (2002) suggest that it is time for a radical rethink. The research was based on a number of case studies centred on a sample of industries, community action groups and other individuals, and involved semi-structured interviews and the scrutiny of key documents. The following conclusions were drawn from the study:

- Pupils need to know and understand the principle concepts of evidence, and how to apply these concepts. They need to be able to examine evidence and make judgements that will inform their personal decision-making.
- Access to scientific information is very easy, and most of the conceptual understanding for people working in industry is obtained when it is needed. A future

curriculum should restrict conceptual understanding to a limited number of basic concepts. Greater emphasis should be given to accessing knowledge that is directly relevant to topical issues and knowing how to apply that knowledge in 'real' situations.

A study of teachers' views of the future of the science curriculum indicated some dissatisfaction with the present situation and made some tentative suggestions for change (Leach, 2002). Three issues were discussed:

1 **Aim and relevance.** The teachers were of the opinion that the NC did not meet the needs of all pupils, in particular those at the top and those at the bottom of the ability range. A future NC should prepare pupils to become consumers and users of science.
2 **Content of the NC.** The teachers suggested that a future NC should contribute to a more general education of pupils, rather than being focussed on pupils who wished to study the subject further.
3 **Motivational factors.** Current provision was seen as being broadly demotivating for teachers and pupils. The teachers suggested that in future teachers should be given more flexibility and autonomy in selecting curriculum content.

Overall the teachers were supportive of change, but they were unable to come up with a common vision of what a new science curriculum should look like.

Rising from continued dissatisfaction with the science curriculum, a number of science educators organised a series of nationwide seminars to consider the possible nature of future courses. The result of their deliberations was a report, *Beyond 2000* (Millar and Osborne, 1998), which made 10 recommendations:

1 The science curriculum from 5–16 should be seen primarily as a course to enhance general 'scientific literacy'.
2 At KS4, the structure of the science curriculum needs to differentiate more explicitly between those elements designed to enhance scientific literacy and those designed as the earlier stages of specialist training in science, so that the requirement of the latter does not come to distort the former.
3 The science curriculum needs to contain a clear statement of its aims – making it clear why teachers consider it valuable for all young people to study science, and what teachers would wish them to gain from the experience. (Gott and Johnson (1999) suggest that a future NC should list a much smaller number of key areas in terms of ideas pupils need to learn, and greater autonomy should be given to teachers.)
4 The curriculum needs to be presented clearly and simply, and its content needs to follow from the aims. Scientific knowledge can best be presented in the curriculum as a number of key explanatory stories. In addition, the curriculum should introduce pupils to a number of important ideas about science.
5 Work should be undertaken to explore how aspects of technology and the applications of science currently omitted could be incorporated within a science curriculum designed to enhance scientific literacy.

6 The science curriculum should provide pupils with an understanding of some key ideas about science – i.e. ideas about the ways in which reliable knowledge of the natural world has been, and is being, obtained.

7 The science curriculum should encourage the use of a wide variety of teaching methods and approaches, and there should be variation in the pace at which new ideas are introduced. In particular, case studies of historical and current issues should be used to consolidate understanding of the explanatory stories and of the key ideas about science, and to make it easier for teachers to match work to the needs and interests of learners.

8 The assessment approaches used to report on pupils' performance should encourage teachers to focus on pupils' ability to understand and interpret scientific information and to discuss controversial issues, as well as on their knowledge and understanding of scientific ideas.

9 In the short term, the aims of the existing NC should be clearly stated with an indication how the proposed content is seen as achieving those aims. Those aspects of the general requirements that deal with the NoS and with systematic inquiry in science should be incorporated into Sc1 to give more stress to the teaching of ideas about science, and new forms of assessment need to be developed to reflect such an emphasis

10 In the medium to long term, a formal procedure should be established whereby innovative approaches in science education are trialled on a restricted scale in a representative range of schools for a fixed period. Such innovations would then be evaluated and the outcomes used to inform subsequent changes at national level. No significant changes should be made to the NC or its assessment unless they have been previously piloted in this way.

The initial significant development following the report was the production of an AS-level specification called *Science for Public Understanding*. The specification, published by AQA, aims to consolidate post-16 pupils' understanding of science by focussing learning on issues that pupils will meet and have to deal with as citizens. Millar and Hunt (2002) explain that the course closely follows the structure proposed in *Beyond 2000*, and links together a series of science explanations (theories) with a set of ideas about science (e.g. data and explanations, social influences on science and technology). Unlike 'normal' science courses, the coursework component does not involve practical work. Two pieces of written work are required. The larger component requires pupils to study a topical scientific issue, and the second component requires pupils to read a piece of popular science writing.

In 2003 we saw the first step of a radical reform of the curriculum, with proposals for a much broader curriculum for the 14–19-year-old age group involving schools and colleges working together in partnership (DfES, 2002). In this new vision, science remains one of the core subjects that all pupils must study, but the nature of the science courses will be significantly different from the existing curriculum. OCR is currently developing a specification, along with staff from the University of York Science Teacher Education Group and the Nuffield Foundation, that consists of a single award to be taken by all pupils, designed to enhance pupils' scientific literacy (QCA, 2003).

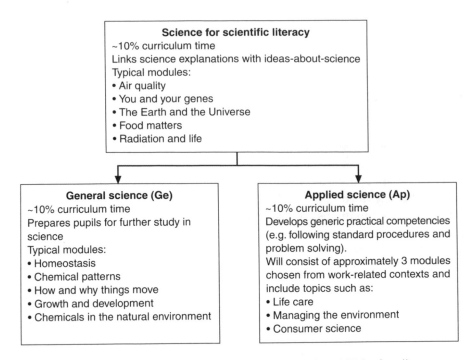

Figure 12.3 *Proposed GCSE science courses for the twenty-first century from OCR (see http://www. 21stcenturyscience.org/home/)*

It would then be possible for pupils to choose between a more academic course, general science, or a work-related course (applied science), if they so wished (Figure 12.3). The course has been devised to eliminate the problems and criticisms mentioned above, and to meet the demands of a world where an understanding of scientific principles is crucial in helping future citizens to make decisions.

Will we get it right next time?

The answer is yes, possibly, but success is only likely to be achieved if teachers make their views known and if curriculum designers listen. Unfortunately, teachers tend to bury themselves in their day to day work and allow changes in educational practice to sweep them along. Changes in the science curriculum are only going to be successful if they have the full support of those who are going to deliver them.

References

Bennett, J. (2001) 'Science with attitude: the perennial problem of pupils' responses to science', *School Science Review*, **82**(300), 59–70.

Campbell, P. (2002a) 'The citizenship agenda', *Education in Science*, **200**, 17.

Campbell, P. (2002b) 'Citizenship education and science at key stage 3', *School Science Review*, **83**(305), 125–130 (further examples of teaching ideas for citizenship education can be found at the Science Year website, http://www.sycd.co.uk).

Chapman, B. (1991) 'The overselling of science education in the eighties', *School Science Review*, **72**(260), 47–63.

DES and WO (1985) (Department for Education and Science and the Welsh Office) *Science 5–16: a Statement of Policy*, London: HMSO.

DfES (2002) 14–19: Opportunity and Excellence, London: DfES (available at http://www.dfes.gov.uk/14-19/main.shtml).

Duggan, S. and Gott, R. (2002) 'What sort of science education do we really need?', *International Journal of Science Education*, **24**(7), 661–679.

Gott, R. and Johnson, P. (1999) 'Science in schools: time to pause for thought?', *School Science Review*, **81**(295), 21–34.

Greatorex, D. and Turner, C.R. (1977) 'A report of a mode 3 project-based O-level chemistry course – part 1', *School Science Review*, **58**(205), 780–783.

Hendley, D., Stables, S. and Stables, A. (1996) 'Pupils' subject preferences at key stage 3 in South Wales', *Educational Studies*, **22**(2), 177–187.

Jarman, R. and McClune, B. (2002) 'A survey of the use of newspapers in science instruction by secondary teachers in Northern Ireland', *International Journal of Science Education*, **24**(10), 997–1020.

Jenkins, E.W. (1999) 'School science, citizenship and the public understanding of science', *International Journal of Science Education*, **21**(7), 703–710.

Jenkins, E.W. (2002) 'Science education from 14–19: practice and standards'. Paper presented to the House of Commons Science and Technology Select Committee on 9 January 2002 (available at: http://www.leeds.ac.uk/educol/documents/00001935.doc).

Langdon, L. and Harrison, W. (1980) 'The development of a mode 3 CSE limited grade science course – based mainly on the LAMP project', *School Science Review*, **61**(216), 560–562.

Laugksch, R. (2000) 'Scientific literacy: a conceptual overview', *Science Education*, **84**, 71–94.

Leach, J. (2002) 'Teachers' views on the future of the secondary science curriculum', *School Science Review*, **83**(304), 43–50.

Levinson, R. (2001) 'Should controversial issues in science be taught through the humanities?', *School Science Review*, **82**(300), 97–102.

Millar, R. (1996) 'Towards a science curriculum for public understanding', *School Science Review*, **77**(280), 7–18.

Millar, R. and Osborne, J. (1998) *Beyond 2000: Science Education for the Future*, London: School of Education, King's College London.

Millar, R. and Hunt, A. (2002) 'Science for public understanding: a different way to teach and learn science', *School Science Review*, **83**(304), 35–42.

Murphy, C., Beggs, J., Hickey, I., O'Meara, J. and Sweeney, J. (2001) 'National Curriculum: compulsory school science – is it improving scientific literacy', *Educational Research*, **43**(2), 189–199.

Ofsted (2000) *Progress in Key Stage 3 Science*, London: Office for Standards in Education.

Parkinson, J., Hendley, D. and Tanner, H. (1998) 'Pupils' attitudes to science in key stage 3 of the National Curriculum: a study of pupils in South Wales', *Research in Science & Technological Education*, **16**(2), 165–176.

QCA (2001) *Schemes of Work: Key Stage 3 Citizenship*, London: QCA (available at: http://www.standards.dfes.gov.uk/schemes2/citizenship/?view=Units).

QCA (2003) *GCSE in the Sciences: QCA's Pilot Qualification for the Study of Science in the 21st Century*, London: QCA (available at: http://www.qca.org.uk/printable. php?p=/nq/framework/content/pilot_gcse_sciences.htm).

Ratcliffe, M. (1998) 'Discussing socio-scientific issue in science lessons – pupils' actions and the teachers' role', *School Science Review*, **79**(288), 55–59.

Solomon, J. (2001) 'Teaching for scientific literacy: what could it mean?', *School Science Review*, **82**(300), 93–96.

SSCR (1989) *Better Science: a Directory of Resources*, London: Heinemann.

Tate, N. (1999) 'What is education for?', *English in Education*, **33**(2), 5–18.

5. Promoting pupils' learning

1 Examples of PRTs are available on the *Thinking Science* CD-ROM (Adey *et al.*, 2001a), or from Science Reasoning, 16 Fen End, Over, Cambridge, CB4 5NE.
2 Some researchers suggest that Bartlet, writing in the mid-1930s, was the first to propose constructivist ideas (Watts and Bentley, 1991). Oakes' work on alternative conceptions in the late 1940s could be described as constructivism, but it attracted little attention at the time as it did not fit in with the prevailing model of research (White and Mitchell, 1994).
3 The term 'alternative conception' is often used where a single idea differs from the scientifically accepted idea, and 'alternative framework' refers to a number of related ideas (Taber, 2002).
4 Adey and Shayer have subsequently measured the cognitive demand of the 1991 Science National Curriculum (Adey and Shayer, 1994: 35).

6. Dealing with differences

1 For up-to-date information on under-achievement and gender, see the DfES website at www.standards.dfee.gov.uk/genderandachievement.
2 Examples of famous scientists from different cultures can be found at http://www.upei.ca/~xliu/multi-culture/main.htm.

7. Making use of information from assessment

1 For further information on Bloom's taxonomy of educational objectives, see, for example, Parkinson, 2002: 137.
2 An example can be found by following the web links from www.sln.org.uk/science.
3 More information can be obtained from: http://www.qca.org.uk/ca/5-14/afl/ and http://www.learntolearn.ac.uk/home.php3.

10. Learning through ICT

1 Labels can be removed or added to diagrams and pictures using software such as Follens' *Diagrams*.

INDEX

eBooks – at www.eBookstore.tandf.co.uk

A library at your fingertips!

eBooks are electronic versions of printed books. You can store them on your PC/laptop or browse them online.

They have advantages for anyone needing rapid access to a wide variety of published, copyright information.

eBooks can help your research by enabling you to bookmark chapters, annotate text and use instant searches to find specific words or phrases. Several eBook files would fit on even a small laptop or PDA.

NEW: Save money by eSubscribing: cheap, online access to any eBook for as long as you need it.

Annual subscription packages

We now offer special low-cost bulk subscriptions to packages of eBooks in certain subject areas. These are available to libraries or to individuals.

For more information please contact webmaster.ebooks@tandf.co.uk

We're continually developing the eBook concept, so keep up to date by visiting the website.

www.eBookstore.tandf.co.uk